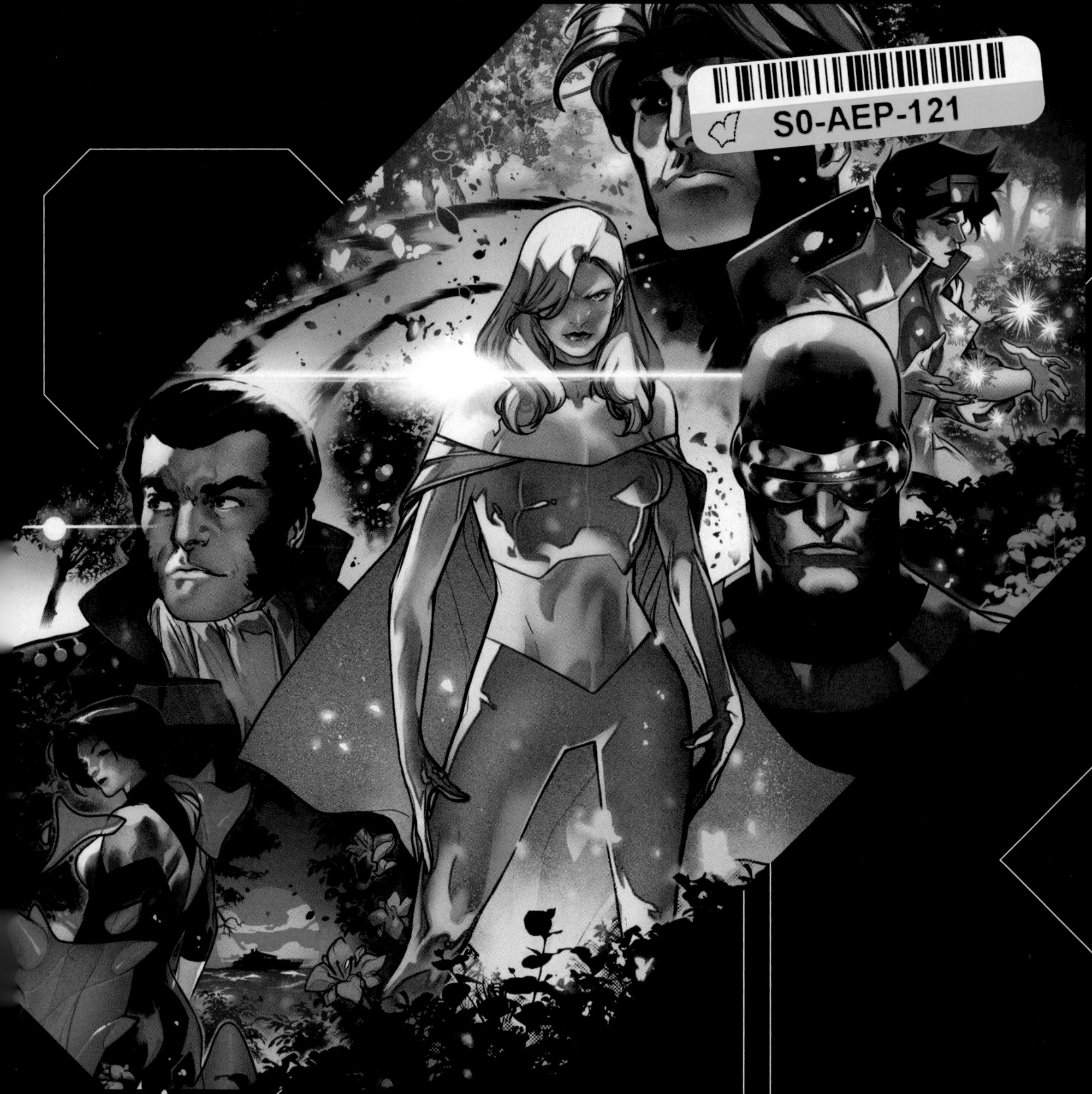

DAWN OF X

Volume
03

X-Men created by Stan Lee & Jack Kirby

Writers:	**Jonathan Hickman, Gerry Duggan, Tini Howard, Ed Brisson, Benjamin Percy & Bryan Hill**
Artists:	**Leinil Francis Yu & Gerry Alanguilan; Michele Bandini & Elisabetta D'Amico; Marcus To; Flaviano; Joshua Cassara; and Szymon Kudranski**
Color Artists:	**Sunny Gho, Federico Blee, Erick Arciniega, Carlos Lopez, Guru-eFX & Frank D'Armata**
Letterers:	**VC's Clayton Cowles, Cory Petit, Travis Lanham, Joe Caramanga & Joe Sabino**
Cover Art:	**Leinil Francis Yu & Sunny Gho; Russell Dauterman & Matthew Wilson; Mahmud Asrar & Matthew Wilson; Rod Reis; Dustin Weaver & Edgar Delgado; and Ashley Witter**
Head of X:	**Jonathan Hickman**
Design:	**Tom Muller**
Assistant Editors:	**Annalise Bissa & Chris Robinson**
Editor:	**Jordan D. White**
Collection Cover Art:	**R.B. Silva & Marte Gracia**
Collection Editor:	**Jennifer Grünwald**
Assistant Managing Editor:	**Maia Loy**
Assistant Managing Editor:	**Lisa Montalbano**
Associate Managing Editor:	**Kateri Woody**
Editor, Special Projects:	**Mark D. Beazley**
VP Production & Special Projects:	**Jeff Youngquist**
SVP Print, Sales & Marketing:	**David Gabriel**
Editor in Chief:	**C.B. Cebulski**

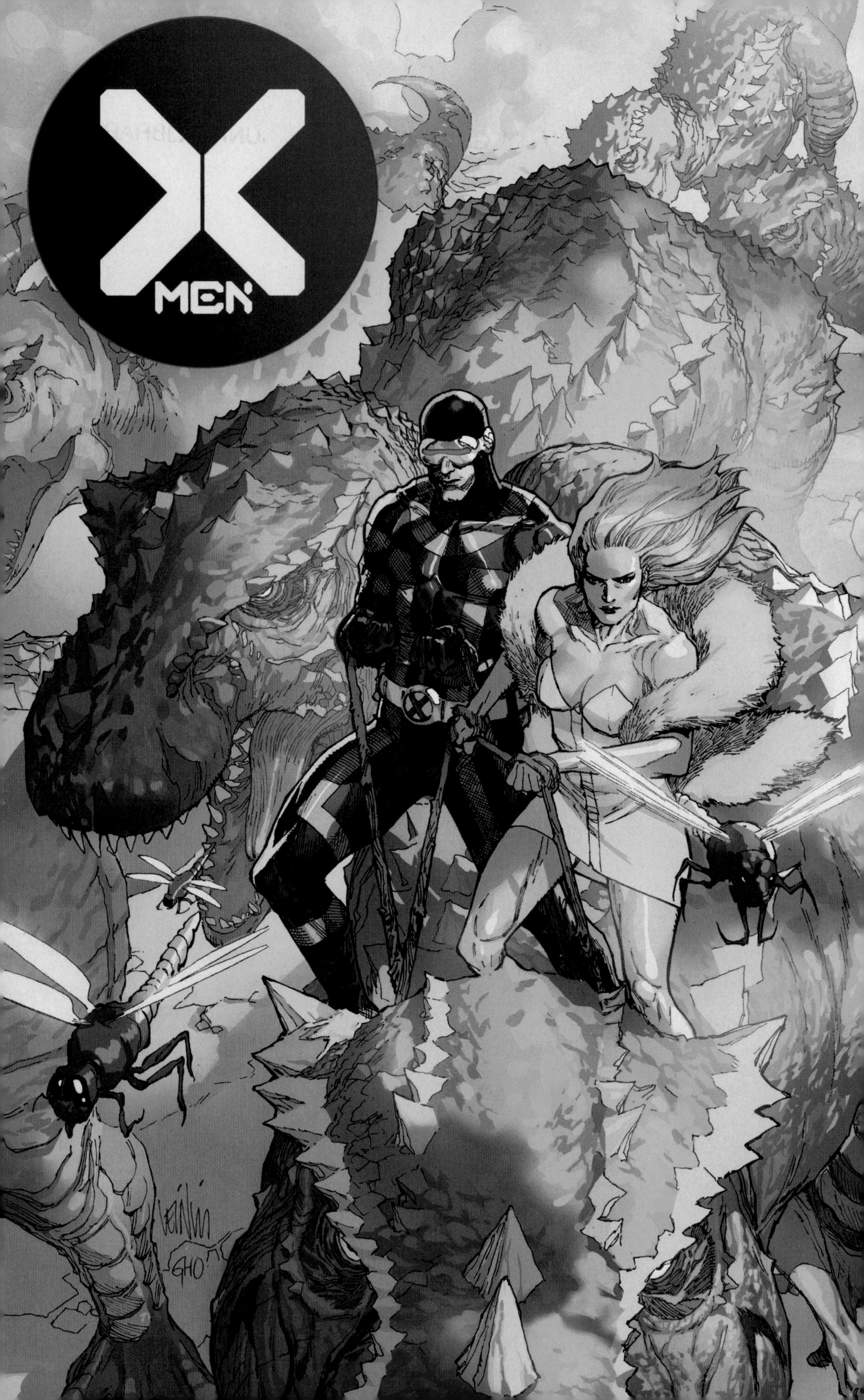
X
MEN

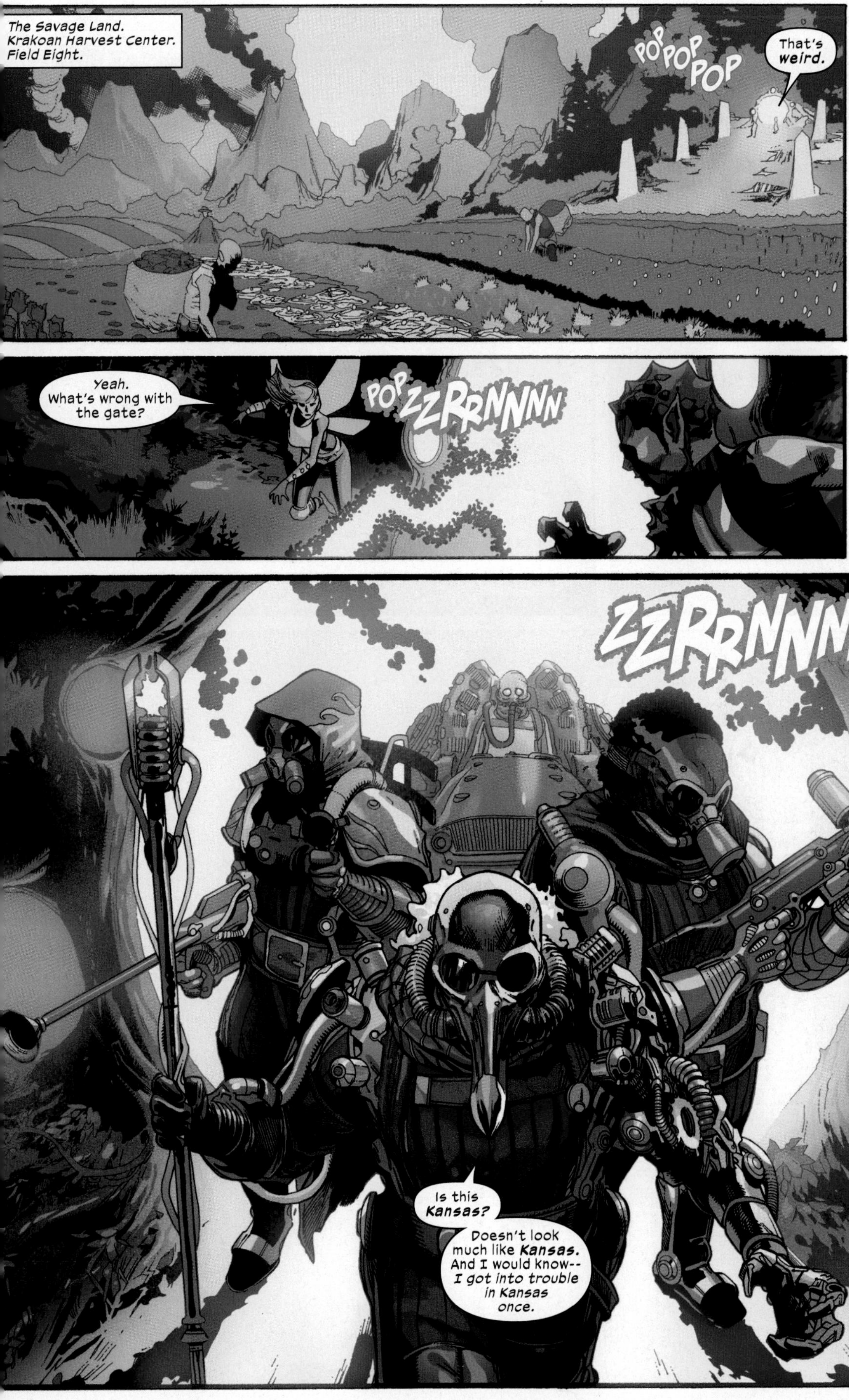
The Savage Land.
Krakoan Harvest Center.
Field Eight.
POP POP POP POP
That's weird.
Yeah. What's wrong with the gate?
POP ZZRRNNNN
ZZRRNNNNN
Is this Kansas?
Doesn't look much like Kansas. And I would know-- I got into trouble in Kansas once.

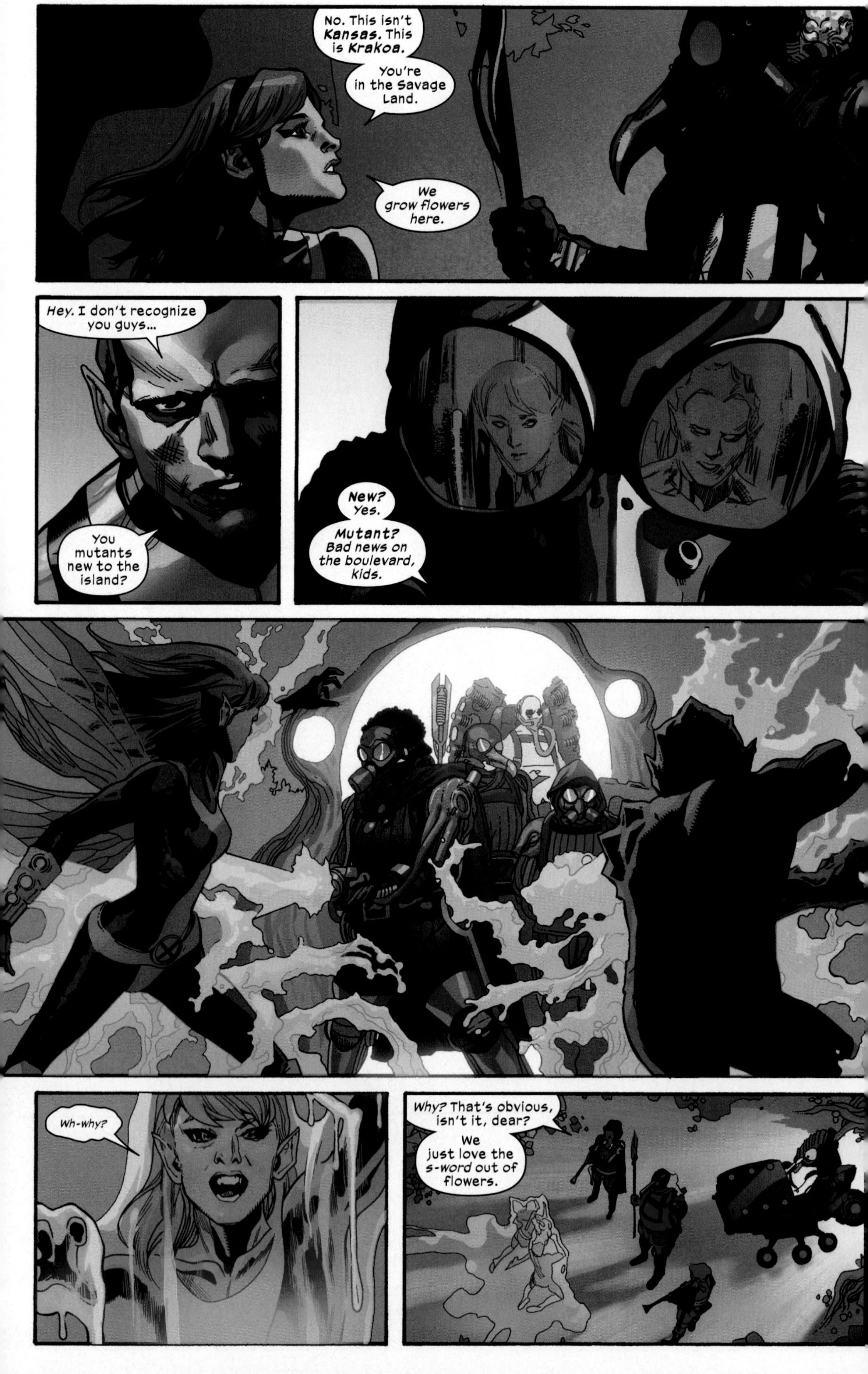

No. This isn't Kansas. This is Krakoa.
You're in the Savage Land.
We grow flowers here.
Hey. I don't recognize you guys...
You mutants new to the island?
New? Yes.
Mutant? Bad news on the boulevard, kids.
Wh-why?
Why? That's obvious, isn't it, dear?
We just love the s-word out of flowers.

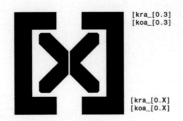

[kra_[0.3]
[koa_[0.3]

[kra_[0.X]
[koa_[0.X]

GROWTH MINDSET

Mutants around the world are flocking to the island-nation of Krakoa to be a part of the first mutant society--but a new nation means new threats...

White
Queen

Cyclops

Magneto

Marvel Girl

Black King

[kra_[0.3]...]
[koa_[0.3]...]

[A._New_World]

[00_mutants_of_X]
[00_the_world__X]

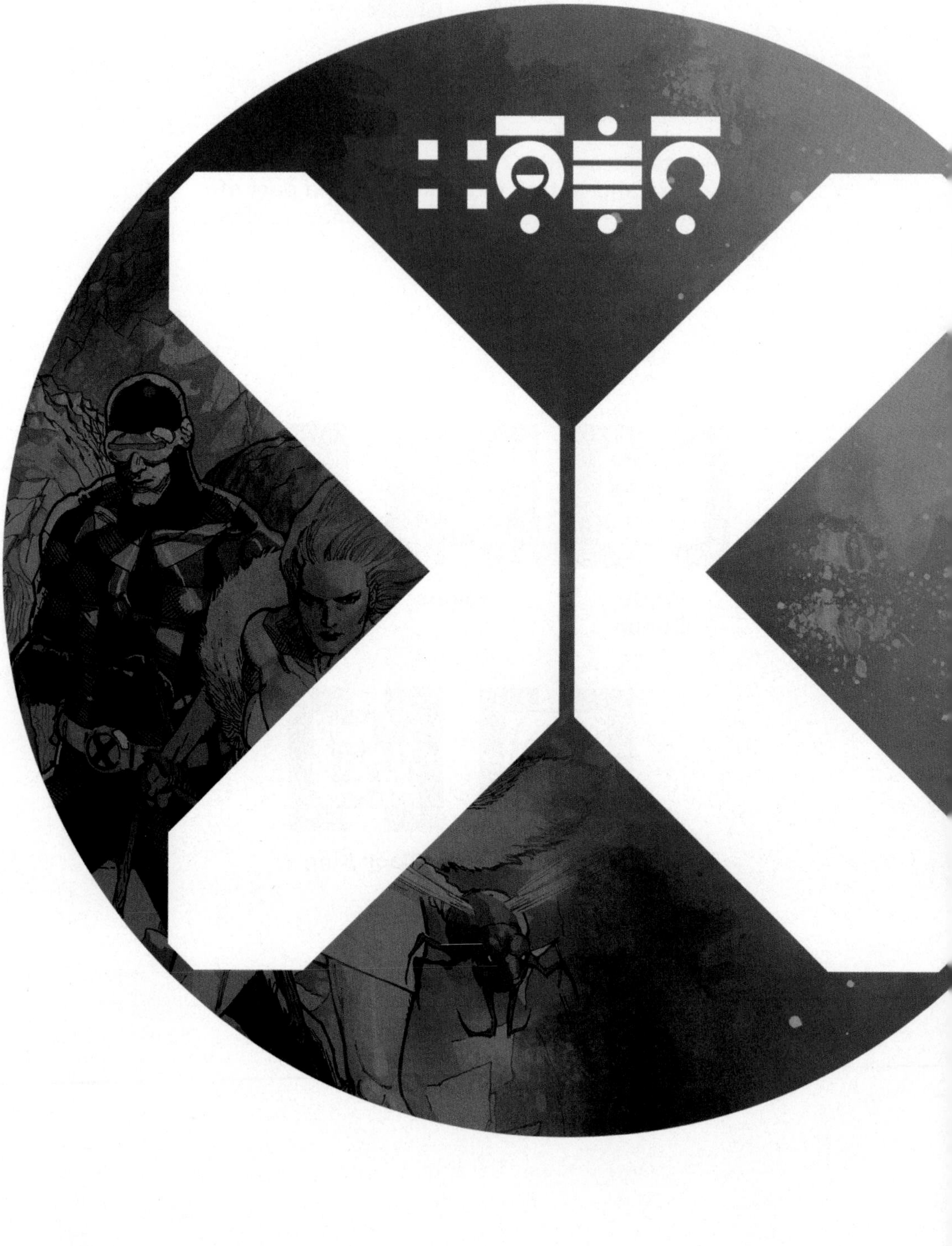

JONATHAN HICKMAN.............................[WRITER]
LEINIL FRANCIS YU ....[ARTIST]
GERRY ALANGUILAN & LEINIL FRANCIS YU..........[INKERS]
SUNNY GHO & RAIN BEREDO.................[COLOR ARTISTS]
VC's CLAYTON COWLES.........................[LETTERER]
TOM MULLER..................................[DESIGN]

LEINIL FRANCIS YU & SUNNY GHO...........[COVER ARTISTS]

ALEX ROSS; MIKE McKONE & RACHELLE ROSENBERG............
.................................[VARIANT COVER ARTISTS]

ANNALISE BISSA.......................[ASSISTANT EDITOR]
JORDAN D. WHITE...............................[EDITOR]
C.B. CEBULSKI........................[EDITOR IN CHIEF]
JOE QUESADA....................[CHIEF CREATIVE OFFICER]
DAN BUCKLEY................................[PRESIDENT]
ALAN FINE.........................[EXECUTIVE PRODUCER]

[03]X-MEN

[ISSUE THREE]................HORDECULTURE
X-MEN CREATED BY...................STAN LEE & JACK KIRBY

[00_mutants_of_X]
[00_the_world__X]

[00_00...0]
[00_00...3]

[00_unite_]
[00_____]

[00_____]

[00_____X]

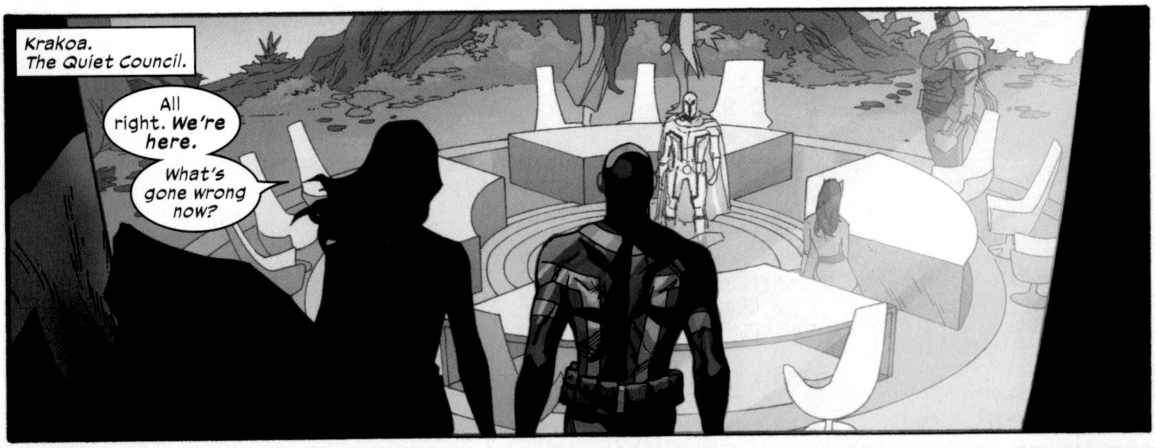

Krakoa.
The Quiet Council.
All right. **We're here.**
What's gone wrong now?

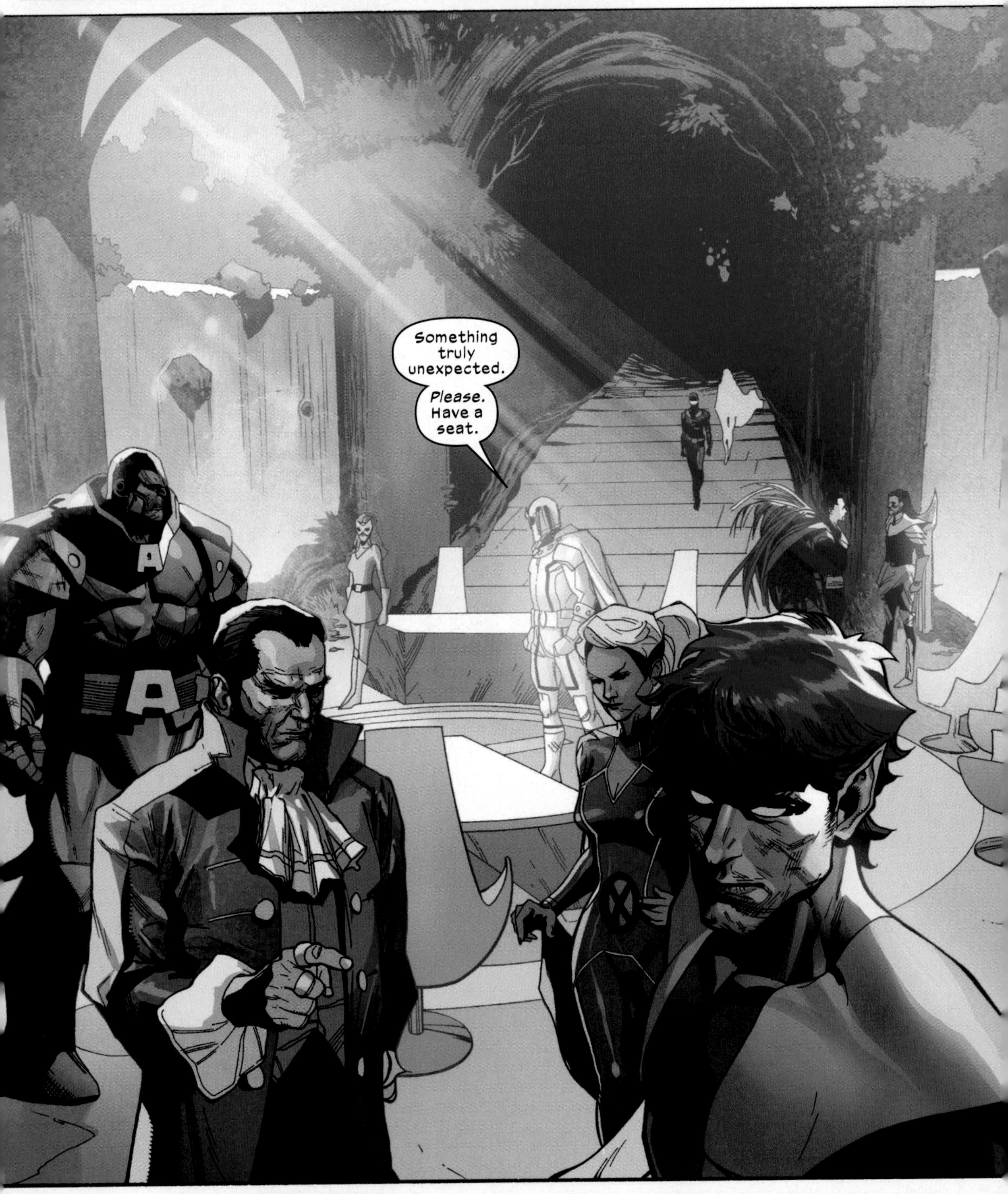

Something truly unexpected.
Please. Have a seat.

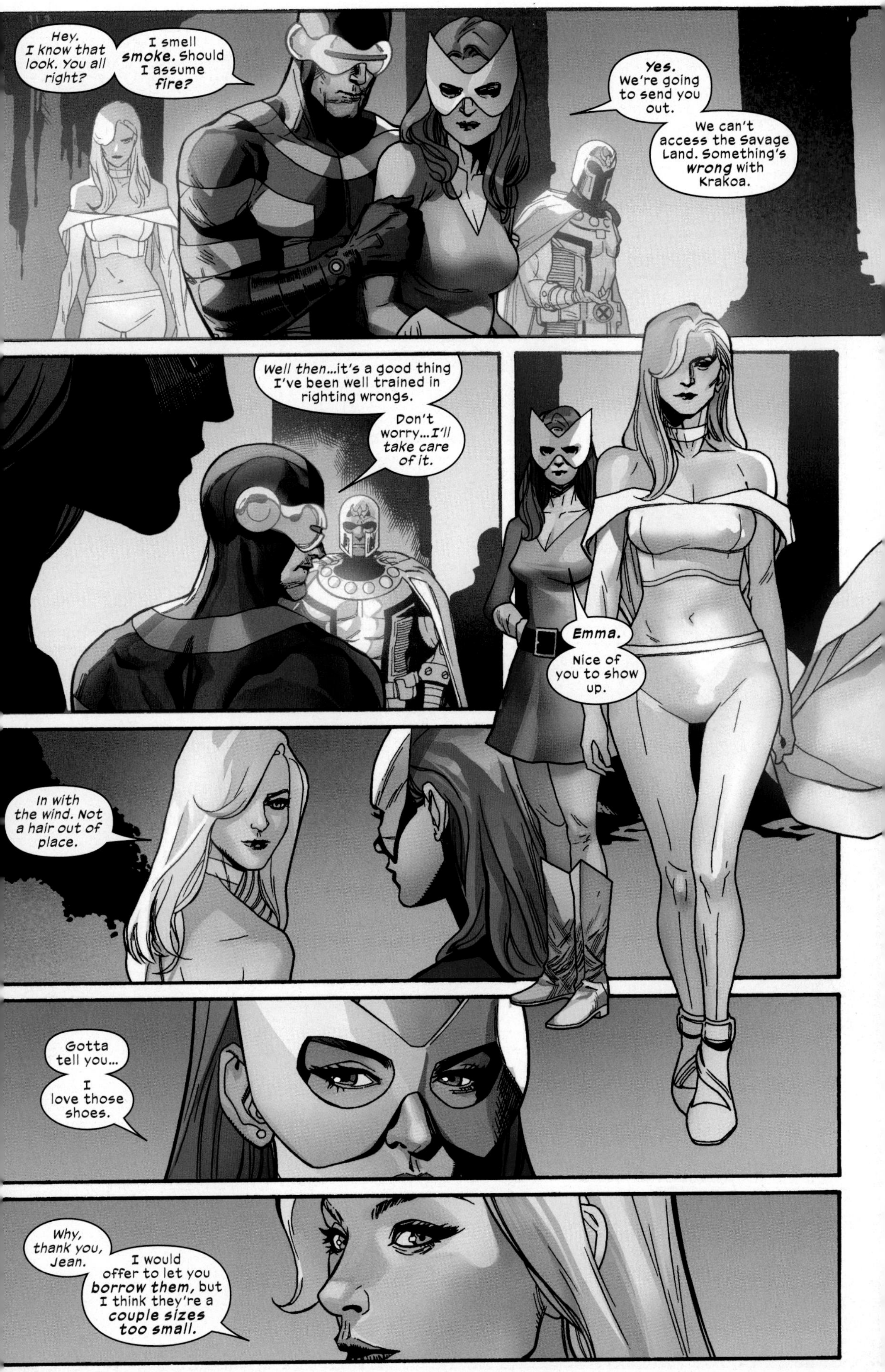
Hey. I know that look. You all right?
I smell smoke. Should I assume fire?
Yes. We're going to send you out.
We can't access the Savage Land. Something's wrong with Krakoa.
Well then...it's a good thing I've been well trained in righting wrongs.
Don't worry...I'll take care of it.
Emma.
Nice of you to show up.
In with the wind. Not a hair out of place.
Gotta tell you...
I love those shoes.
Why, thank you, Jean.
I would offer to let you borrow them, but I think they're a couple sizes too small.

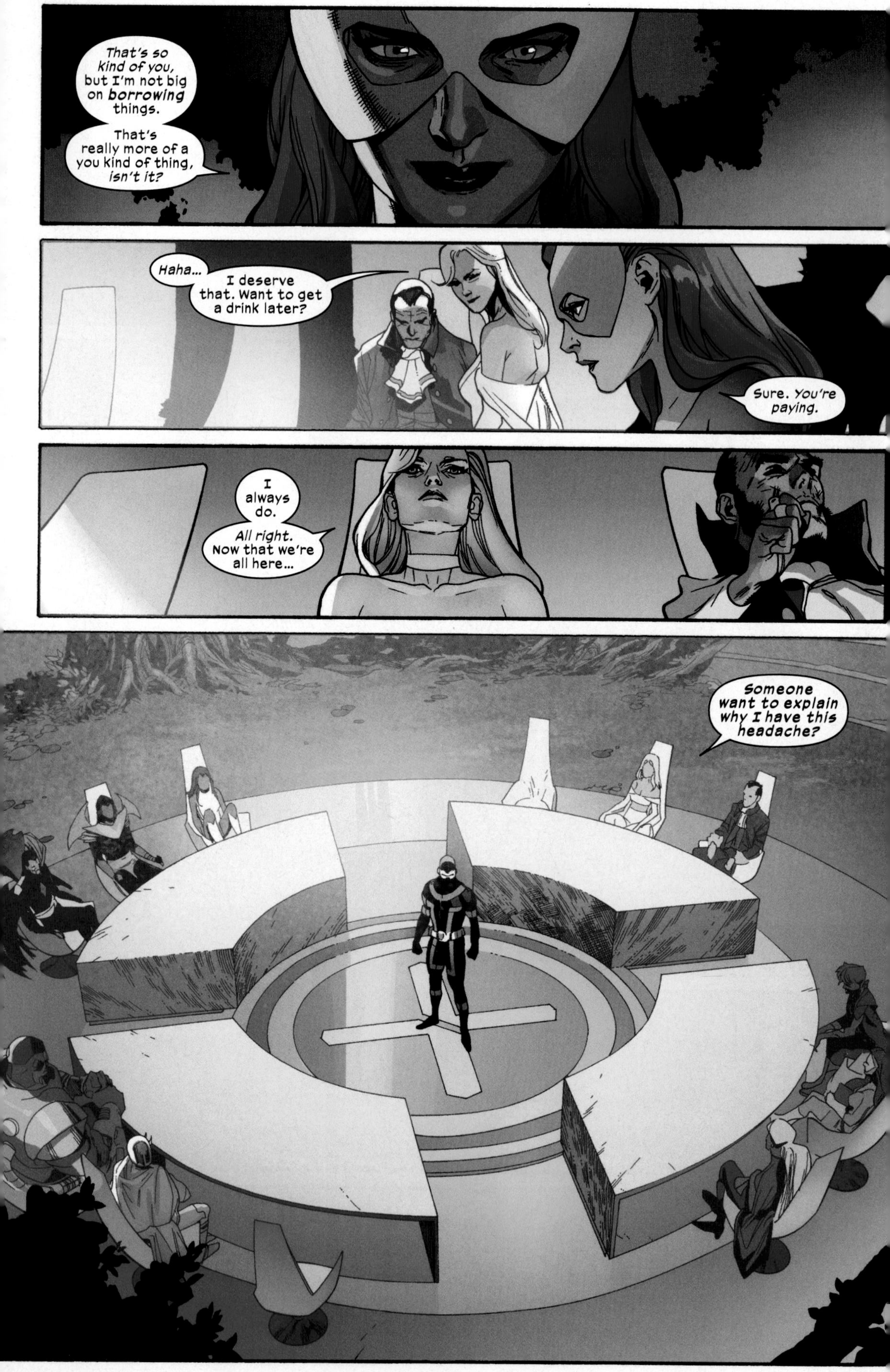
That's so kind of you, but I'm not big on borrowing things.
That's really more of a you kind of thing, isn't it?
Haha...
I deserve that. Want to get a drink later?
Sure. You're paying.
I always do.
All right. Now that we're all here...
Someone want to explain why I have this headache?

KRAKOA IS SCREAMING

SAVAGE LAND GATEWAY NONRESPONSIVE
—

The [suspected] forced seizure of a Krakoan gate has caused Krakoa itself incredible discomfort -- this has resulted in several unexpected, abnormal island disturbances:

— Krakoan wildlife has gotten more aggressive. After a period of over a month with no reported incidences with the island's wildlife, there have been six in the last hour.

— Undetectable to most mutants, Black Tom Cassidy has noted a decrease in island mass. Beast has confirmed this and noted a decrease of .0001 percent, or roughly 158 square feet.

— Finally, all telepaths within the localized manifestation of the island are currently experiencing an increased level of psychic assault/consumption.*

An action team has been tasked with discovering what has happened to the gate and, if possible, re-establishing its connection to Krakoa.

FEED THE ISLAND
—

*As most know, Krakoa "feeds" on the psychic energy of mutants. When the island is at maximum growth [not the contracted, pre-nation state, "winter" version], Krakoa needs to consume two mutants a year to maintain a stable environment. However, the current population of Krakoa means that only a minimal amount of psychic energy is needed from each citizen to maintain the health of the island -- something each mutant is happy to give.

There are aggressive protocols in place to ensure that Krakoa is not exceeding its minimal psychic draw. Two mutants who share similar limitations as the island [mutants who feed on mutants], Selene and Emplate, have been tasked to observe the levels of psychic depletion among the island's mutant population. [Similar protocols are used for the two of them as well.]

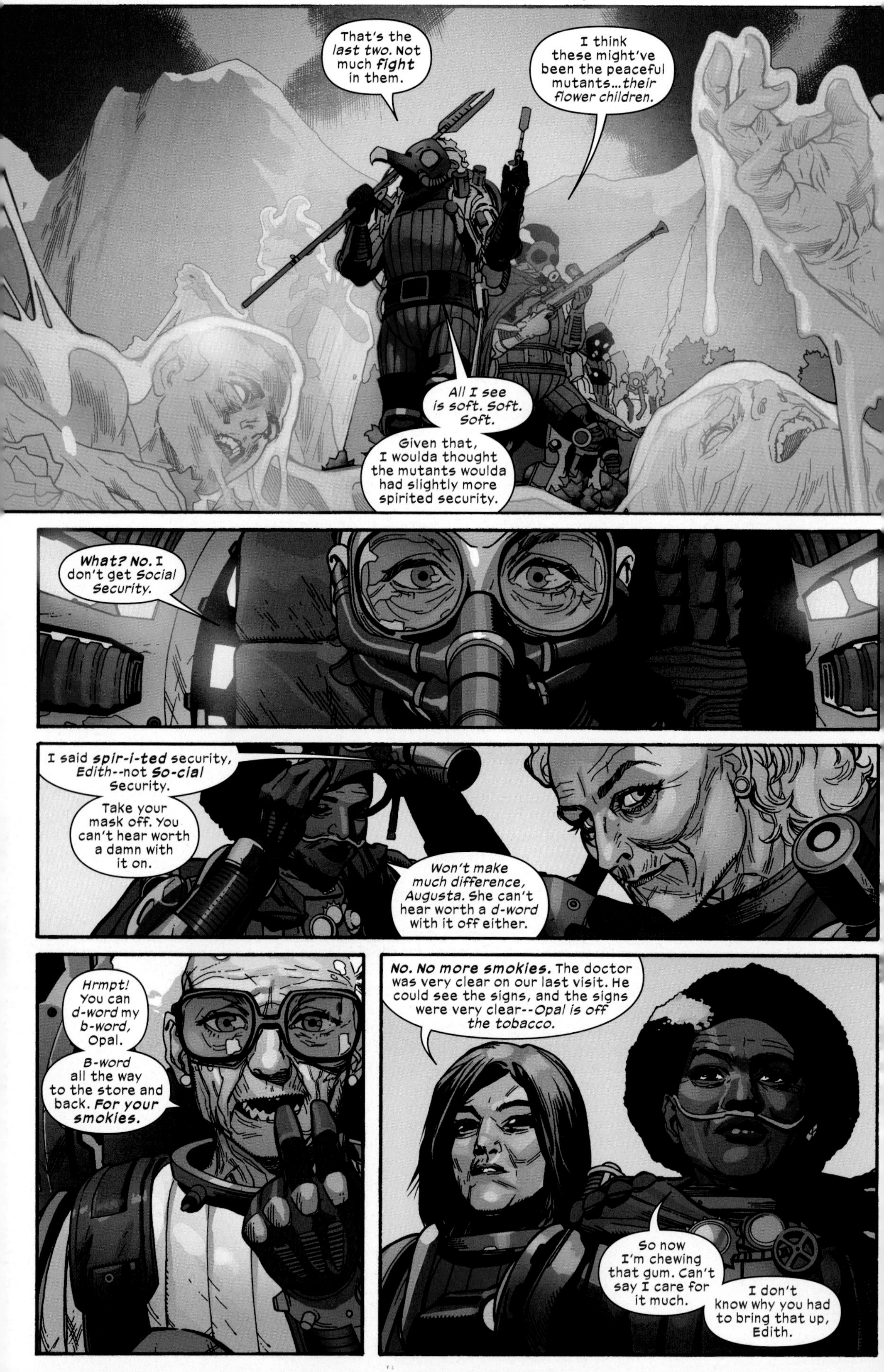
That's the *last two.* Not much ***fight*** in them.
I think these might've been the peaceful mutants...*their flower children.*
All I see is soft. Soft. Soft.
Given that, I woulda thought the mutants woulda had slightly more spirited security.
What? No. I don't get *Social Security.*
I said ***spir-i-ted*** security, *Edith*--not ***So-cial*** Security.
Take your mask off. You can't hear worth a damn with it on.
Won't make much difference, Augusta. She can't hear worth a *d-word* with it off either.
Hrmpt! You can *d-word* my *b-word,* Opal.
B-word all the way to the store and back. ***For your smokies.***
No. No more smokies. The doctor was very clear on our last visit. He could see the signs, and the signs were very clear--*Opal is off the tobacco.*
So now I'm chewing that gum. Can't say I care for it much.
I don't know why you had to bring that up, Edith.

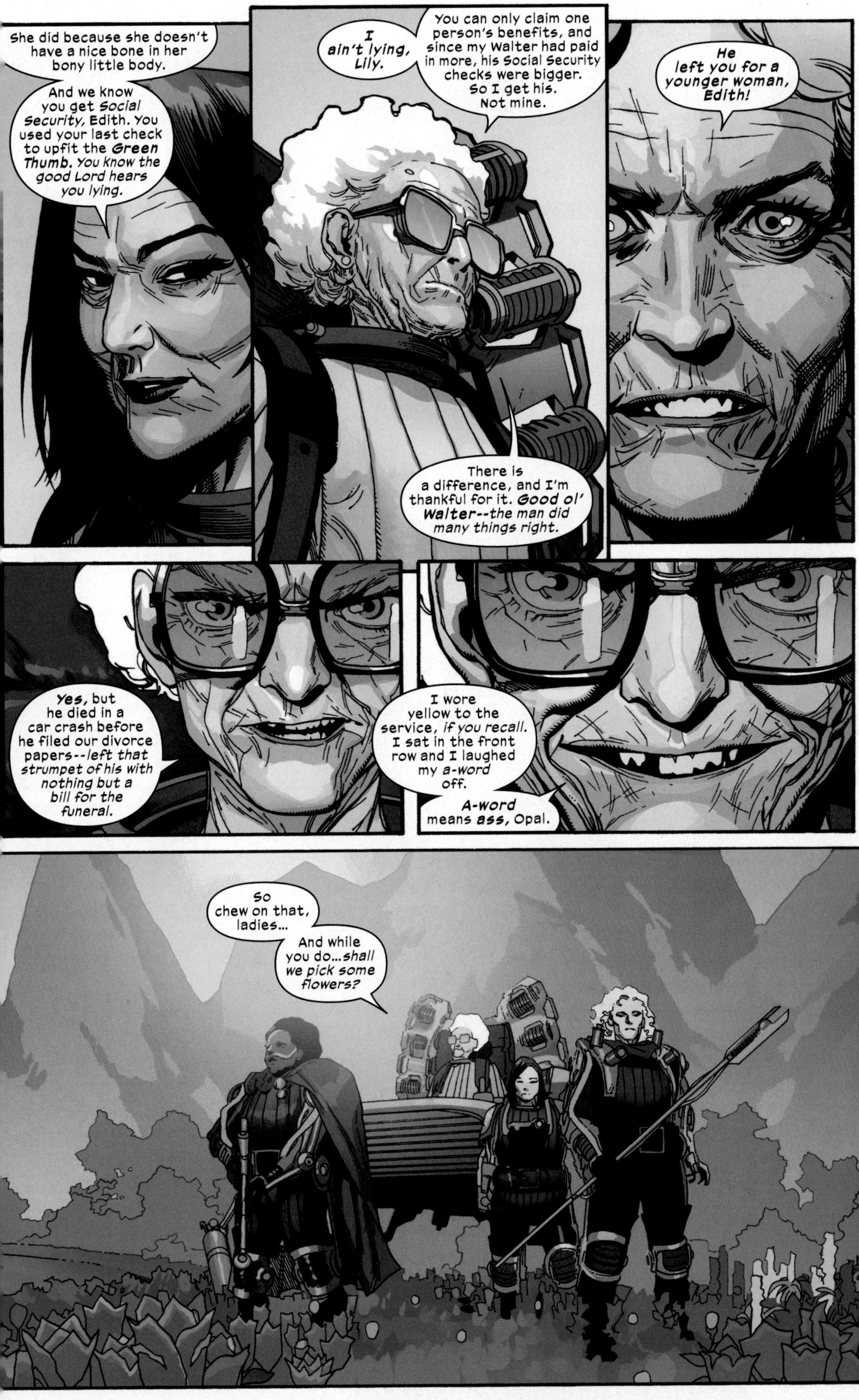
She did because she doesn't have a nice bone in her bony little body.
And we know you get Social Security, Edith. You used your last check to upfit the Green Thumb. You know the good Lord hears you lying.
I ain't lying, Lily.
You can only claim one person's benefits, and since my Walter had paid in more, his Social Security checks were bigger. So I get his. Not mine.
There is a difference, and I'm thankful for it. Good ol' Walter--the man did many things right.
He left you for a younger woman, Edith!
Yes, but he died in a car crash before he filed our divorce papers--left that strumpet of his with nothing but a bill for the funeral.
I wore yellow to the service, if you recall. I sat in the front row and I laughed my a-word off.
A-word means ass, Opal.
So chew on that, ladies...
And while you do...shall we pick some flowers?

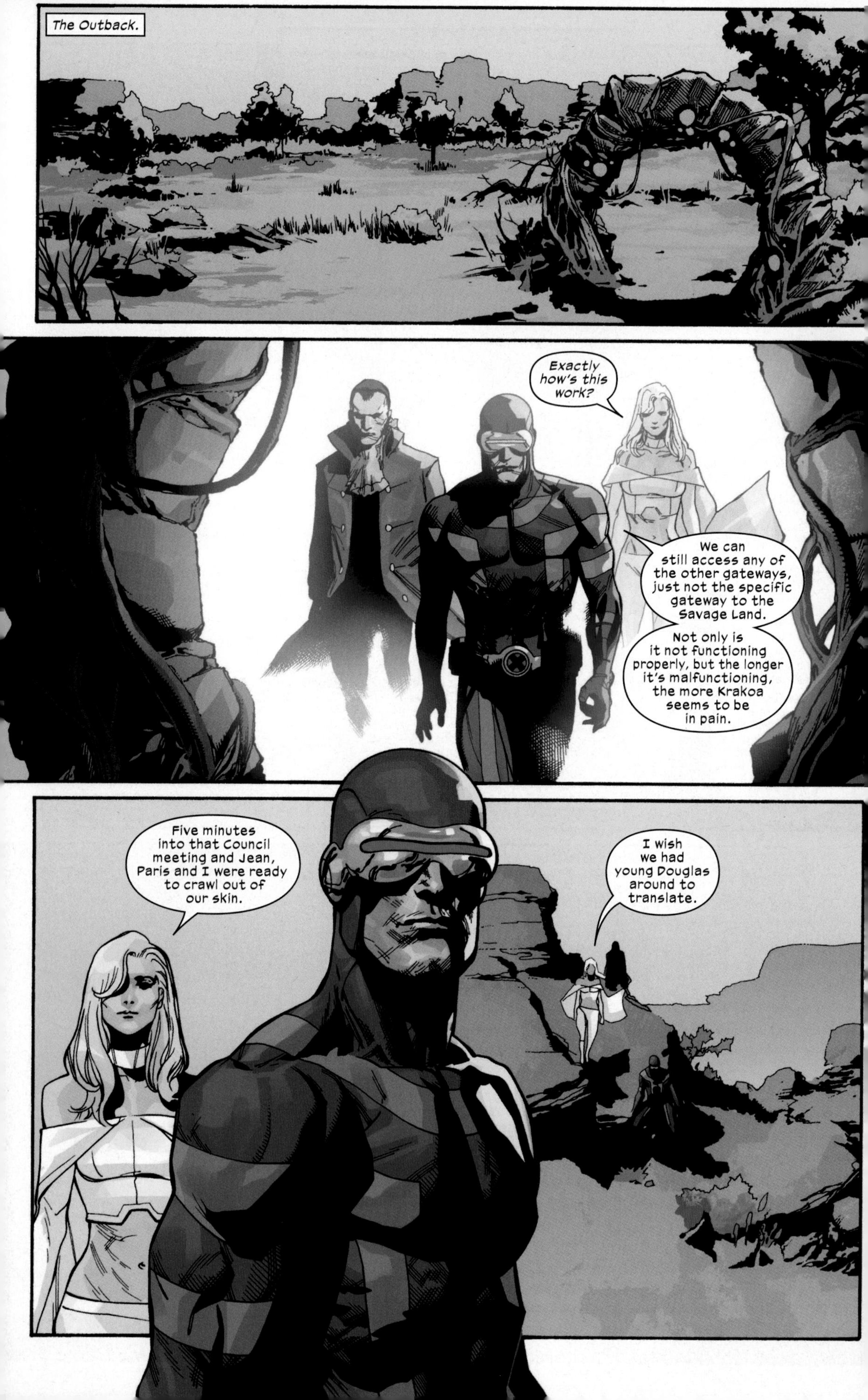
The Outback.
Exactly how's this work?
We can still access any of the other gateways, just not the specific gateway to the Savage Land.
Not only is it not functioning properly, but the longer it's malfunctioning, the more Krakoa seems to be in pain.
Five minutes into that Council meeting and Jean, Paris and I were ready to crawl out of our skin.
I wish we had young Douglas around to translate.

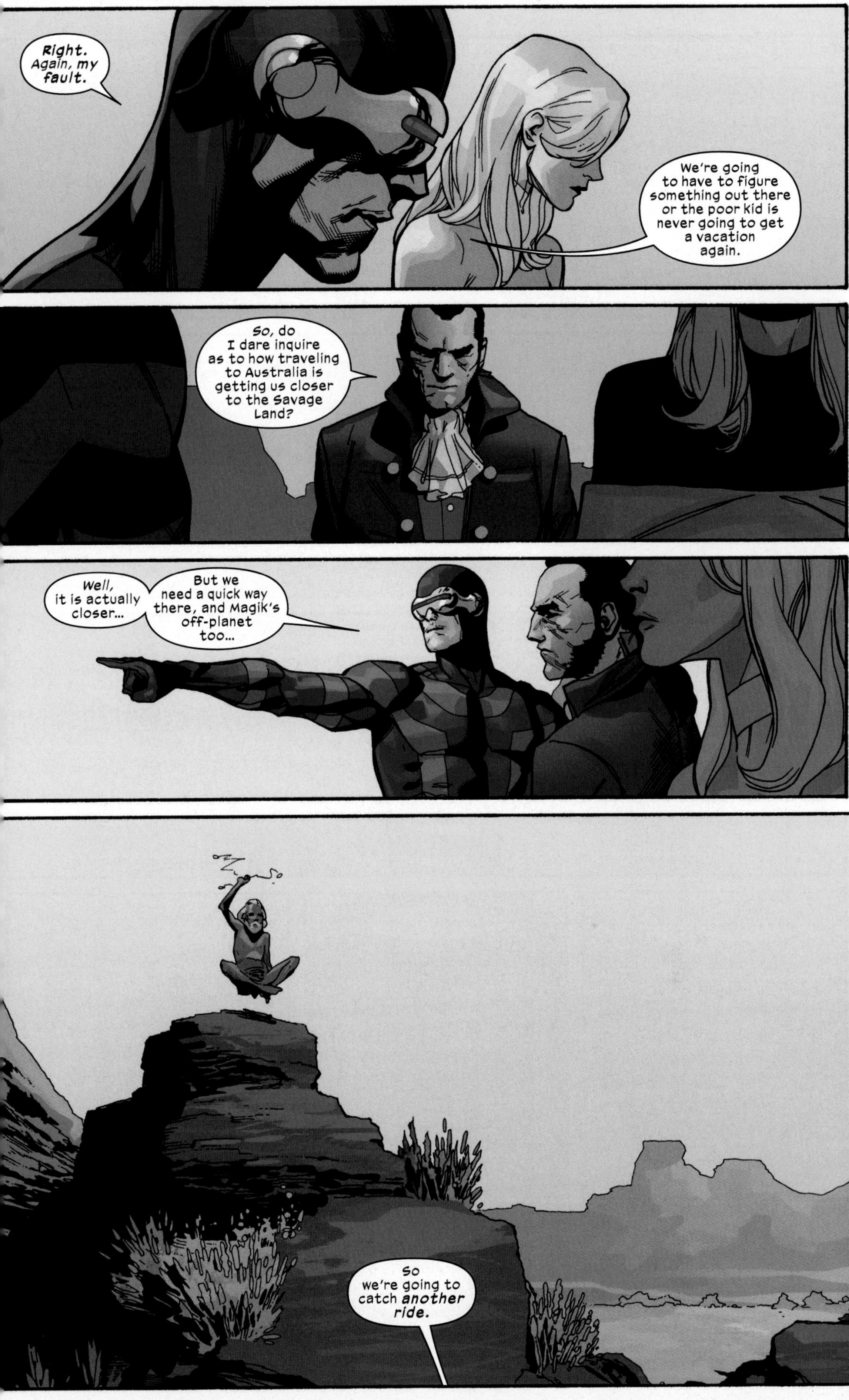
Right. Again, my fault.
We're going to have to figure something out there or the poor kid is never going to get a vacation again.
So, do I dare inquire as to how traveling to Australia is getting us closer to the Savage Land?
Well, it is actually closer...
But we need a quick way there, and Magik's off-planet too...
So we're going to catch another ride.

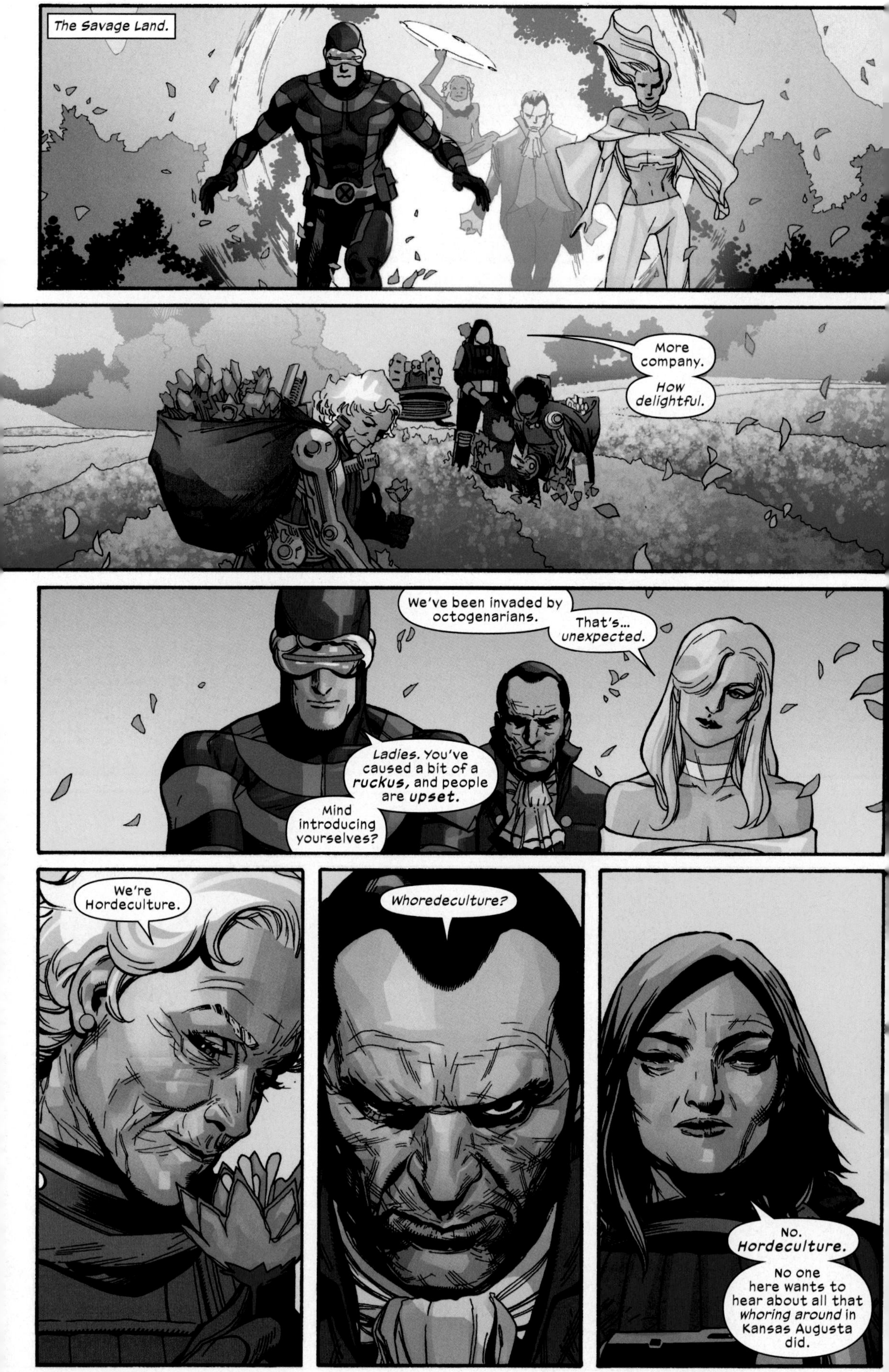
The Savage Land.
More company.
How delightful.
We've been invaded by octogenarians.
That's... unexpected.
Ladies. You've caused a bit of a ruckus, and people are upset.
Mind introducing yourselves?
We're Hordeculture.
Whoredeculture?
No. Hordeculture.
No one here wants to hear about all that whoring around in Kansas Augusta did.

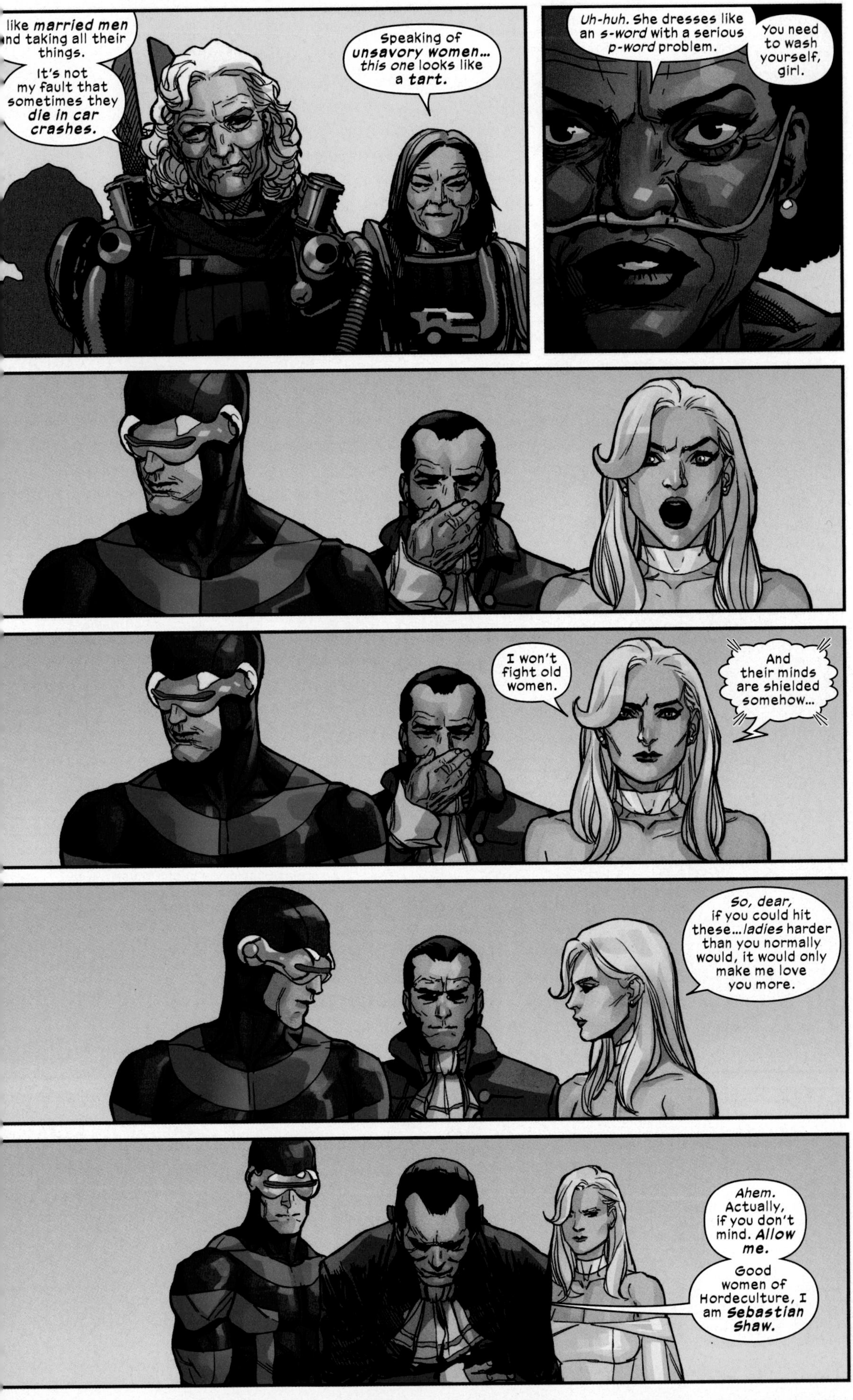

like married men
nd taking all their things.
It's not my fault that sometimes they die in car crashes.
Speaking of unsavory women... this one looks like a tart.
Uh-huh. She dresses like an s-word with a serious p-word problem.
You need to wash yourself, girl.
I won't fight old women.
And their minds are shielded somehow...
So, dear, if you could hit these...ladies harder than you normally would, it would only make me love you more.
Ahem. Actually, if you don't mind. Allow me.
Good women of Hordeculture, I am Sebastian Shaw.

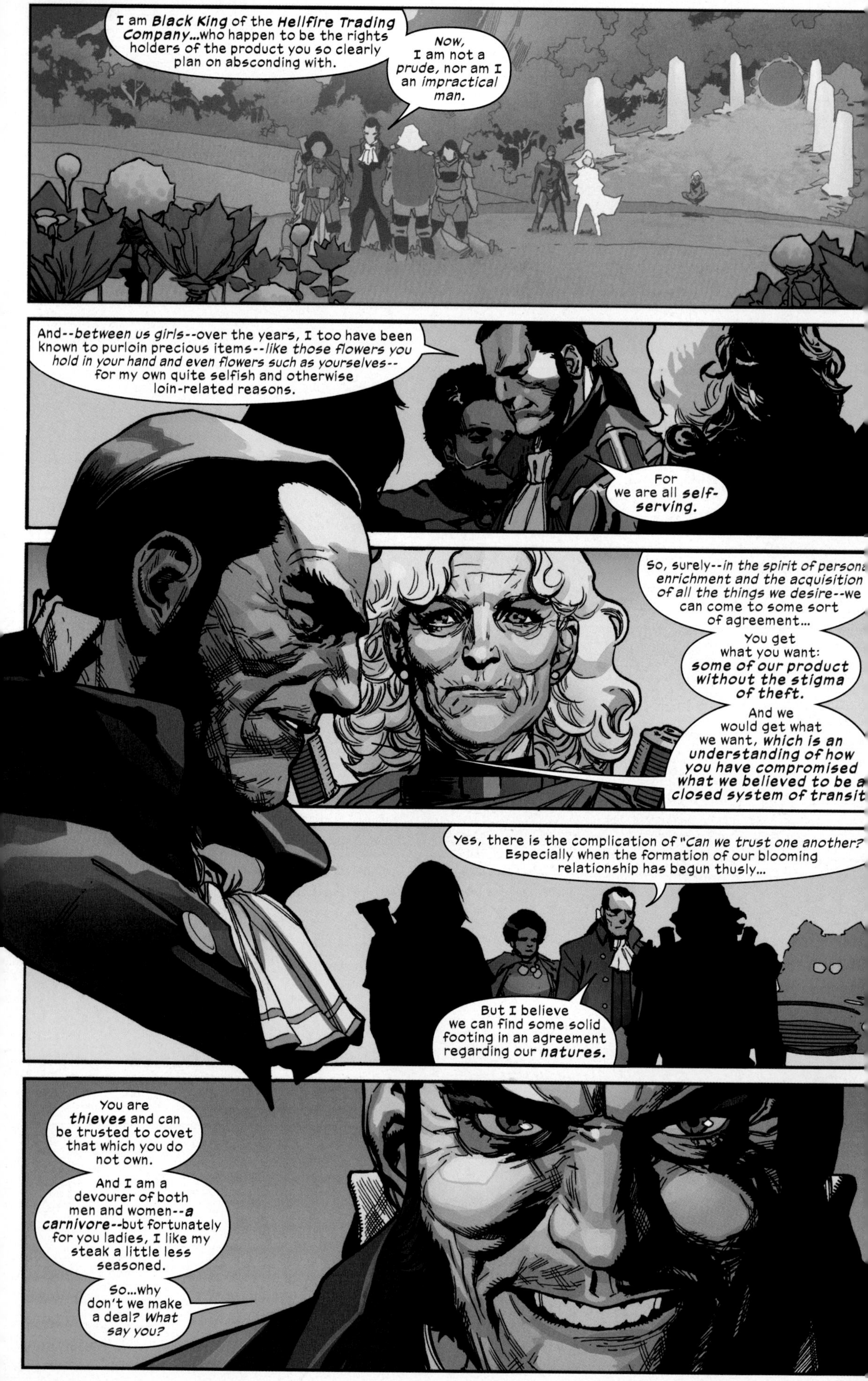
I am Black King of the Hellfire Trading Company...who happen to be the rights holders of the product you so clearly plan on absconding with.
Now, I am not a prude, nor am I an impractical man.
And--between us girls--over the years, I too have been known to purloin precious items--like those flowers you hold in your hand and even flowers such as yourselves--for my own quite selfish and otherwise loin-related reasons.
For we are all self-serving.
So, surely--in the spirit of persona enrichment and the acquisition of all the things we desire--we can come to some sort of agreement...
You get what you want: some of our product without the stigma of theft.
And we would get what we want, which is an understanding of how you have compromised what we believed to be a closed system of transit
Yes, there is the complication of "Can we trust one another? Especially when the formation of our blooming relationship has begun thusly...
But I believe we can find some solid footing in an agreement regarding our natures.
You are thieves and can be trusted to covet that which you do not own.
And I am a devourer of both men and women--a carnivore--but fortunately for you ladies, I like my steak a little less seasoned.
So...why don't we make a deal? What say you?

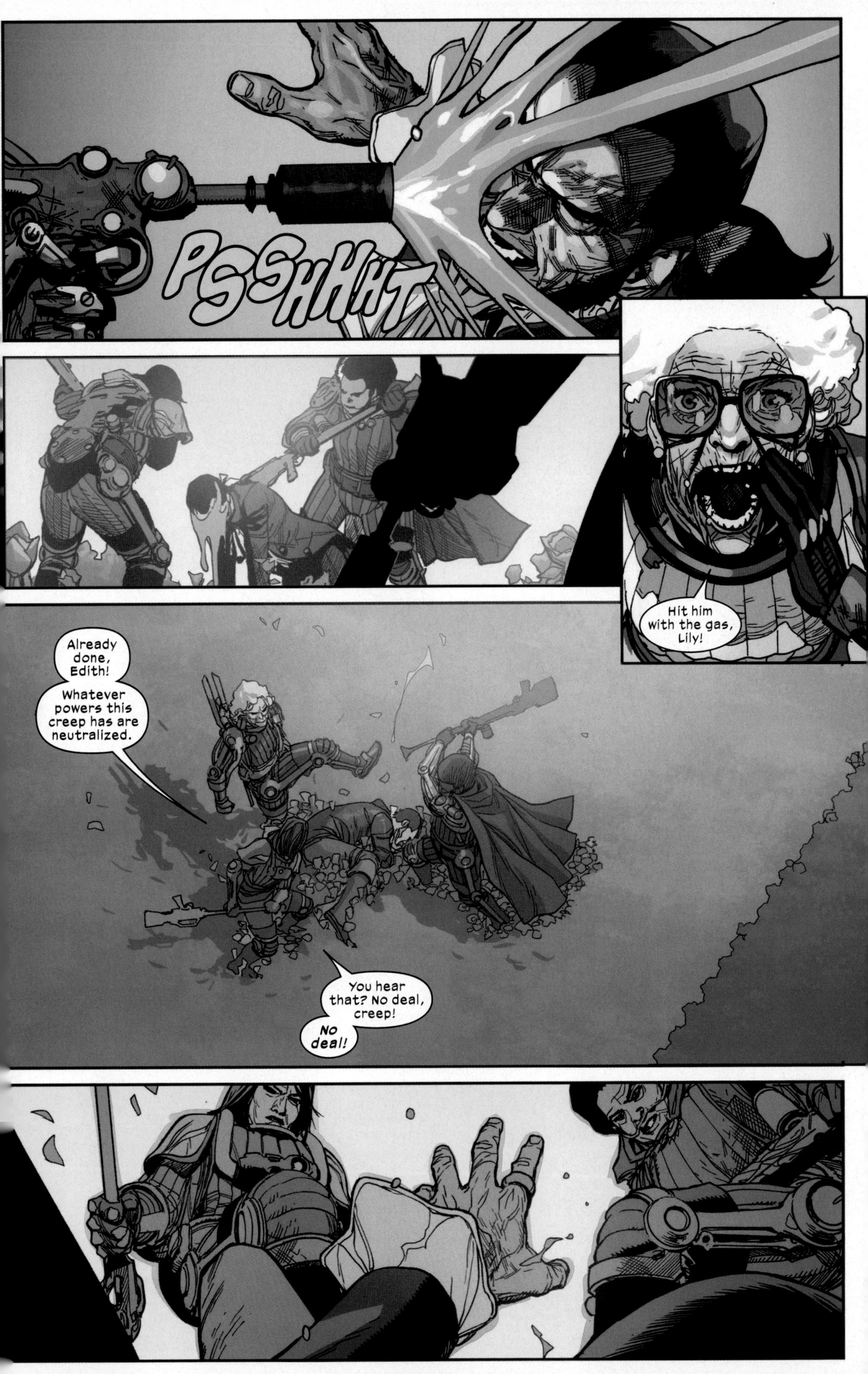
PSSHHHT
Hit him with the gas, Lily!
Already done, Edith!
Whatever powers this creep has are neutralized.
You hear that? No deal, creep!
No deal!

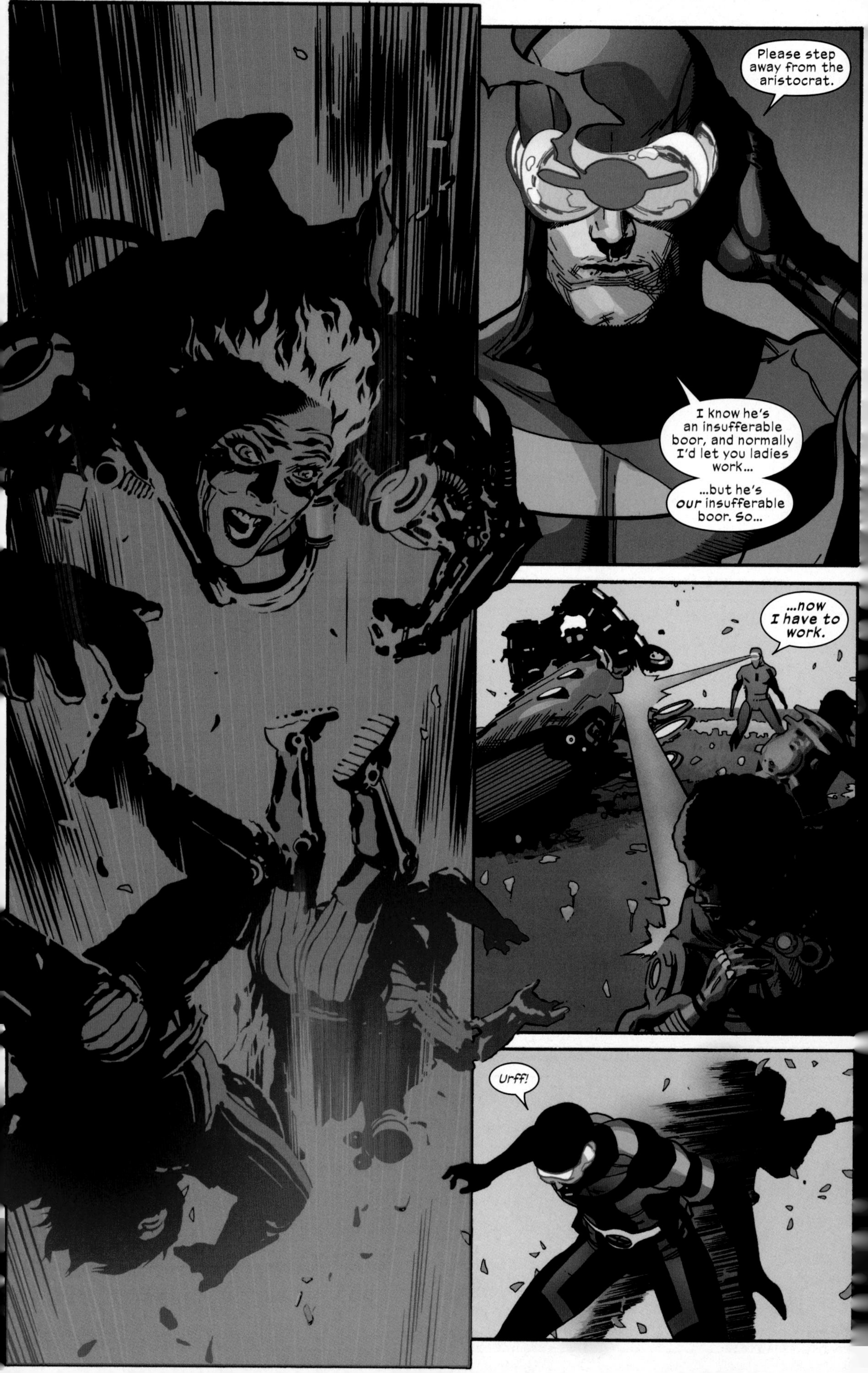
Please step away from the aristocrat.
I know he's an insufferable boor, and normally I'd let you ladies work...
...but he's *our* insufferable boor. So...
...now I have to work.
Urff!

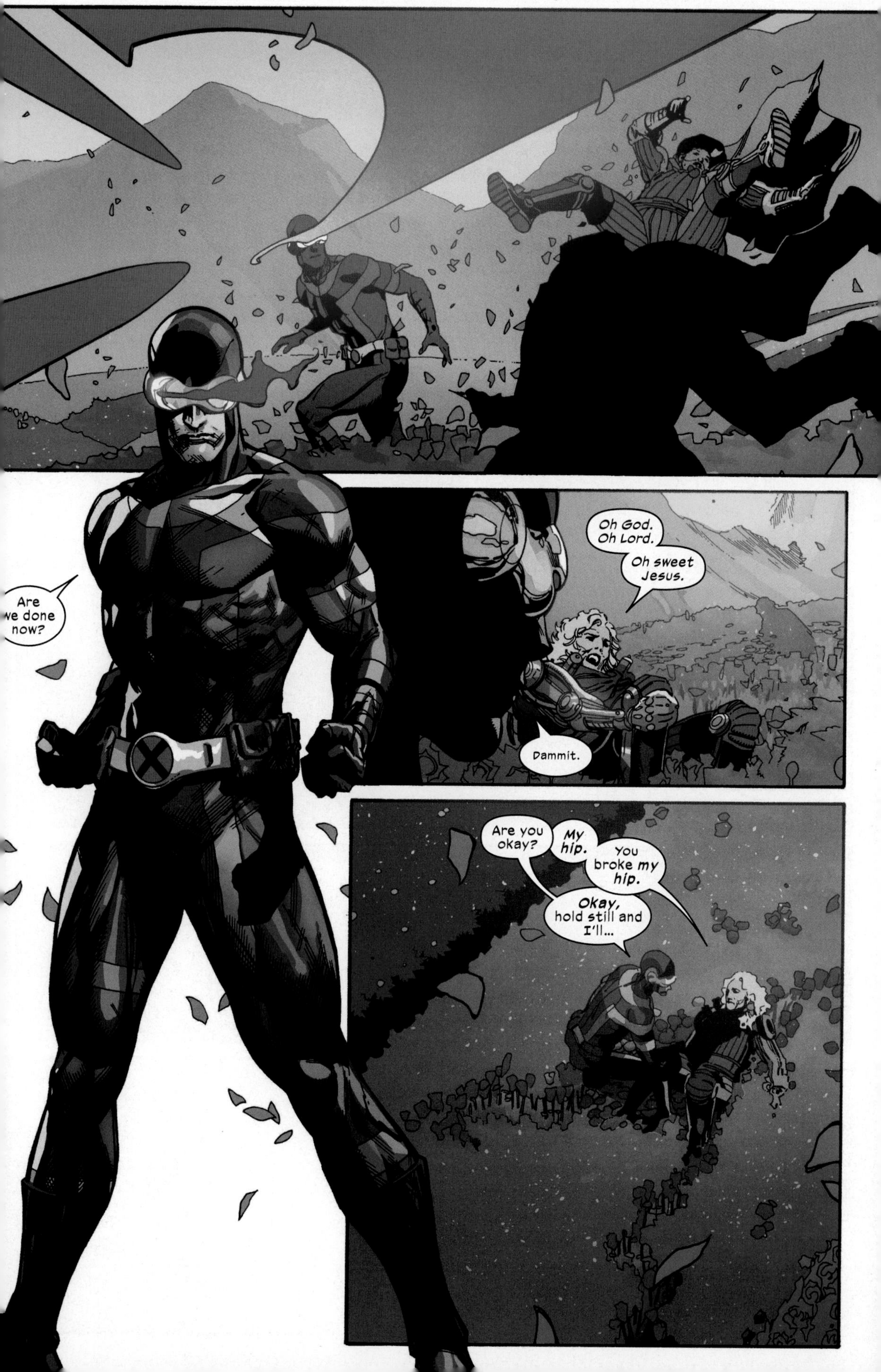
Are we done now?
Oh God. Oh Lord.
Oh sweet Jesus.
Dammit.
Are you okay?
My hip.
You broke my hip.
Okay, hold still and I'll...

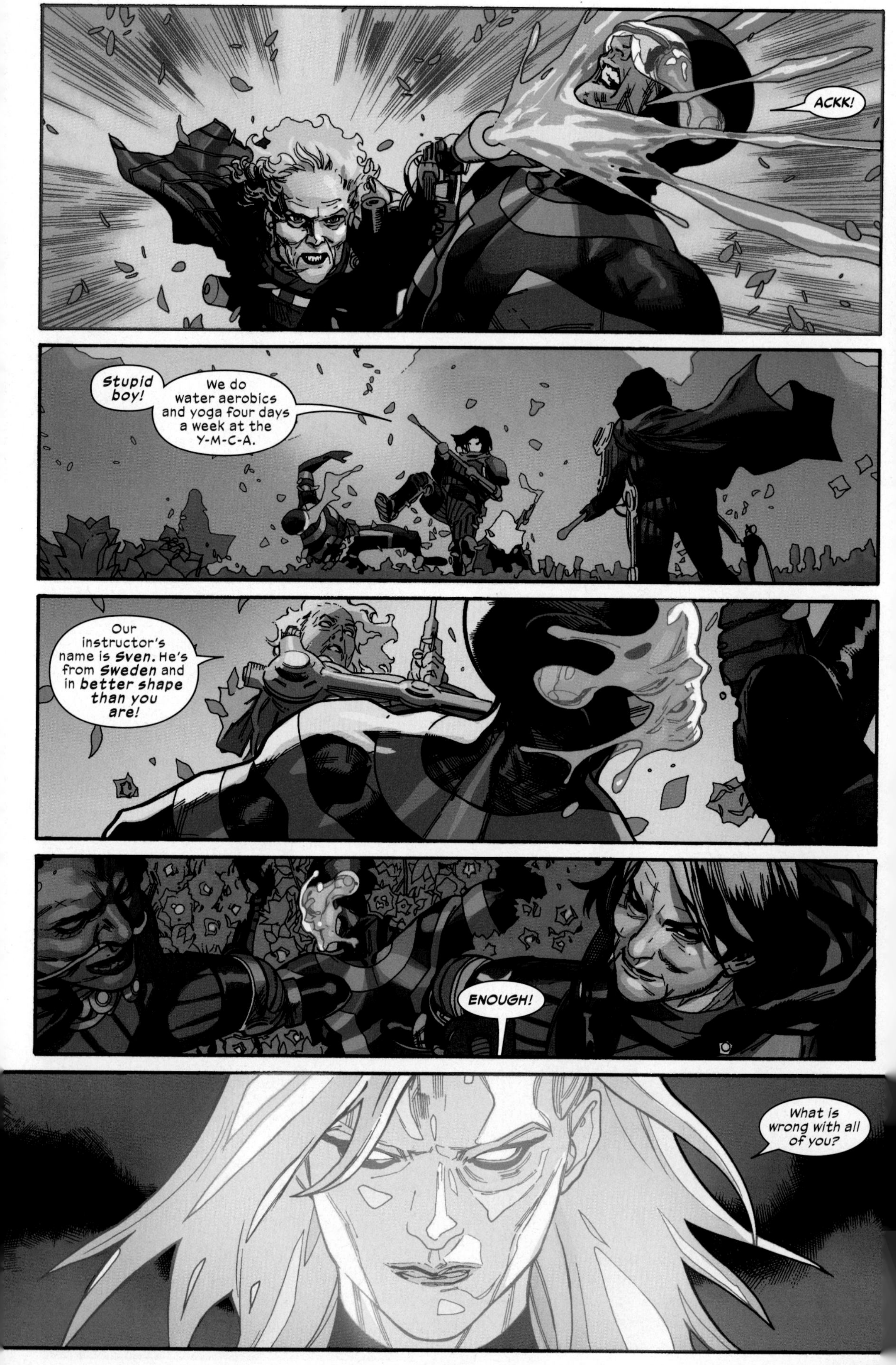

ACKK!
Stupid boy!
We do water aerobics and yoga four days a week at the Y-M-C-A.
Our instructor's name is Sven. He's from Sweden and in better shape than you are!
ENOUGH!
What is wrong with all of you?

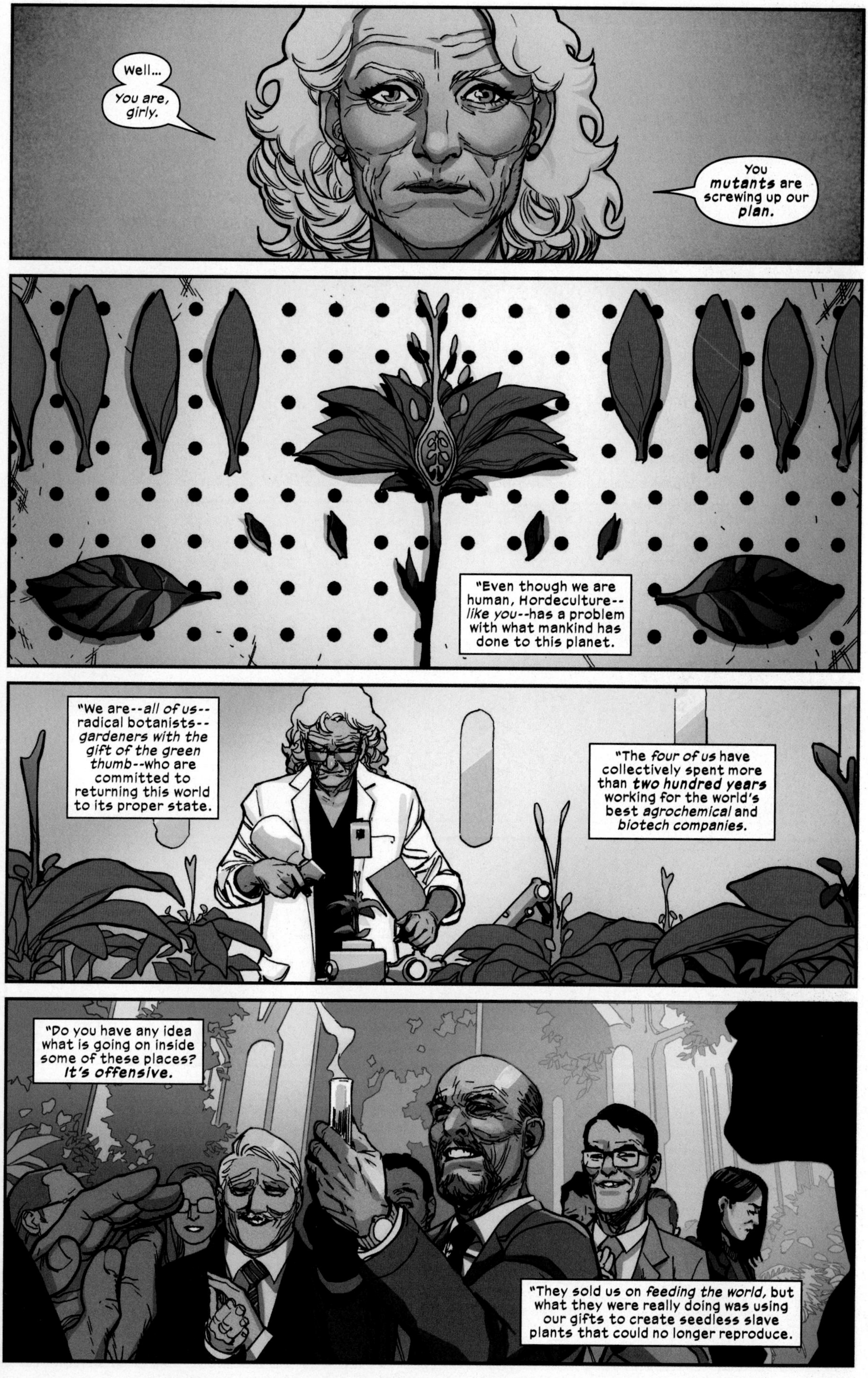
Well...
You are, girly.
You mutants are screwing up our plan.
"Even though we are human, Hordeculture--like you--has a problem with what mankind has done to this planet.
"We are--all of us--radical botanists--gardeners with the gift of the green thumb--who are committed to returning this world to its proper state.
"The four of us have collectively spent more than two hundred years working for the world's best agrochemical and biotech companies.
"Do you have any idea what is going on inside some of these places? It's offensive.
"They sold us on feeding the world, but what they were really doing was using our gifts to create seedless slave plants that could no longer reproduce.

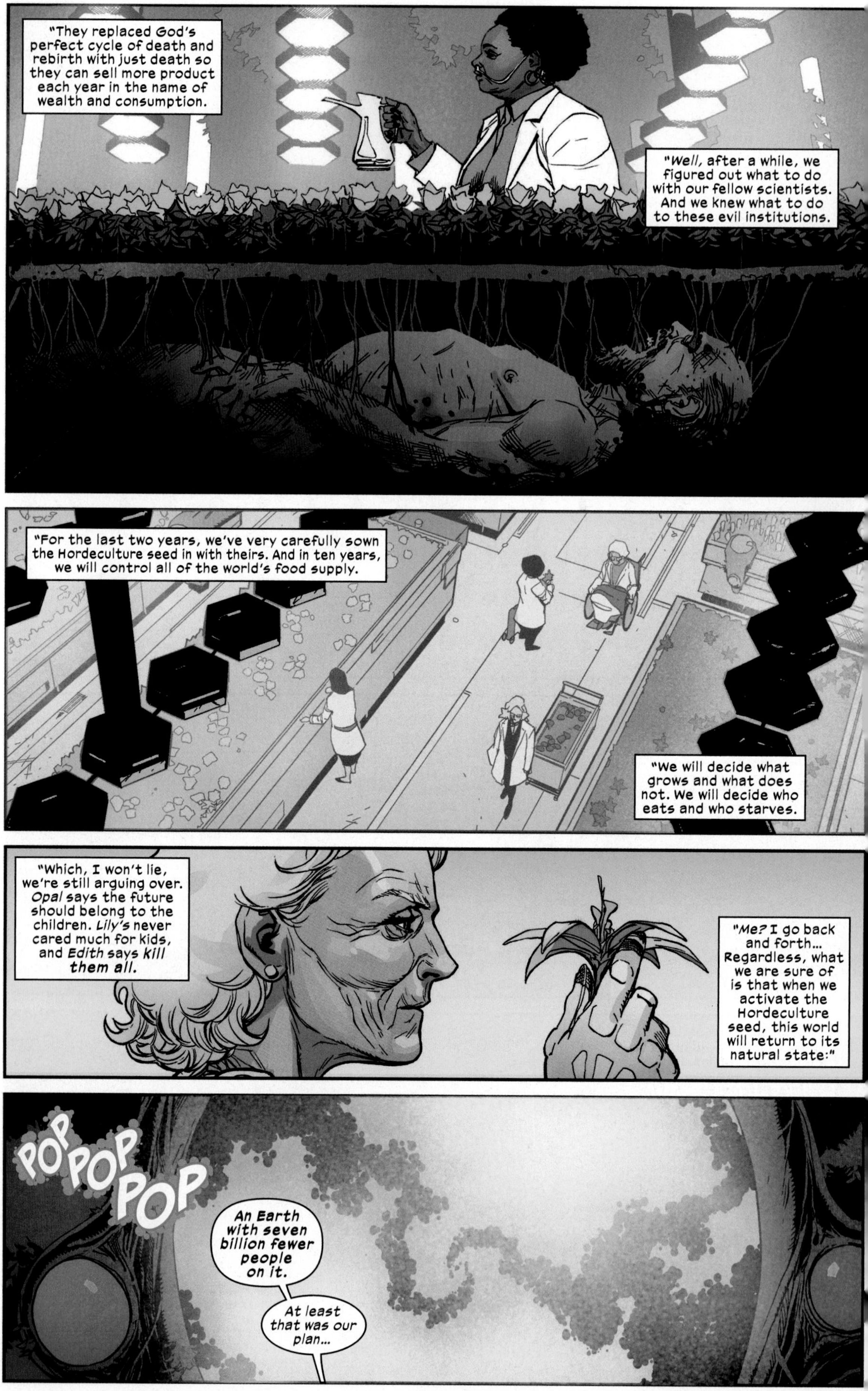
"They replaced God's perfect cycle of death and rebirth with just death so they can sell more product each year in the name of wealth and consumption.
"Well, after a while, we figured out what to do with our fellow scientists. And we knew what to do to these evil institutions.
"For the last two years, we've very carefully sown the Hordeculture seed in with theirs. And in ten years, we will control all of the world's food supply.
"We will decide what grows and what does not. We will decide who eats and who starves.
"Which, I won't lie, we're still arguing over. Opal says the future should belong to the children. Lily's never cared much for kids, and Edith says kill them all.
"Me? I go back and forth... Regardless, what we are sure of is that when we activate the Hordeculture seed, this world will return to its natural state:"
POP POP POP
An Earth with seven billion fewer people on it.
At least that was our plan...

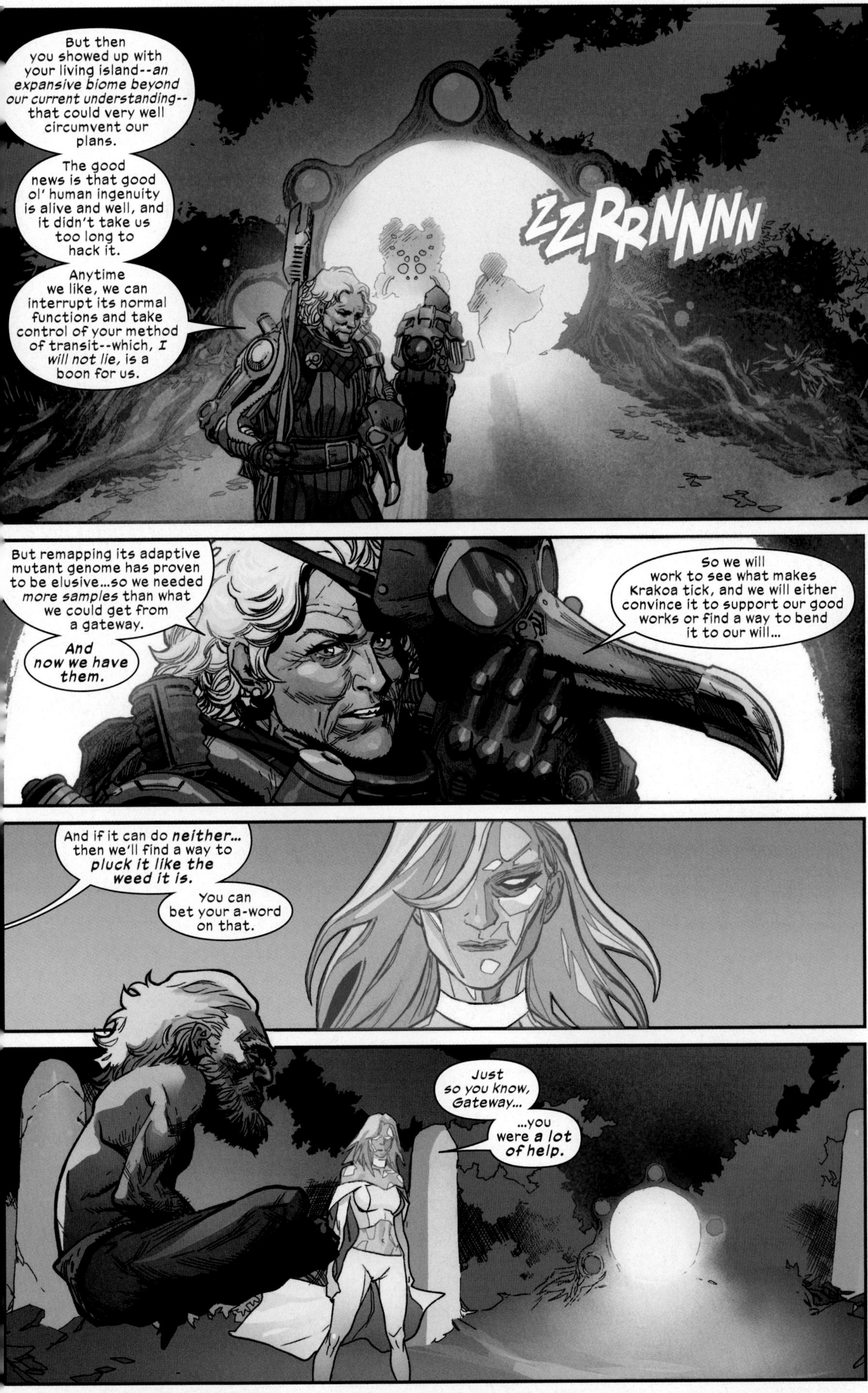

But then you showed up with your living island--*an expansive biome beyond our current understanding*--that could very well circumvent our plans.
The good news is that good ol' human ingenuity is alive and well, and it didn't take us too long to hack it.
Anytime we like, we can interrupt its normal functions and take control of your method of transit--which, *I will not lie,* is a boon for us.
ZZRRRNNNN
But remapping its adaptive mutant genome has proven to be elusive...so we needed *more samples* than what we could get from a gateway.
And now we have them.
So we will work to see what makes Krakoa tick, and we will either convince it to support our good works or find a way to bend it to our will...
And if it can do *neither*... then we'll find a way to *pluck it like the weed it is.*
You can bet your a-word on that.
Just so you know, Gateway...
...you were a *lot of help.*

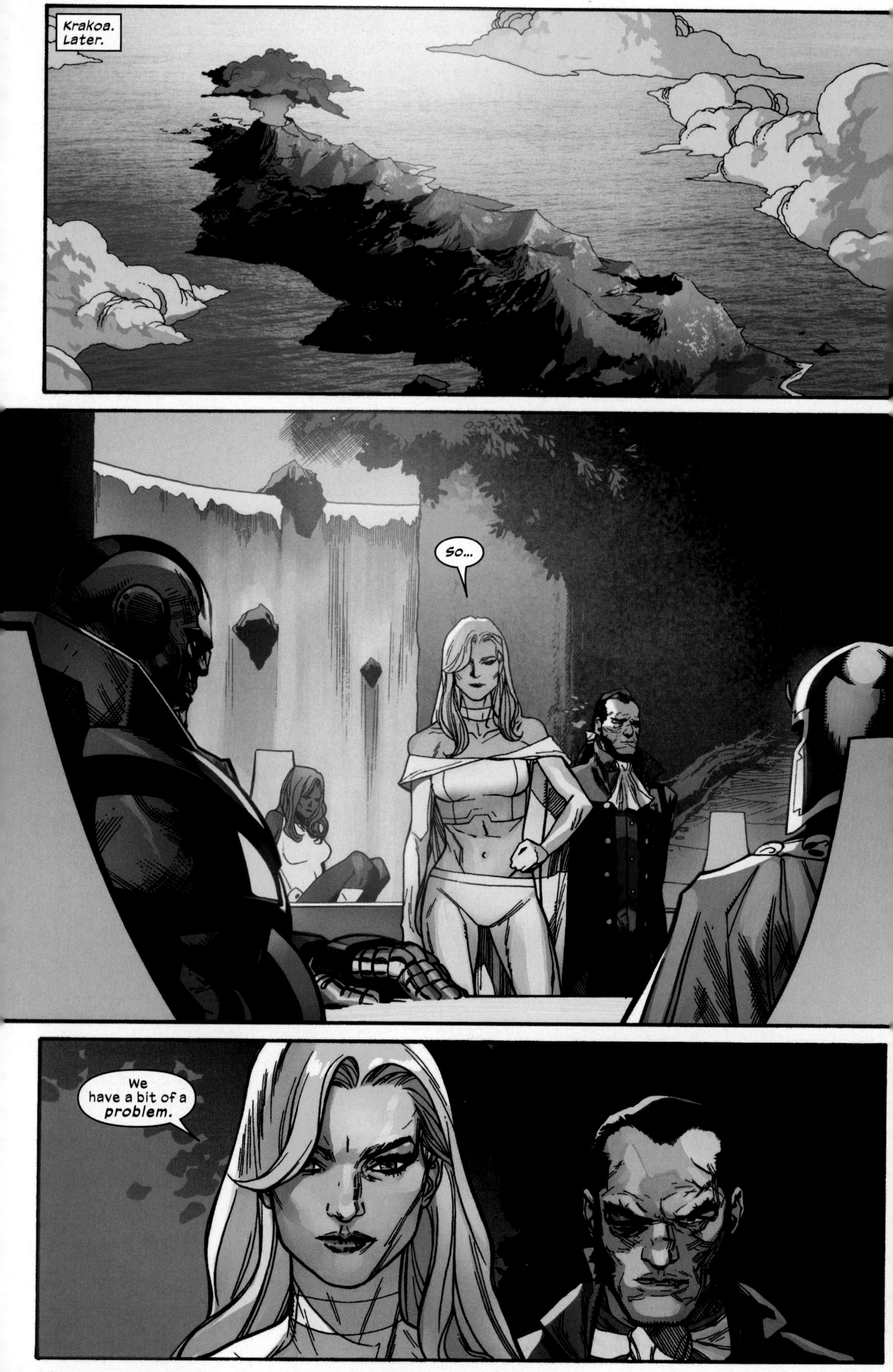

Krakoa. Later.
So...
We have a bit of a problem.

HORDECULTURE IS:

A collaborative group of like-minded agrochemists, biotechnolo-gists and bioengineers who specialize in the genetic manipulation of -- and propagation of -- all things botanical. Their goal is the radical depopulation of humanity and the return of the planet to what they would consider a more pristine state.

Beyond genetic modifications believed to have been made to themselves [unconfirmed outside of a documented resistance to telepathy], the women of Hordeculture are experts at manipulating the environment to suit their extinction agenda.

While it is unknown if there are more than four members of Hordeculture, the known existing members are:

AUGUSTA BROMES
Agrochemist, 64 years old.
Best friends with Opal.

OPAL VETIVER
Bioengineer, 68 years old.
Best friends with Augusta.

LILY LEYMUS
Geneticist, 71 years old.
Thinks she's best friends with Opal but isn't.

EDITH SCUTCH
Botanical engineer, 81 years old.
Don't need friends, don't want 'em.

—

The Green Thumb is a mobile base of operations designed and built by Edith. It is currently located in Sedona, Arizona, but will move when the current lunar cycle completes.

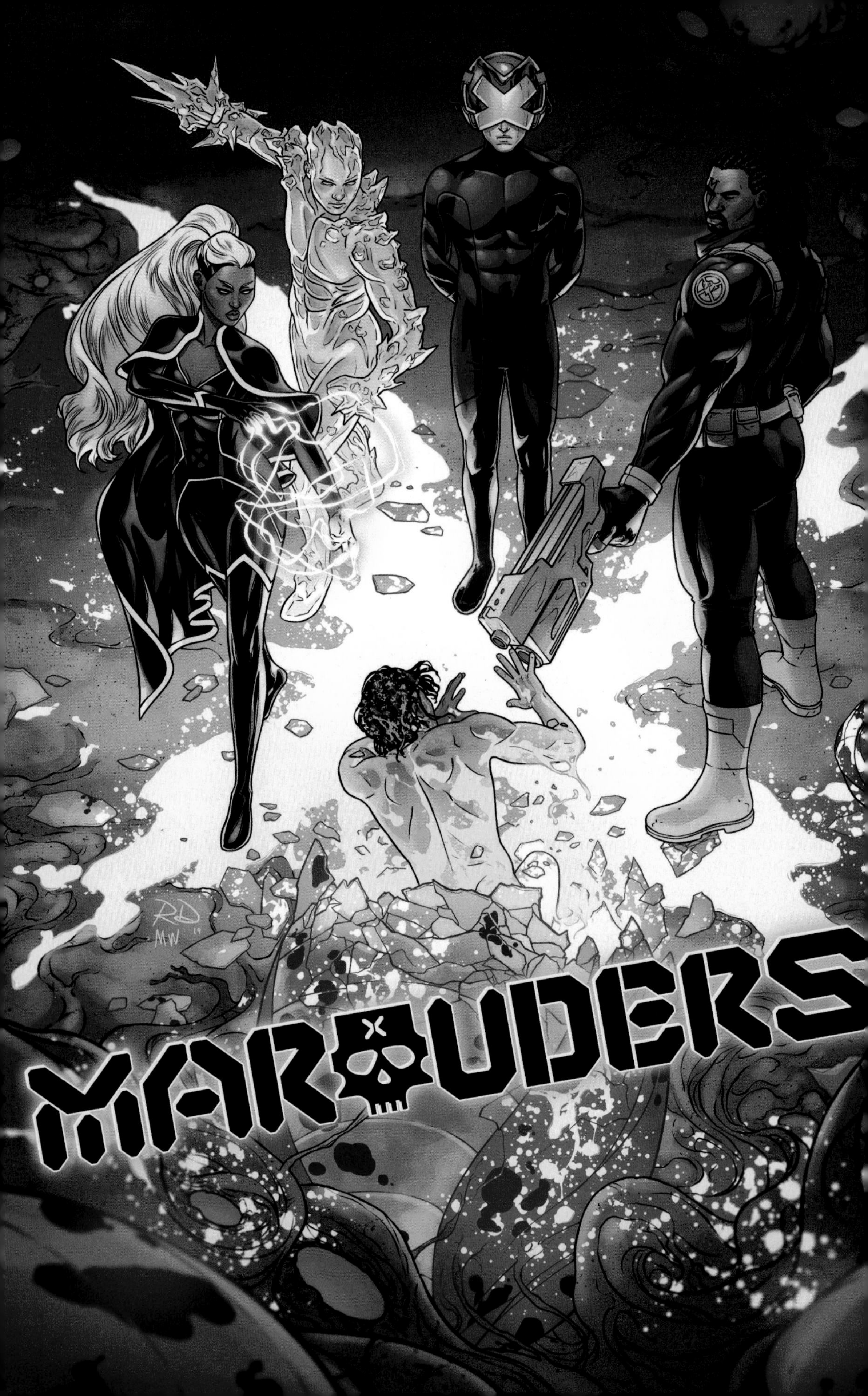
RD
MW '19
MARAUDERS

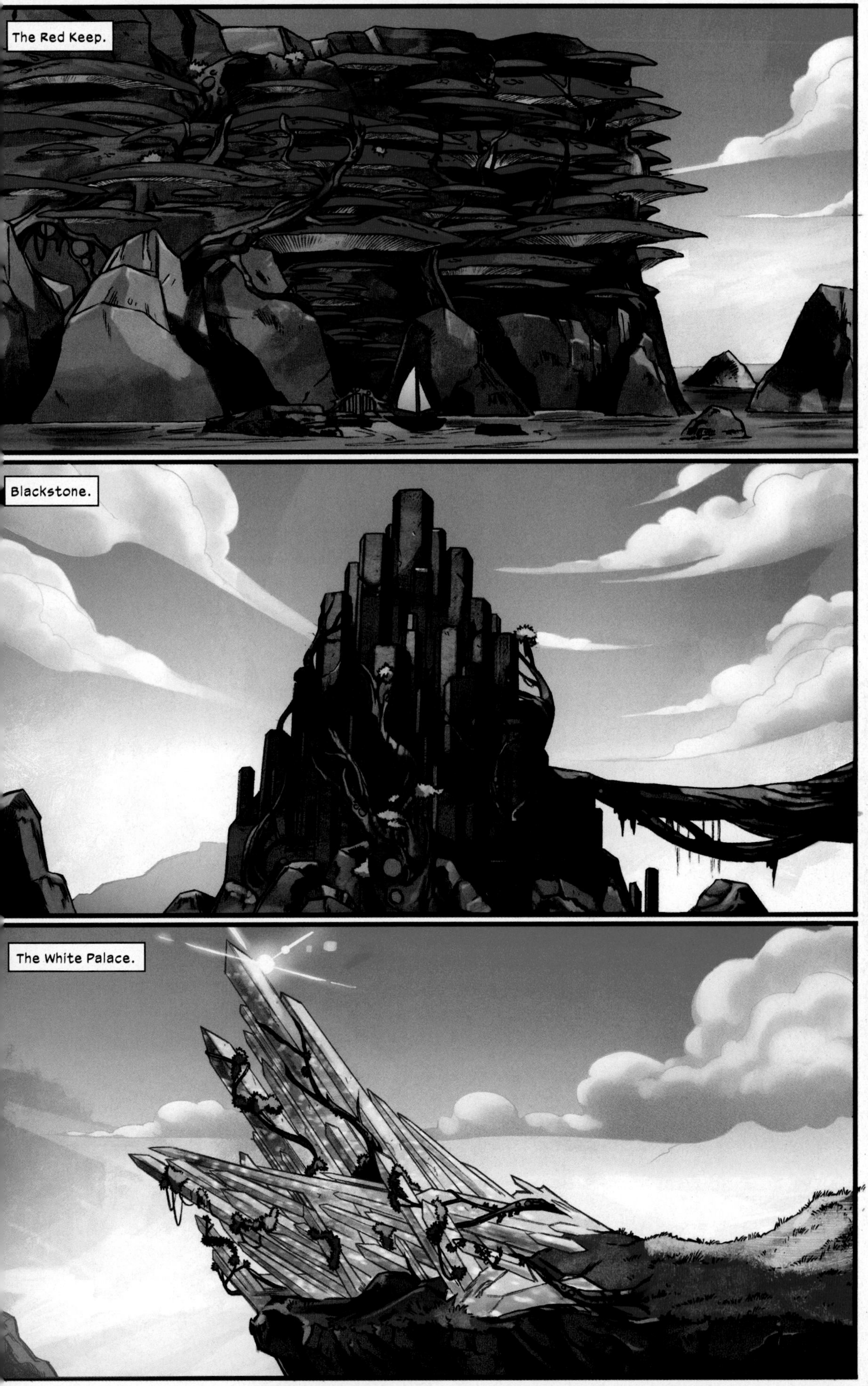
The Red Keep.
Blackstone.
The White Palace.

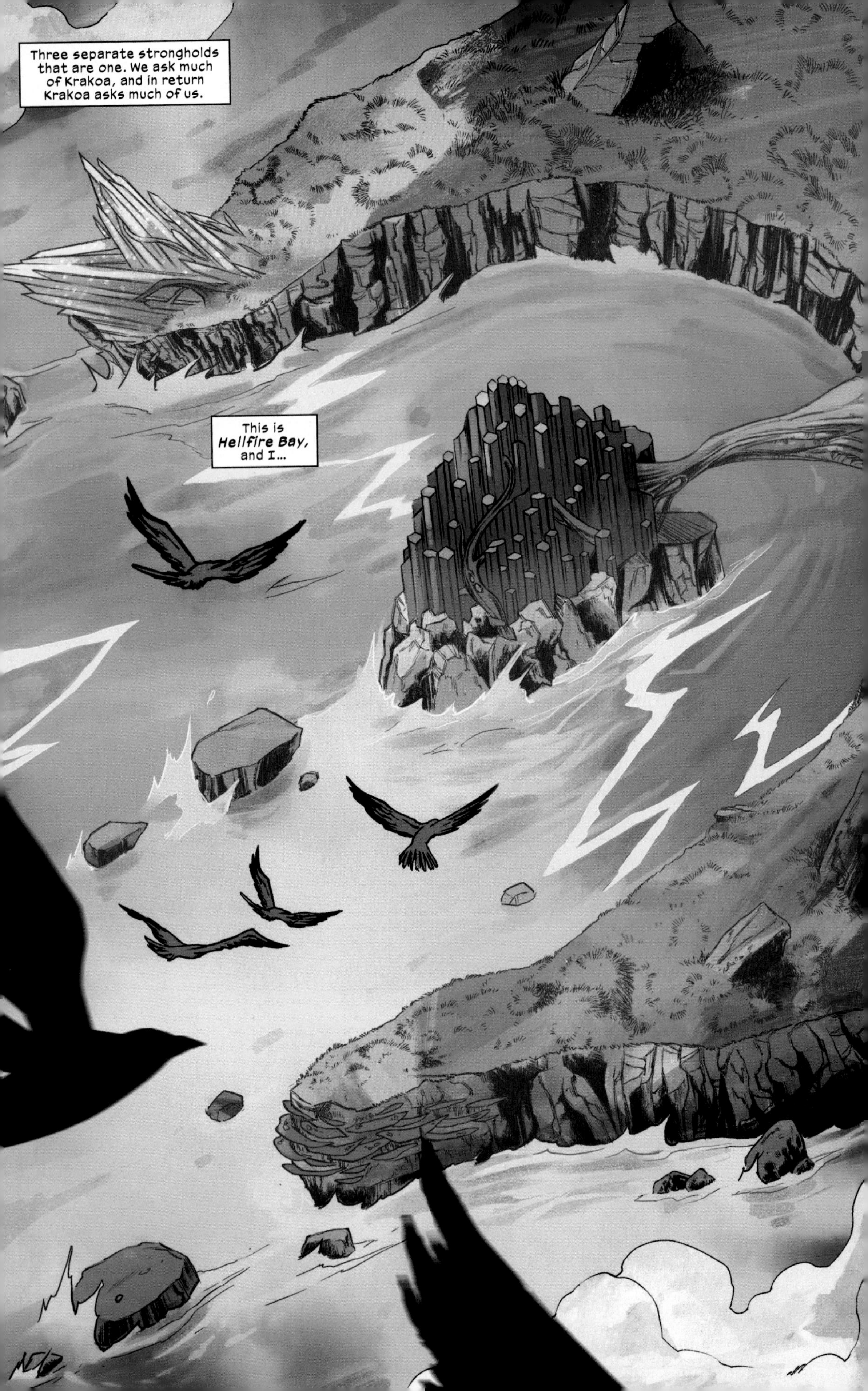
Three separate strongholds that are one. We ask much of Krakoa, and in return Krakoa asks much of us.
This is *Hellfire Bay*, and I...

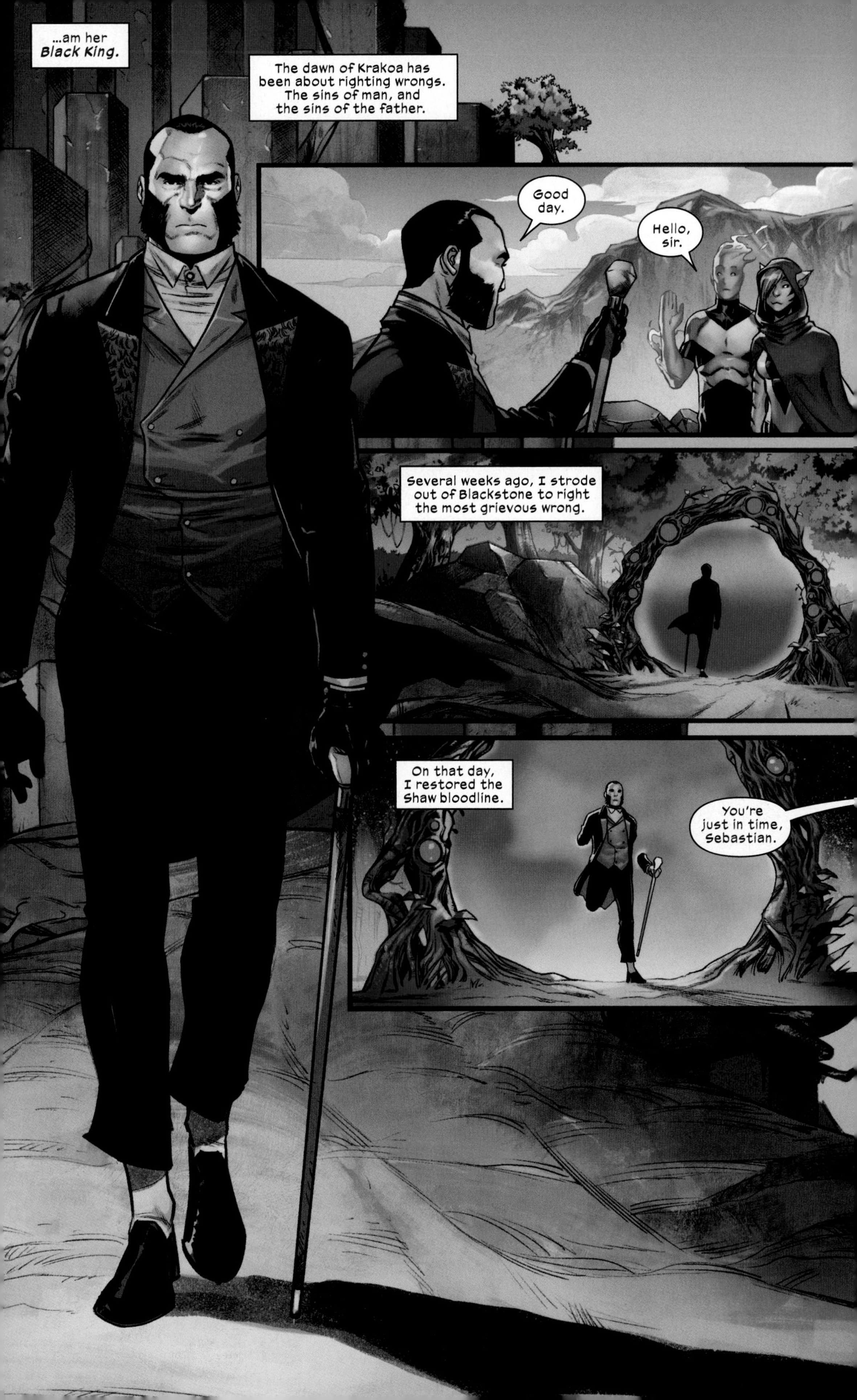

...am her *Black King.*
The dawn of Krakoa has been about righting wrongs. The sins of man, and the sins of the father.
Good day.
Hello, sir.
Several weeks ago, I strode out of Blackstone to right the most grievous wrong.
On that day, I restored the Shaw bloodline.
You're just in time, Sebastian.

[00_mutant_piracy]
[00_sea_shores_X_]

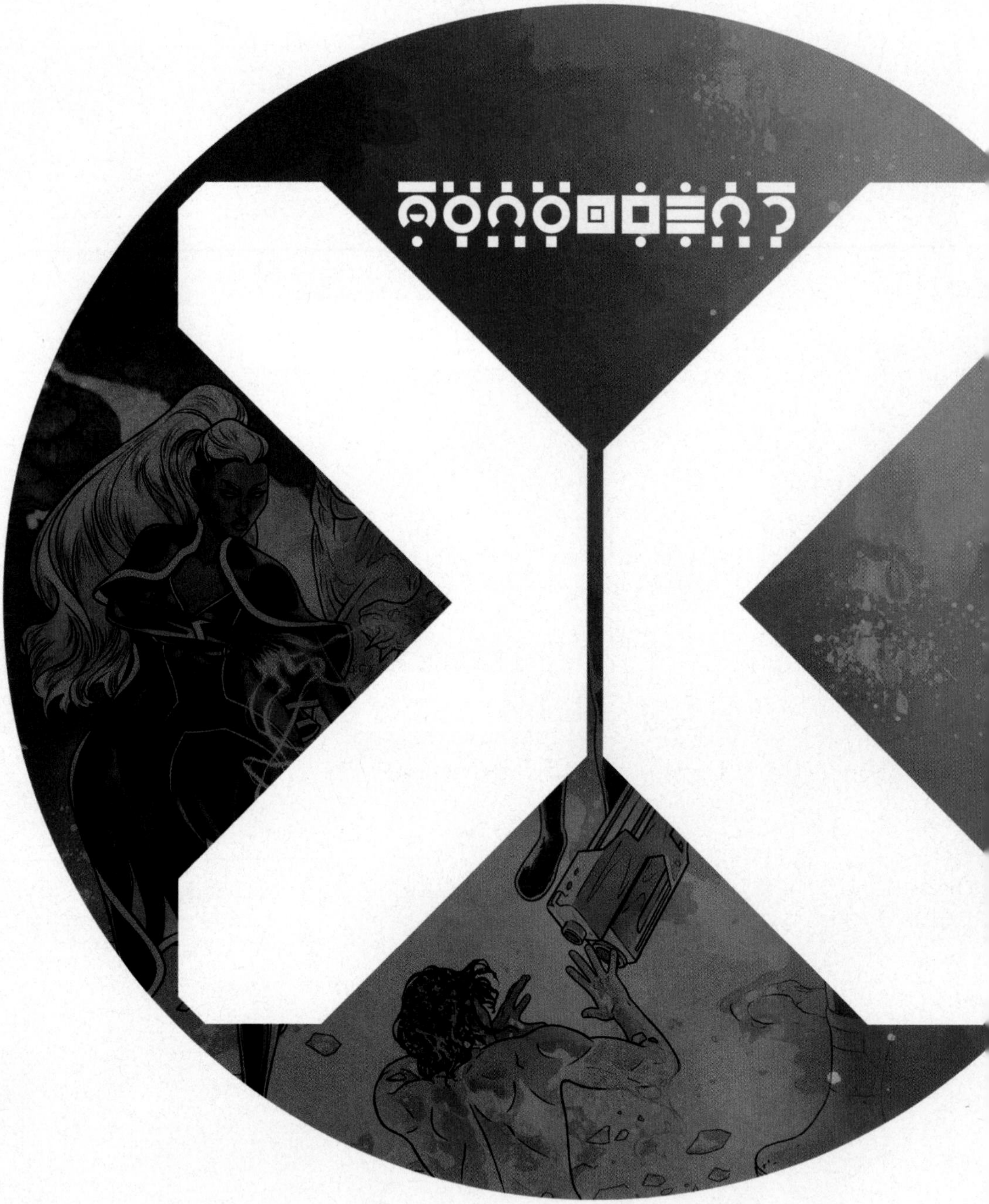

[00_mutant_piracy
[00_sea_shores_X_

GERRY DUGGAN..................................[WRITER]
MICHELE BANDINI...............................[ARTIST]
MICHELE BANDINI & ELISABETTA D'AMICO...........[INKERS]
FEDERICO BLEE...........................[COLOR ARTIST]
VC's CORY PETIT.............................[LETTERER]
TOM MULLER....................................[DESIGN]

RUSSELL DAUTERMAN & MATTHEW WILSON......[COVER ARTISTS]

JEEHYUNG LEE....................[VARIANT COVER ARTIST]

JAY BOWEN.................................[PRODUCTION]

JONATHAN HICKMAN............................[HEAD OF X]
CHRIS ROBINSON.......................[ASSISTANT EDITOR]
JORDAN D. WHITE.................................[EDITOR]
C.B. CEBULSKI.........................[EDITOR IN CHIEF]
JOE QUESADA.....................[CHIEF CREATIVE OFFICER]
DAN BUCKLEY..................................[PRESIDENT]
ALAN FINE.........................[EXECUTIVE PRODUCER]

[03] MARAUDERS

[ISSUE THREE]......THE BISHOP IN BLACK

[00_mutant_piracy]
[00_sea_shores_X_]

[00_00...0]
[00_00...3]

[00_boat__]
[00_______]

[00_______]

[00______X]

[kra_[0.3]
[koa_[0.3]

[kra_[0.X]
[koa_[0.X]

RECLAMATION

Mutants around the world are flocking to the island-nation of Krakoa for safety, security and to be part of the first mutant society.

The Hellfire Trading Company, responsible for distributing Krakoa's pharmaceuticals to friendly nations and smuggling mutants out of unfriendly ones, has just added a third leader to its organization: Red Queen Kate Pryde, captain of the *Marauder*. The Black King, Sebastian Shaw, had different plans for the position, for which his preparations began weeks ago...

Sebastian
Shaw

Egg

Professor X

Pyro

Shinobi
Shaw

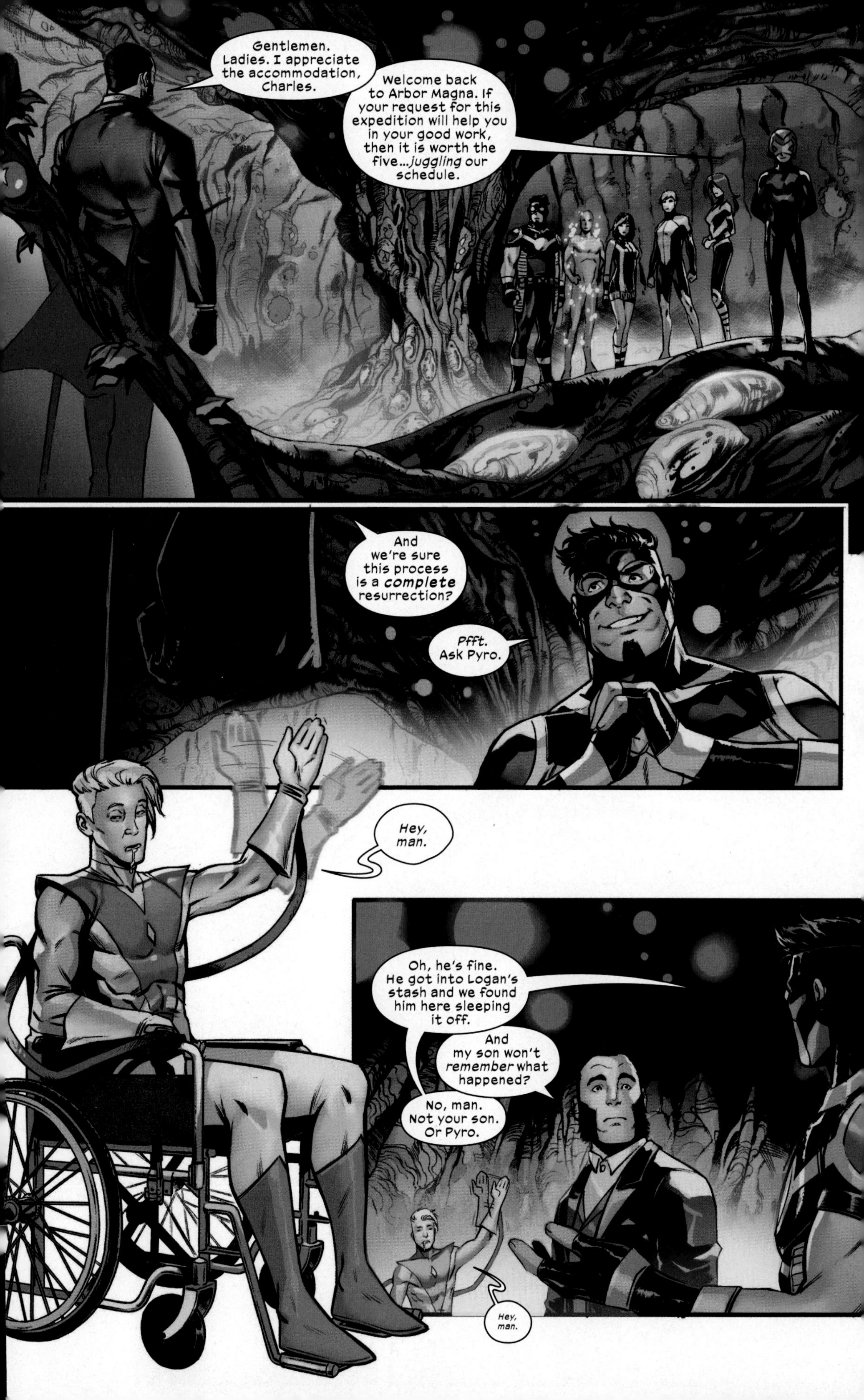
Gentlemen. Ladies. I appreciate the accommodation, Charles.
Welcome back to Arbor Magna. If your request for this expedition will help you in your good work, then it is worth the five...*juggling* our schedule.
And we're sure this process is a *complete* resurrection?
Pfft. Ask Pyro.
Hey, man.
Oh, he's fine. He got into Logan's stash and we found him here sleeping it off.
And my son won't *remember* what happened?
No, man. Not your son. Or Pyro.
Hey, man.

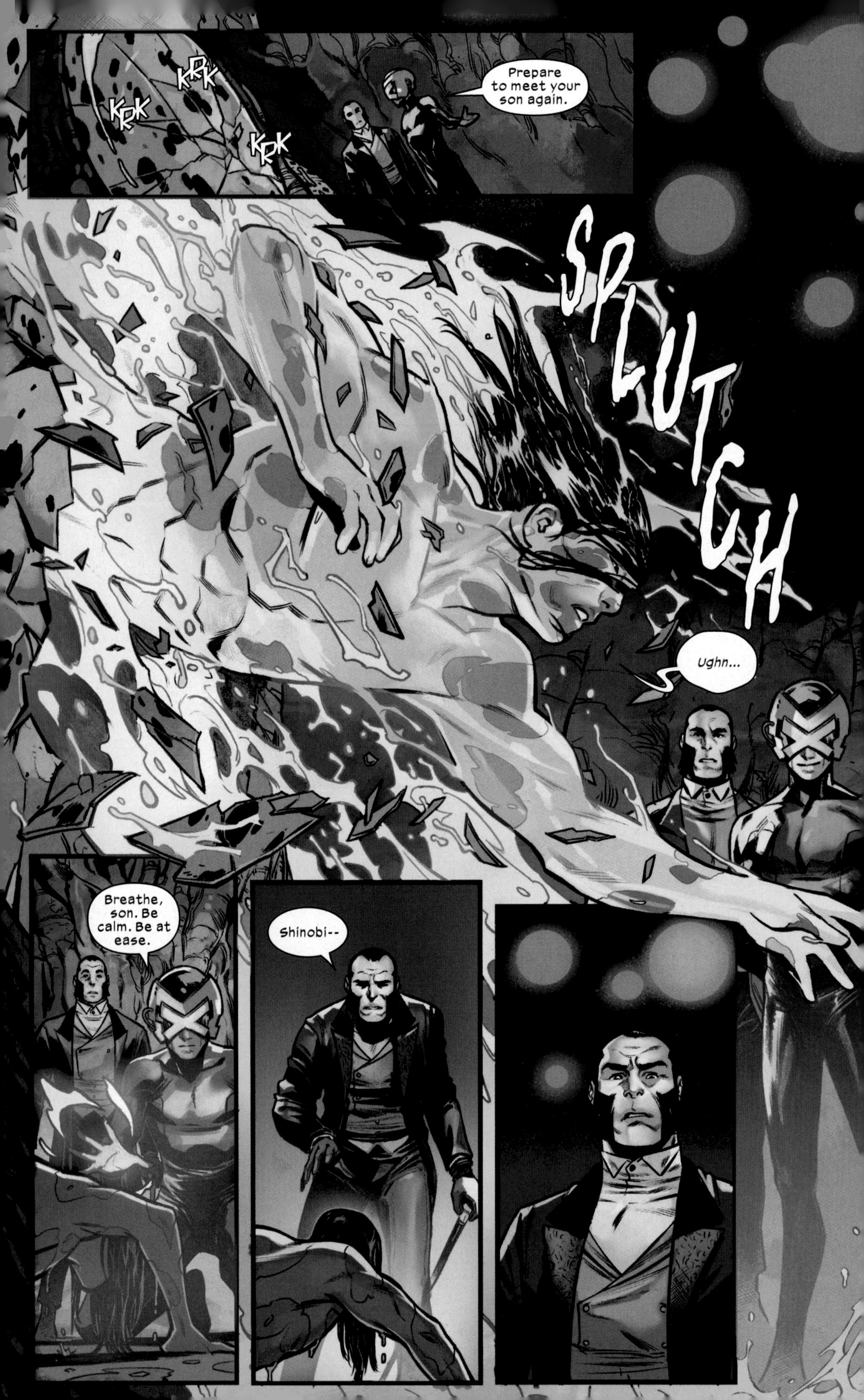
KRK
KRK
KRK
Prepare to meet your son again.
SPLUTCH
Ughn...
Breathe, son. Be calm. Be at ease.
Shinobi--

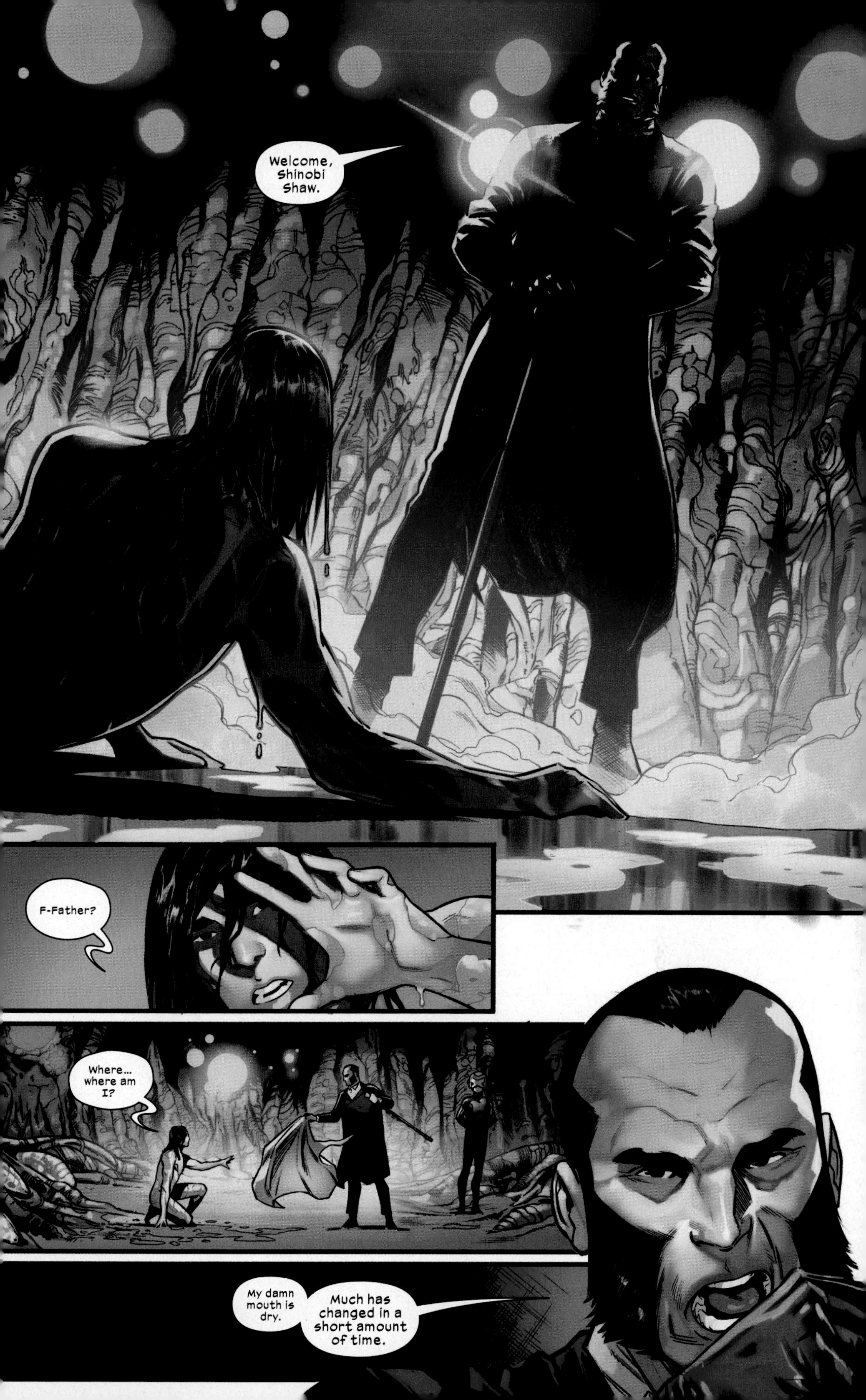
Welcome, Shinobi Shaw.
F-Father?
Where... where am I?
My damn mouth is dry.
Much has changed in a short amount of time.

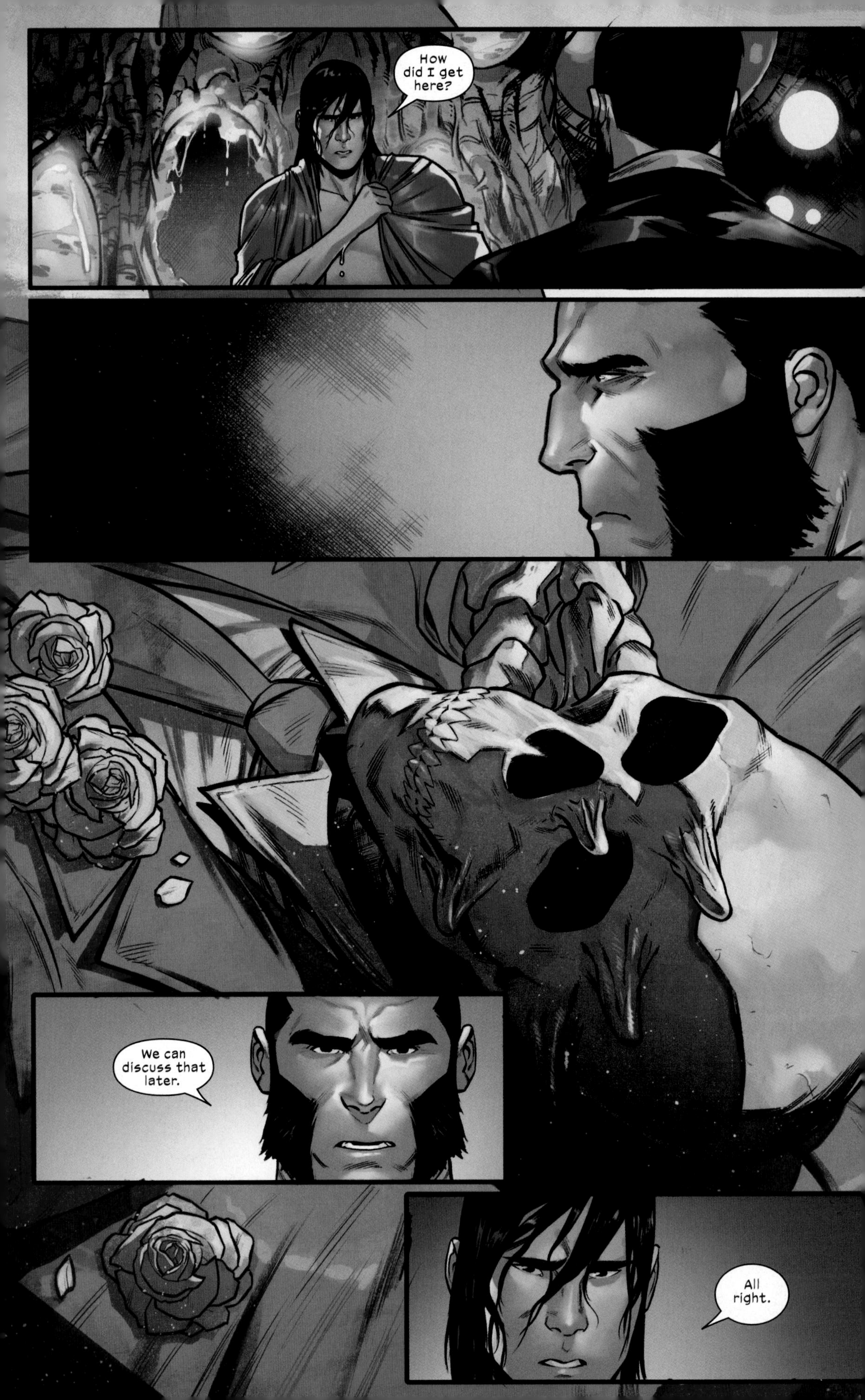
How did I get here?
We can discuss that later.
All right.

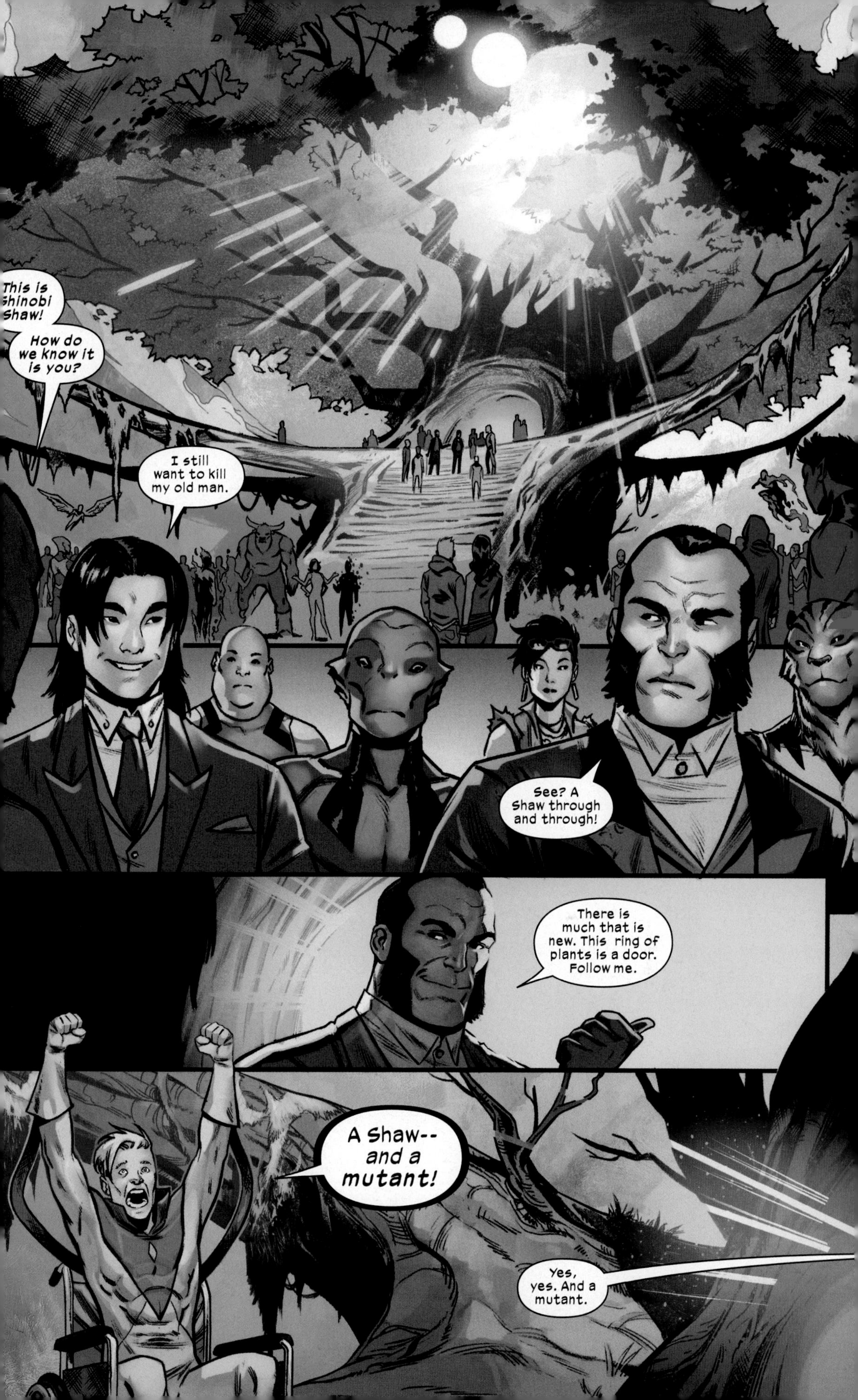
This is Shinobi Shaw!
How do we know it is you?
I still want to kill my old man.
See? A Shaw through and through!
There is much that is new. This ring of plants is a door. Follow me.
A Shaw-- and a mutant!
Yes, yes. And a mutant.

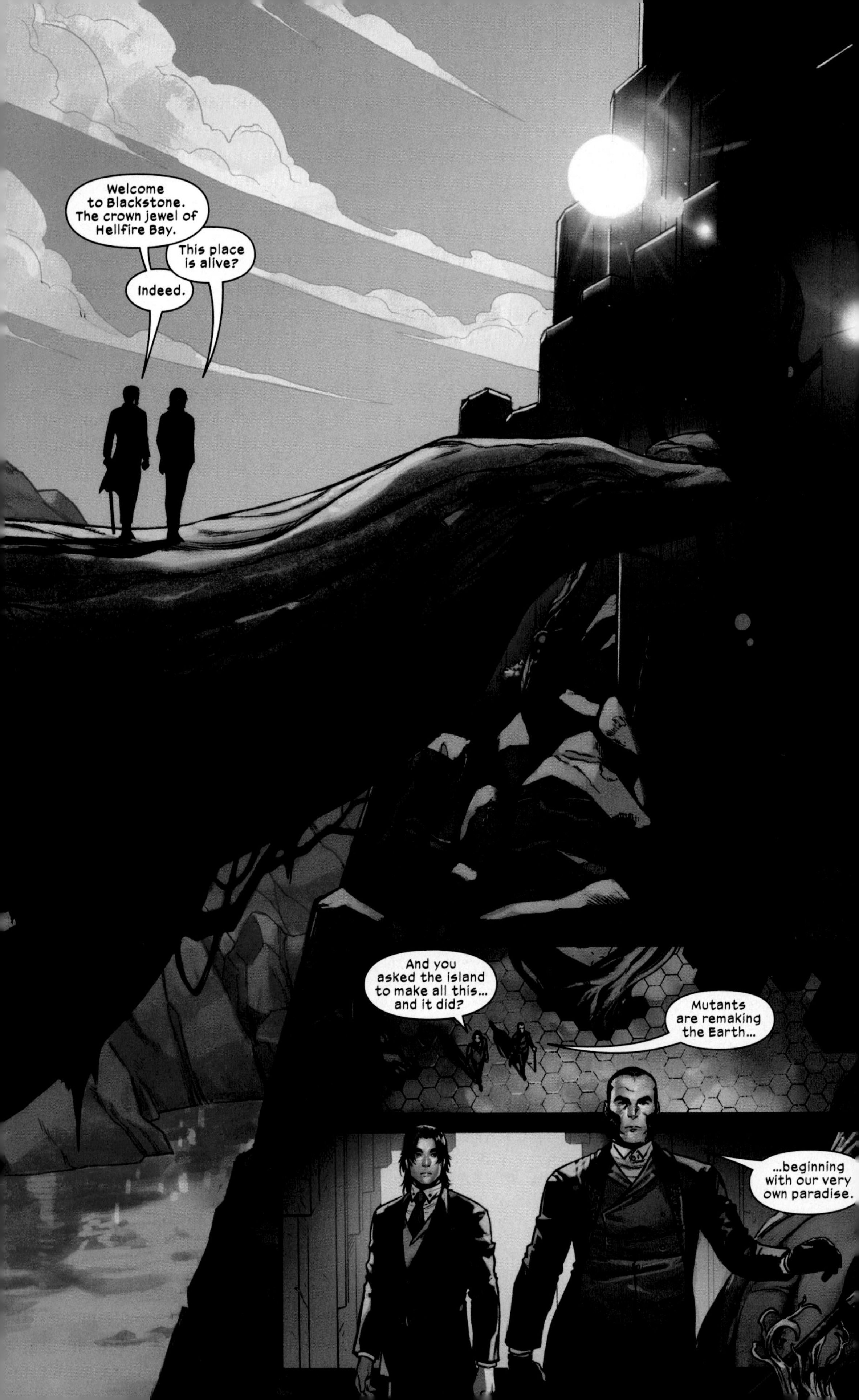
Welcome to Blackstone. The crown jewel of Hellfire Bay.
This place is alive?
Indeed.
And you asked the island to make all this... and it did?
Mutants are remaking the Earth...
...beginning with our very own paradise.

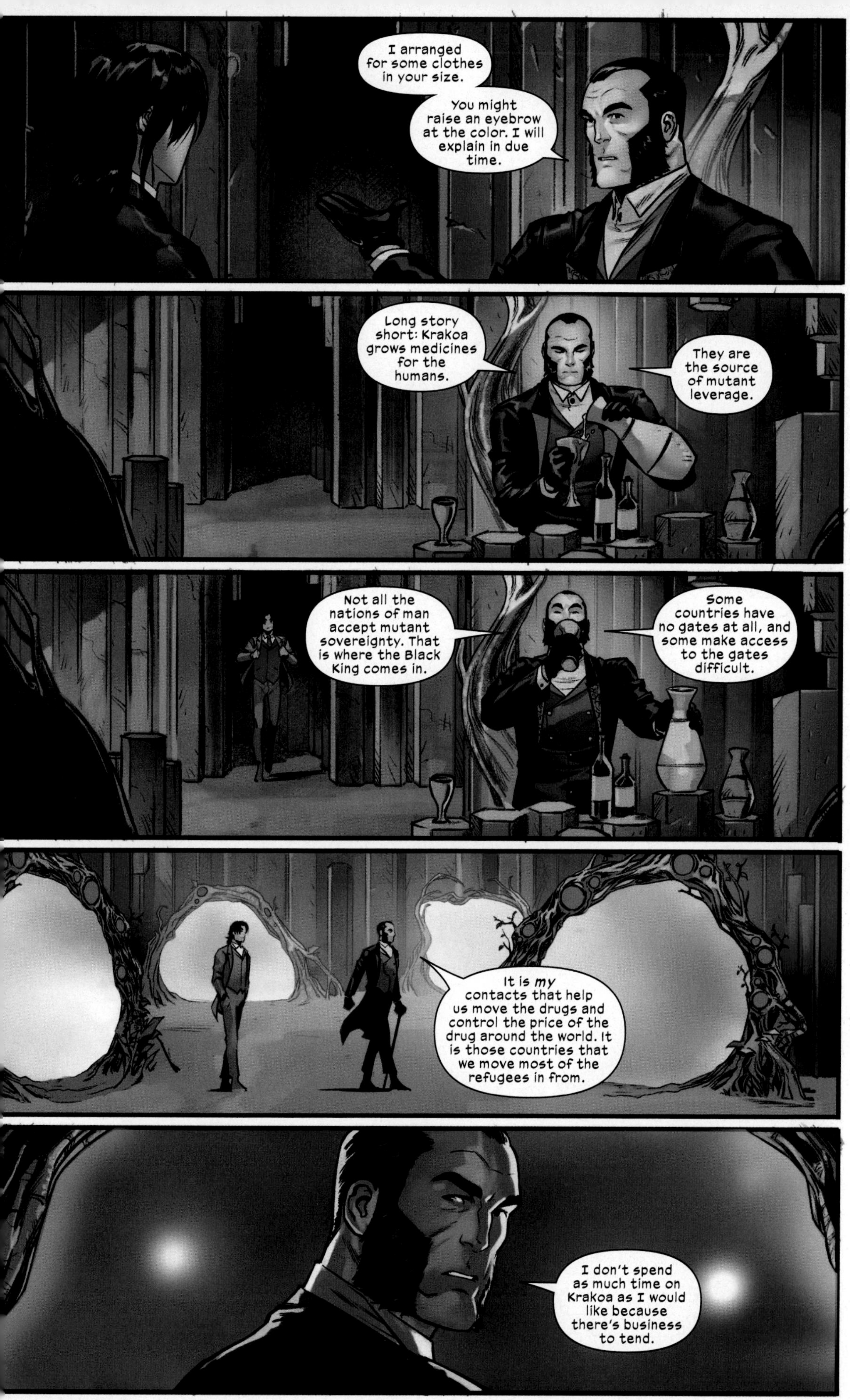
I arranged for some clothes in your size.
You might raise an eyebrow at the color. I will explain in due time.
Long story short: Krakoa grows medicines for the humans.
They are the source of mutant leverage.
Not all the nations of man accept mutant sovereignty. That is where the Black King comes in.
Some countries have no gates at all, and some make access to the gates difficult.
It is *my* contacts that help us move the drugs and control the price of the drug around the world. It is those countries that we move most of the refugees in from.
I don't spend as much time on Krakoa as I would like because there's business to tend.

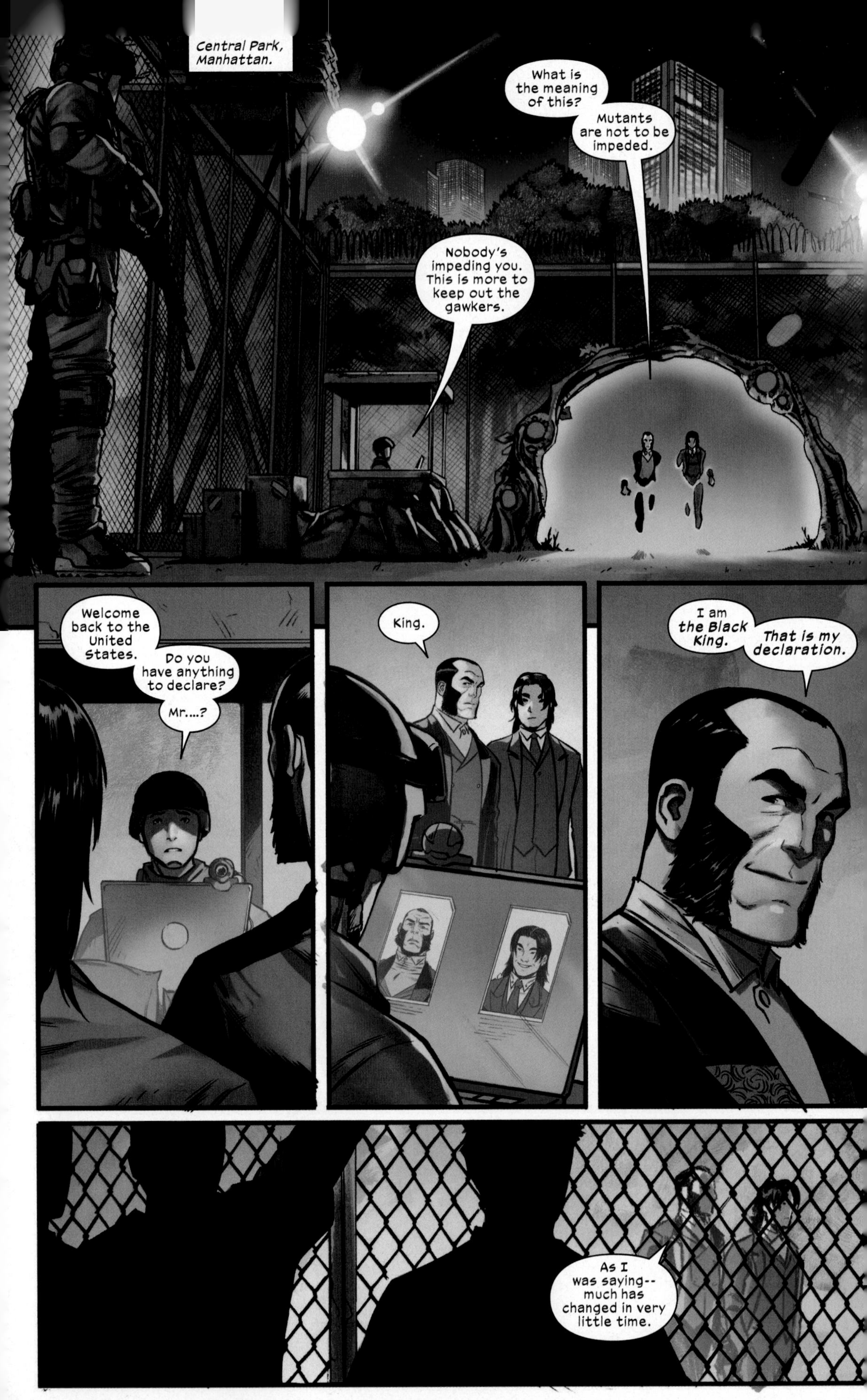
Central Park, Manhattan.
What is the meaning of this?
Mutants are not to be impeded.
Nobody's impeding you. This is more to keep out the gawkers.
Welcome back to the United States.
Do you have anything to declare?
Mr....?
King.
I am the Black King.
That is my declaration.
As I was saying-- much has changed in very little time.

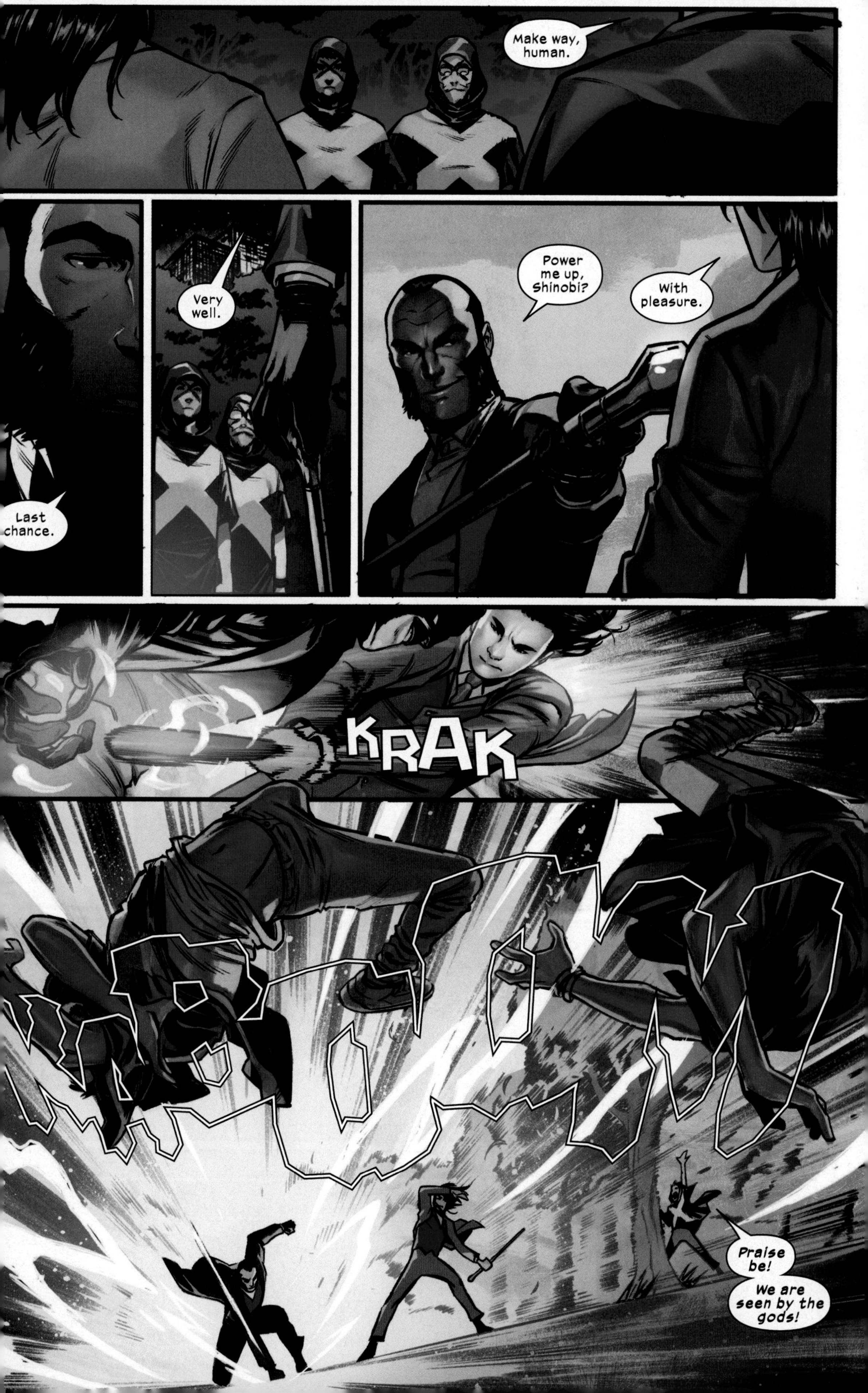

Make way, human.
Last chance.
Very well.
Power me up, Shinobi?
With pleasure.
KRAK
Praise be!
We are seen by the gods!

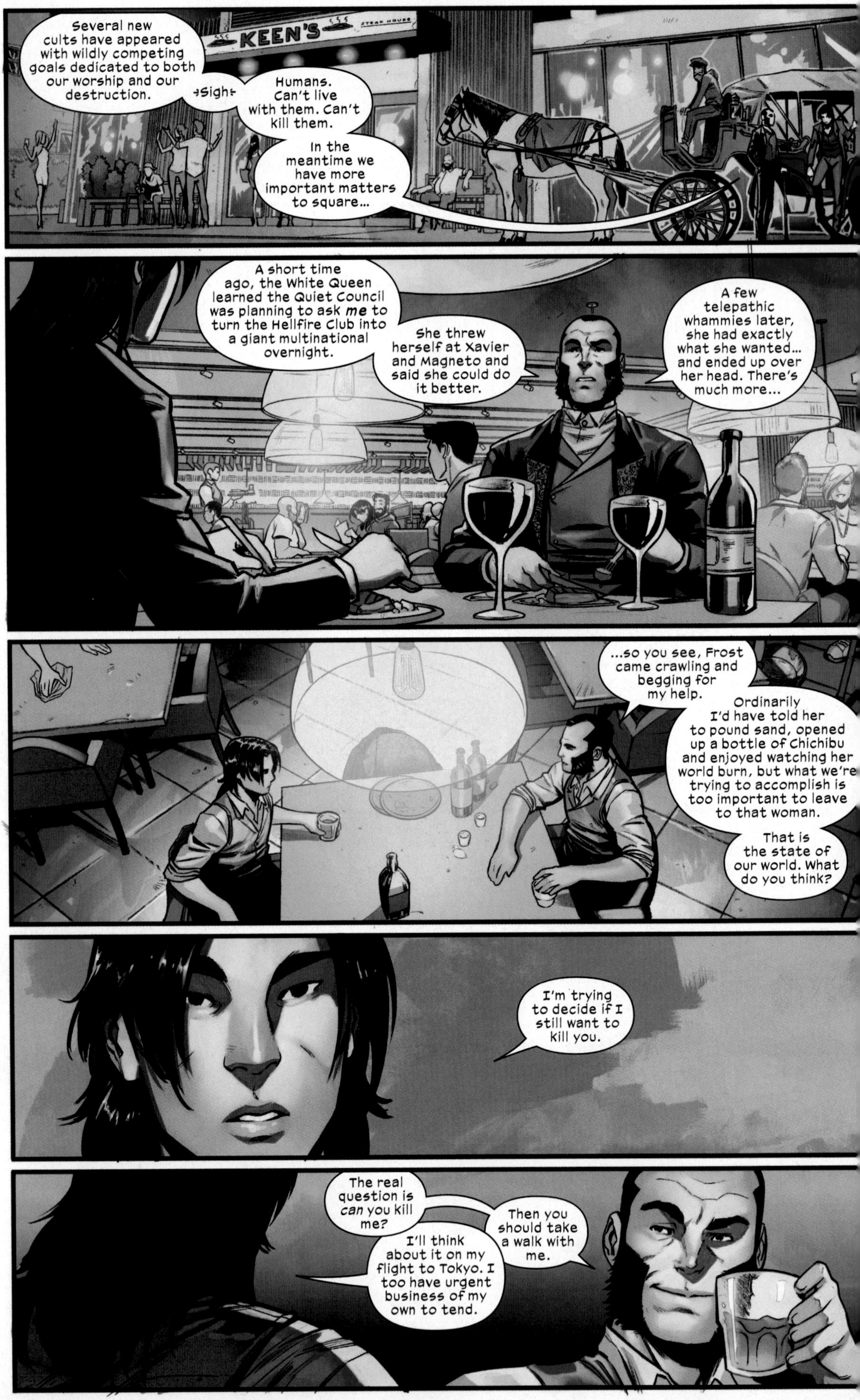
KEEN'S
STEAK HOUSE
Several new cults have appeared with wildly competing goals dedicated to both our worship and our destruction.
+Sigh+
Humans. Can't live with them. Can't kill them.
In the meantime we have more important matters to square...
A short time ago, the White Queen learned the Quiet Council was planning to ask *me* to turn the Hellfire Club into a giant multinational overnight.
She threw herself at Xavier and Magneto and said she could do it better.
A few telepathic whammies later, she had exactly what she wanted... and ended up over her head. There's much more...
...so you see, Frost came crawling and begging for my help.
Ordinarily I'd have told her to pound sand, opened up a bottle of Chichibu and enjoyed watching her world burn, but what we're trying to accomplish is too important to leave to that woman.
That is the state of our world. What do you think?
I'm trying to decide if I still want to kill you.
The real question is *can* you kill me?
Then you should take a walk with me.
I'll think about it on my flight to Tokyo. I too have urgent business of my own to tend.

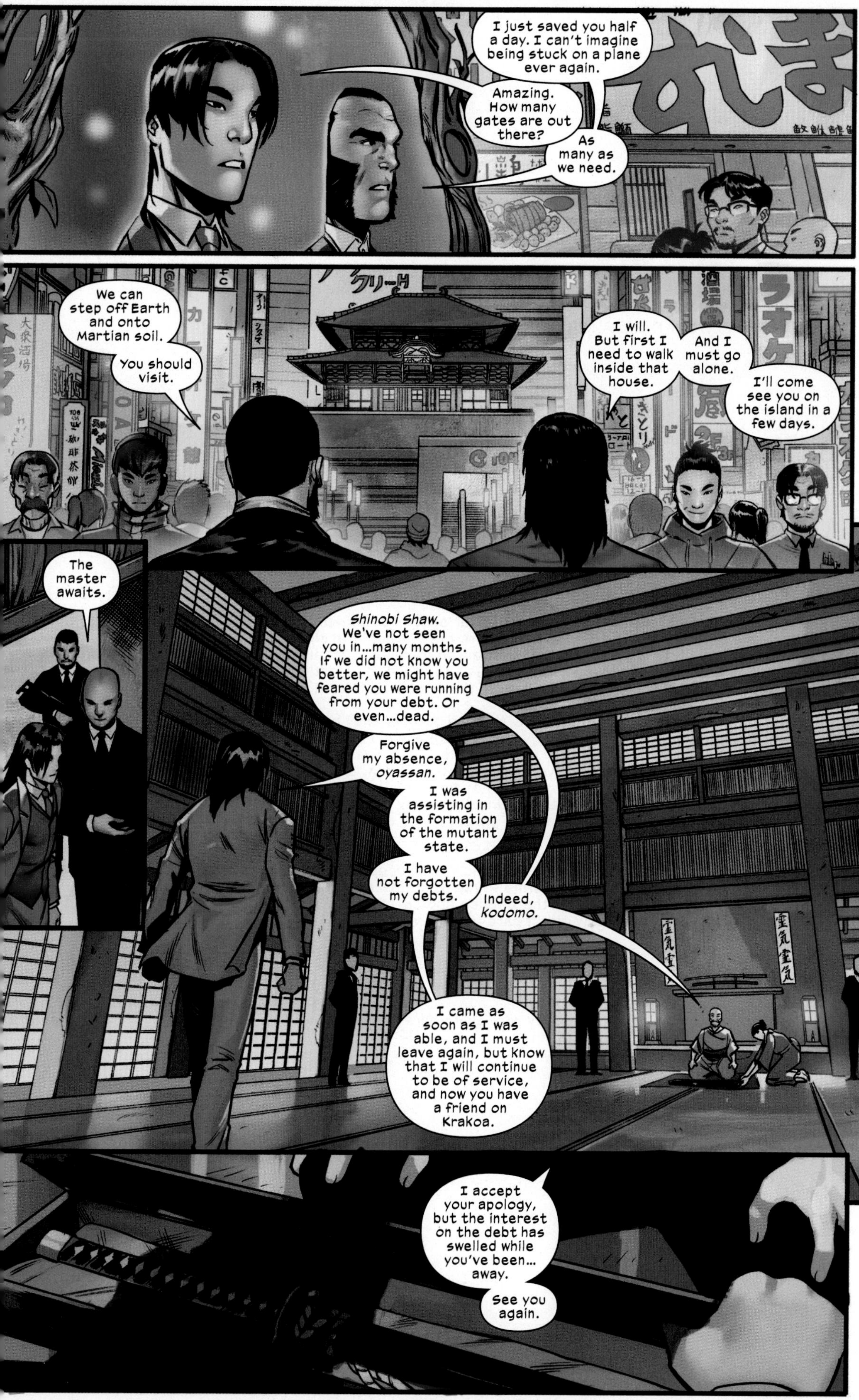
I just saved you half a day. I can't imagine being stuck on a plane ever again.
Amazing. How many gates are out there?
As many as we need.
We can step off Earth and onto Martian soil.
You should visit.
I will. But first I need to walk inside that house.
And I must go alone.
I'll come see you on the island in a few days.
The master awaits.
Shinobi Shaw. We've not seen you in...many months. If we did not know you better, we might have feared you were running from your debt. Or even...dead.
Forgive my absence, *oyassan.*
I was assisting in the formation of the mutant state.
I have not forgotten my debts.
Indeed, *kodomo.*
I came as soon as I was able, and I must leave again, but know that I will continue to be of service, and now you have a friend on Krakoa.
I accept your apology, but the interest on the debt has swelled while you've been... away.
See you again.

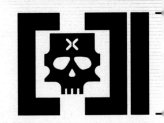

TOP SECRET - EYES ONLY ACCESS

FROM: THE X-DESK
TO: ALL POINTS
SUBJECT: THE KRAKOA MATTER

—

After the Marauders sailed from the U.K. in their new ships, a series of sea trials took place, including a rough weather test courtesy of Ororo Munroe (Storm).

The ship made a stop in the Northern Atlantic at Island M. This is new information on our desk. Is anybody holding back? If the Krakoans are using Island M, are they using any other islands we don't know about? The Hellfire crowd has been using shell companies for years, and now Krakoa is a sovereign nation. We really need to know who owns what. Do we have a list? If not, we'll need to commence on a database of assets and especially islands.

The weather was clear at Island M, and our satellites observed subjects Katherine Pryde and Lucas Bishop disembark the *Marauder* at this location. The new vessel then acted in a very unexpected manner. The mutants went belowdecks, and it cruised away from the island at what we estimate to be 300 knots an hour. If they maintain course they'll shortly land in Brazil.

U.S. Navy intel can confirm the speed, but the boomer they had shadowing the *Marauder* was quickly left in her wake. It's unknown if the mutants knew they were being shadowed or they were just flexing. It seems there is more happening under the hood that we can currently explain. It's possible that former DoD employee and mutant Forge has been busy again giving Krakoa a technical advantage. Someone explain to me how that horse got out of our barn? We should do a full review of what he was doing while he was on our side.

There was one other matter of note this week. We intercepted text messages between burner phones from Katherine Pryde (Shadowcat) & Lucas Bishop. Transcript follows. They dumped the phones shortly after leaving the boat and, as you will see, obviously didn't care the line was not secure.

More as it develops,

■■■■■■■

P.S. If you're coming to the holiday racket, bring a bottle. If we go by the budget, we're dry. Thanks.

—

ADDENDUM TO REPORT FROM X-DESK, LANGLEY

KP It's K.

LB Hey.

KP Gonna need an answer. Lotta action here, I'm holding back my other candidates, but I don't want to kick the can down the road forever.

LB I gave you my answer.

KP I thought you were kidding when you said no.

LB No, I was not, and I believe I said "Hell no"

KP Plus, you'll look great in red.

LB No I won't, Kitty.

KP Fine, Bishy.

LB Sorry. Old habits.

KP You were born to be a real Bishop.

Why don't you want to be in the Hellfire Club?

LB Have you ever met anyone in the Hellfire Club?

KP Be the Red Bishop and I can promise you'll get to observe all the mutants you'd be keeping an eye on anyway, but you'll be in the room.

You're gonna look good in red.

LB No I won't and these are unsecured burners. Now we're gonna need new ones for T.

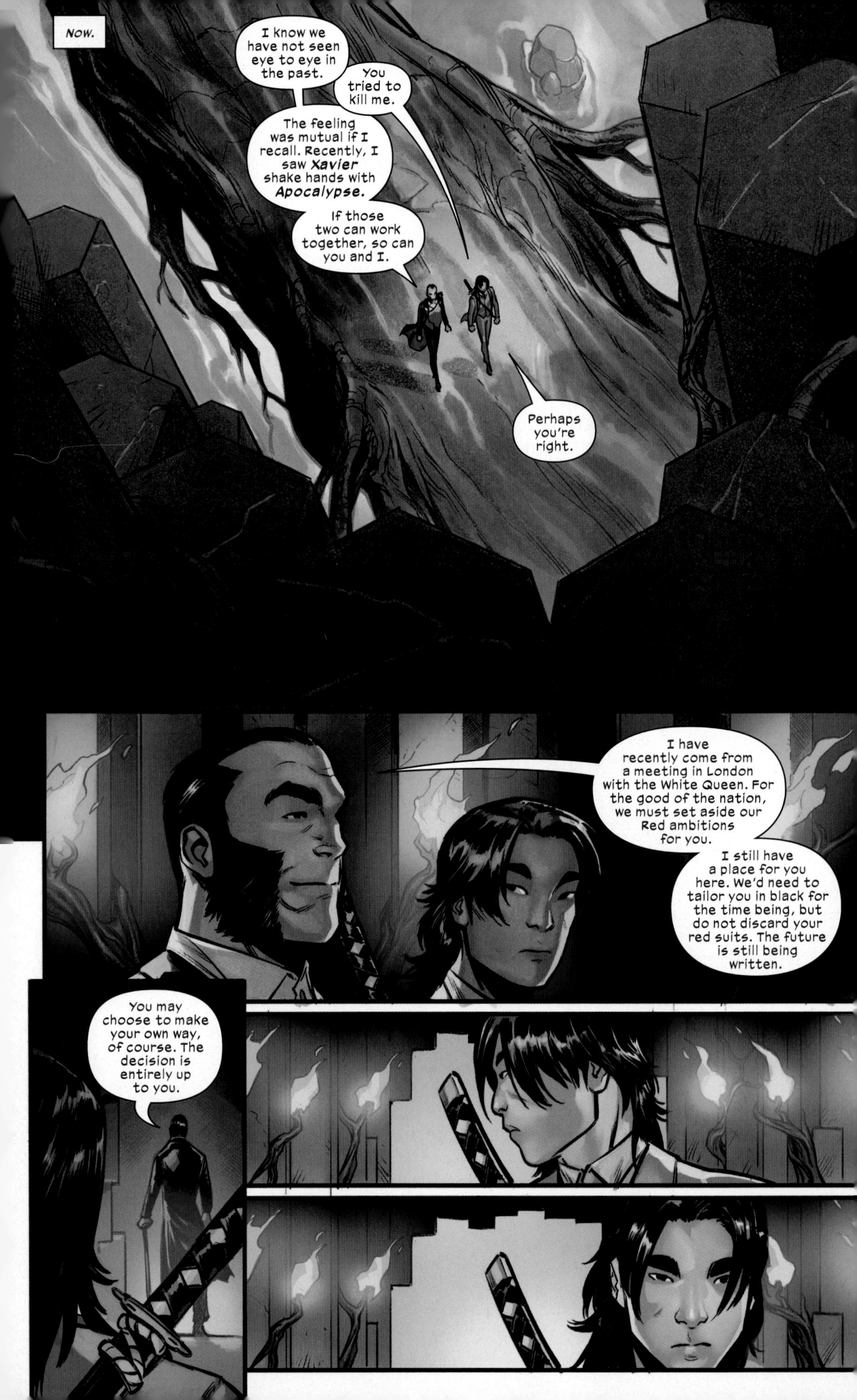
Now.
I know we have not seen eye to eye in the past.
You tried to kill me.
The feeling was mutual if I recall. Recently, I saw Xavier shake hands with Apocalypse.
If those two can work together, so can you and I.
Perhaps you're right.
I have recently come from a meeting in London with the White Queen. For the good of the nation, we must set aside our Red ambitions for you.
I still have a place for you here. We'd need to tailor you in black for the time being, but do not discard your red suits. The future is still being written.
You may choose to make your own way, of course. The decision is entirely up to you.

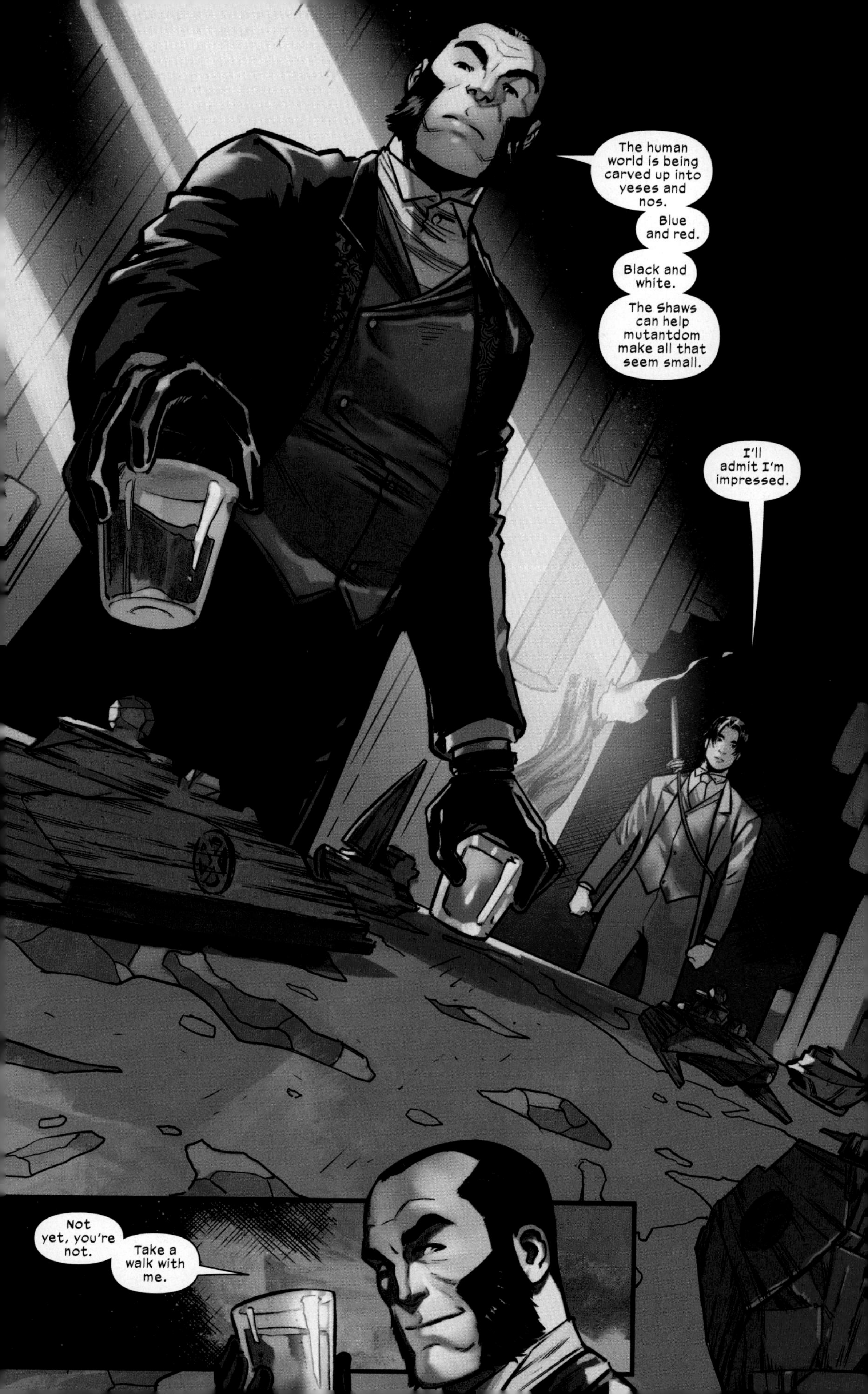
The human world is being carved up into yeses and nos.
Blue and red.
Black and white.
The Shaws can help mutantdom make all that seem small.
I'll admit I'm impressed.
Not yet, you're not.
Take a walk with me.

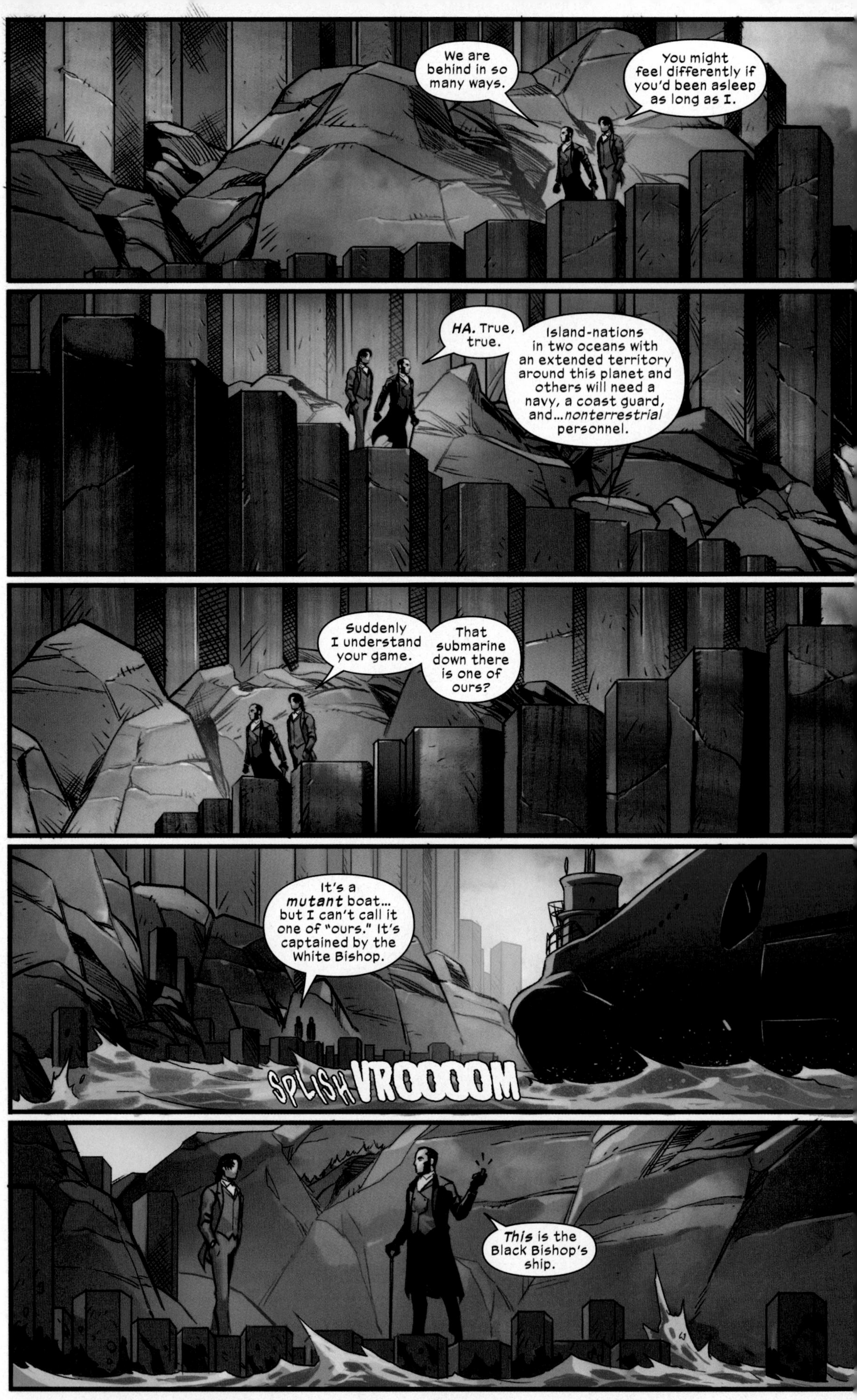
We are behind in so many ways.
You might feel differently if you'd been asleep as long as I.
HA. True, true.
Island-nations in two oceans with an extended territory around this planet and others will need a navy, a coast guard, and...nonterrestrial personnel.
Suddenly I understand your game.
That submarine down there is one of ours?
It's a mutant boat... but I can't call it one of "ours." It's captained by the White Bishop.
SPLISH
VROOOOM
This is the Black Bishop's ship.

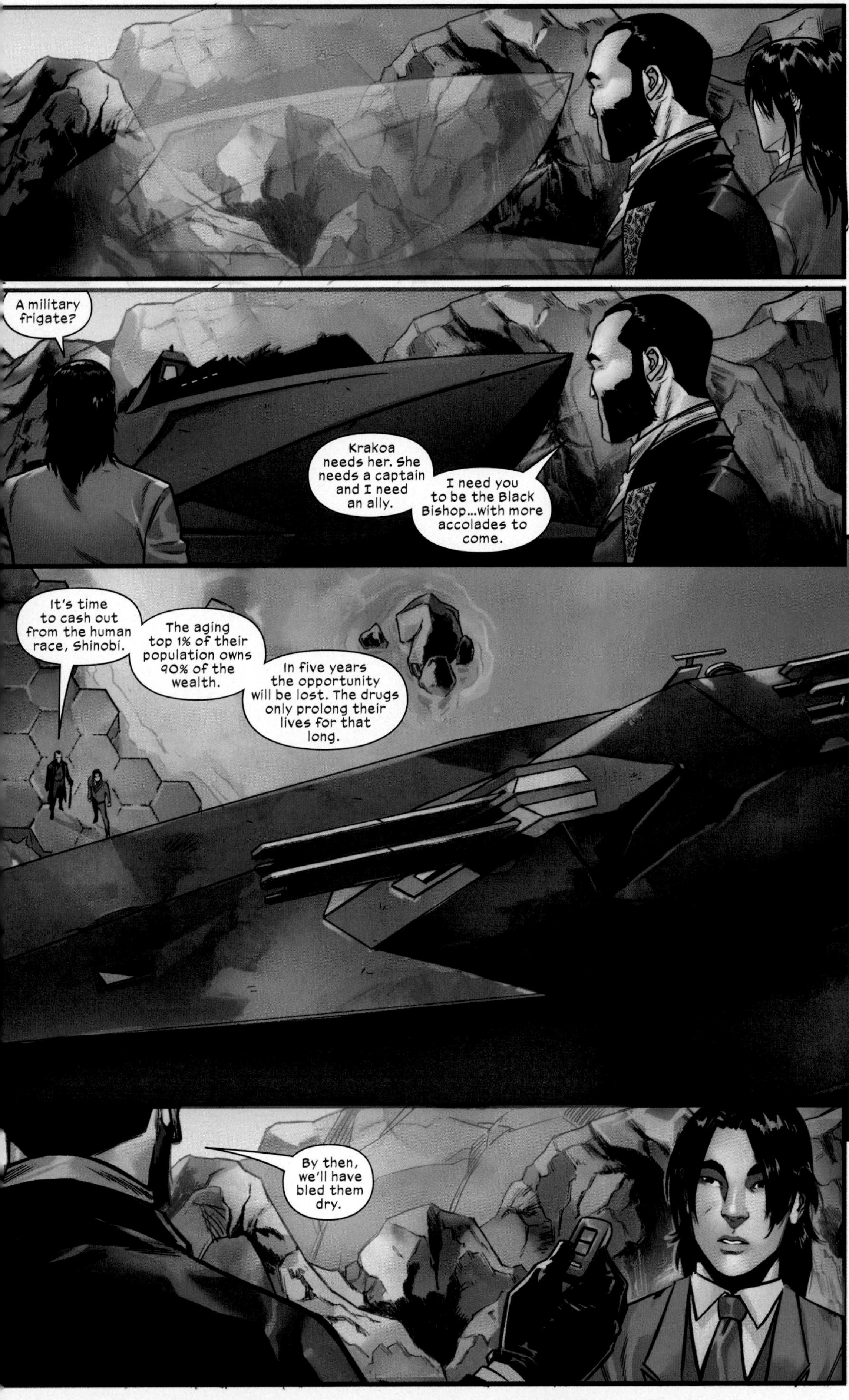
A military frigate?
Krakoa needs her. She needs a captain and I need an ally.
I need you to be the Black Bishop...with more accolades to come.
It's time to cash out from the human race, Shinobi.
The aging top 1% of their population owns 90% of the wealth.
In five years the opportunity will be lost. The drugs only prolong their lives for that long.
By then, we'll have bled them dry.

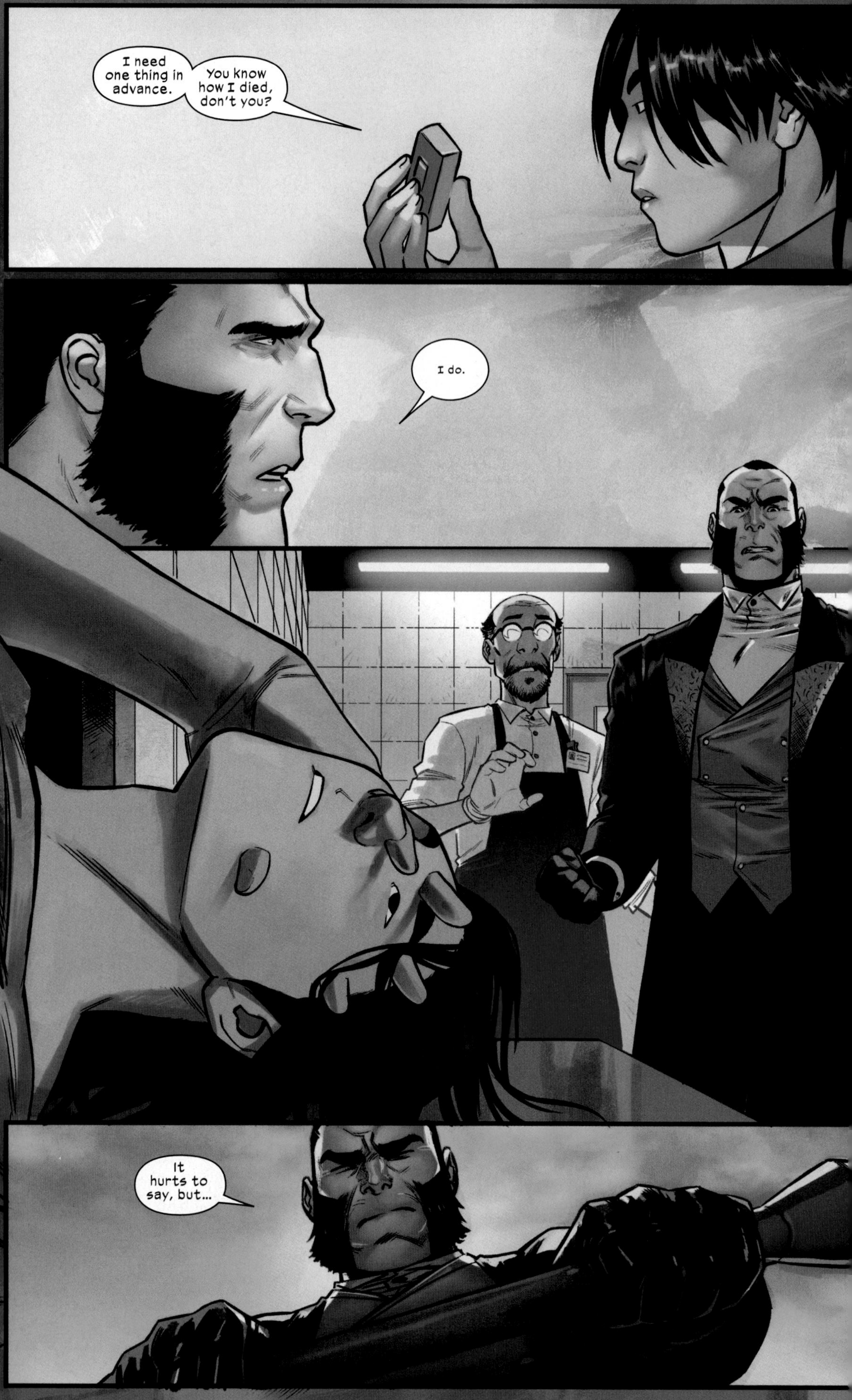
I need one thing in advance.
You know how I died, don't you?
I do.
It hurts to say, but...

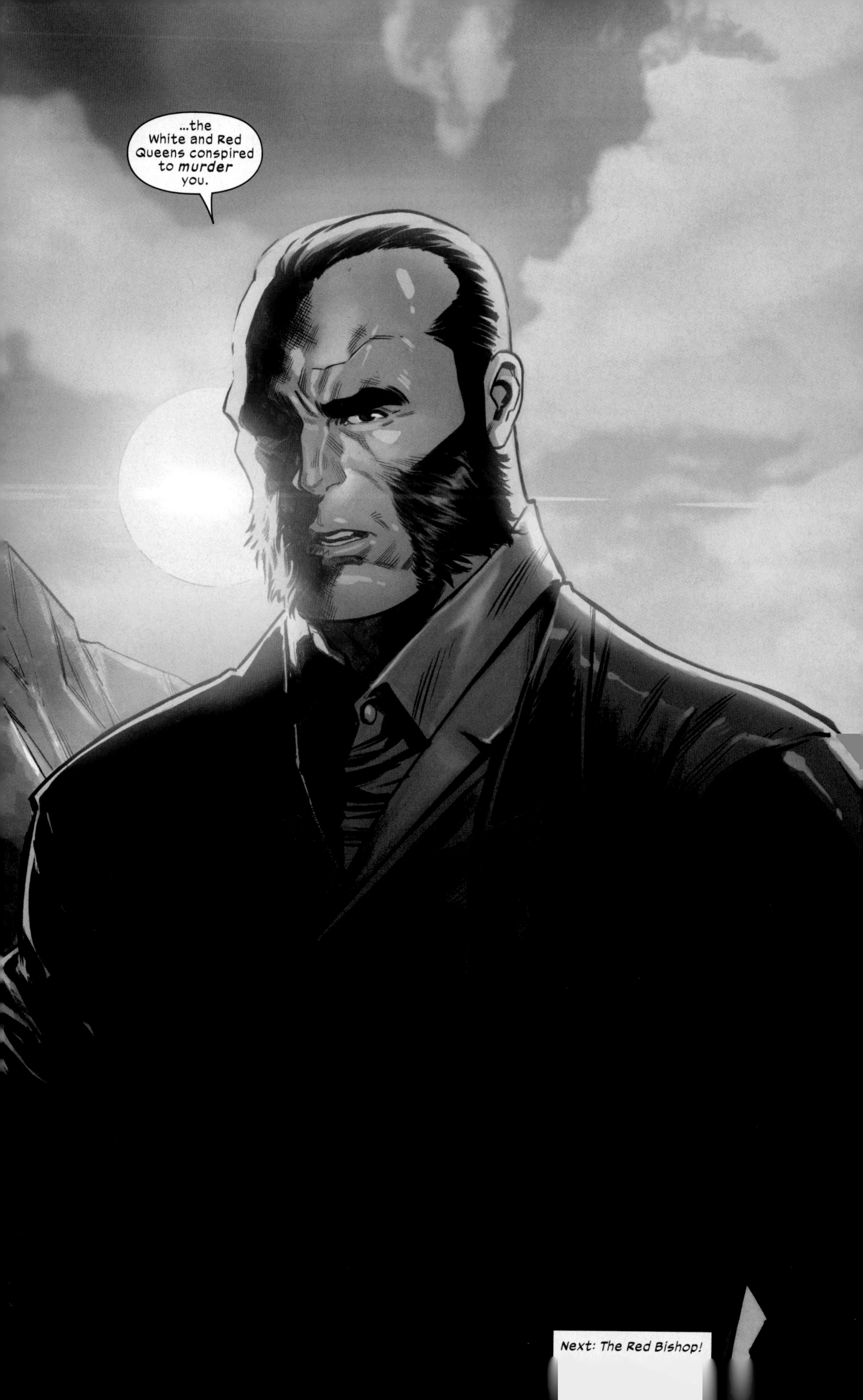
...the White and Red Queens conspired to *murder* you.
Next: The Red Bishop!

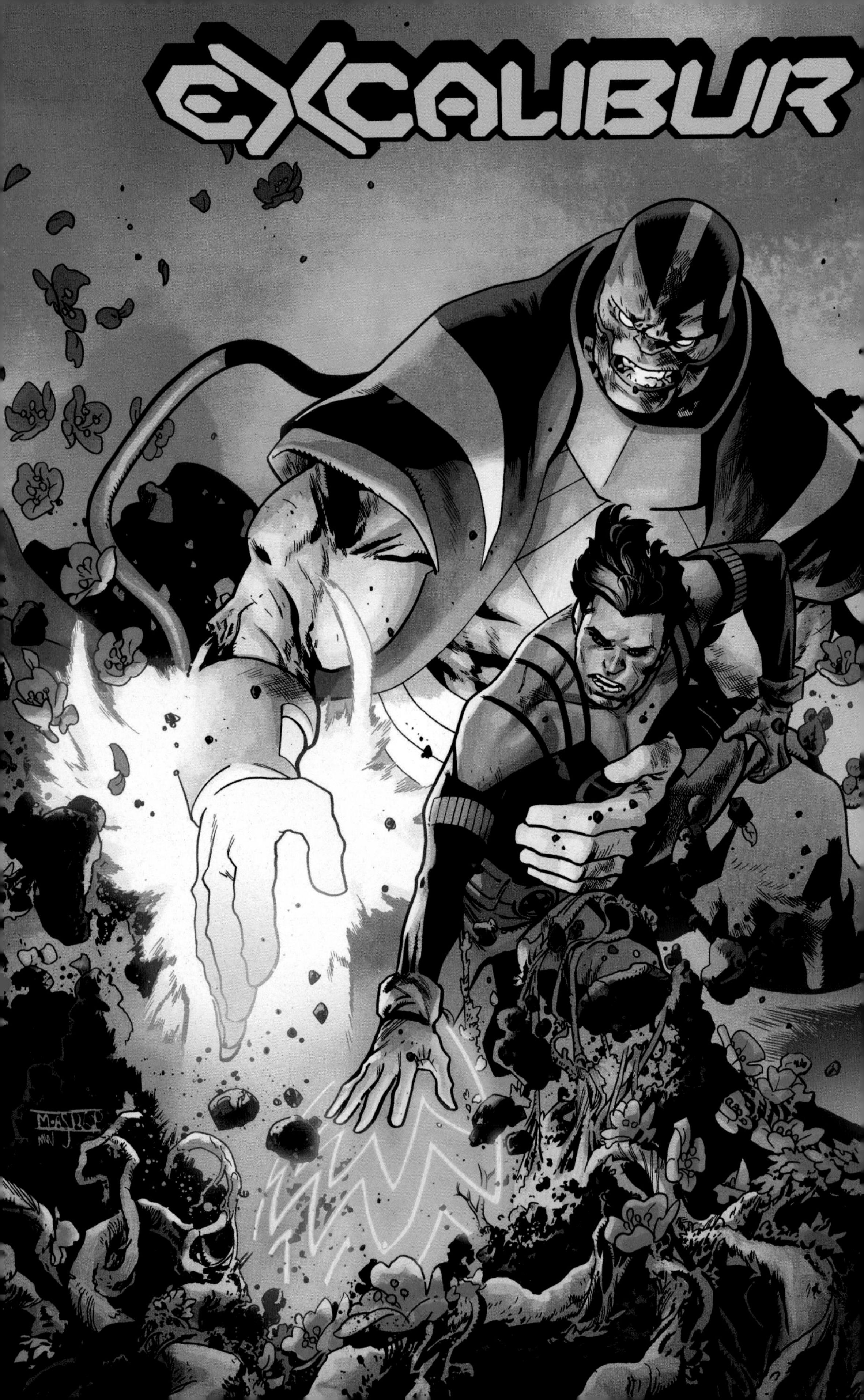
EXCALIBUR

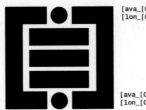

[ava_[0.3]
[lon_[0.3]

[ava_[0.X]
[lon_[0.X]

OTHERWORLD NOW.

The new nation of Krakoa offers a promise of peace to mutantkind, but peace has been hard to come by. Apocalypse has declared his intentions to harness mutant magic, but not everyone is convinced—especially since his experimentation seemed to put Rogue into a mysterious floral coma. And war in Otherworld called Brian Braddock into battle against the sorceress Morgan Le Fay—but when she possessed Brian, he used the last of his strength to bestow upon Betsy the mantle of CAPTAIN BRITAIN. Now, to get Brian back, Captain Britain, Gambit and Jubilee have entered Otherworld... where anything can happen.

Captain Britain    Apocalypse    Jubilee    Rogue

Gambit   Shogo    Rictor

Morgan Le Fay    Marianna Stern    Brian Braddock

[ava_[0.3]...]
[lon_[0.3]...]

[All....HAIL.]

[00_so_below_X]
[00_as_above_X]

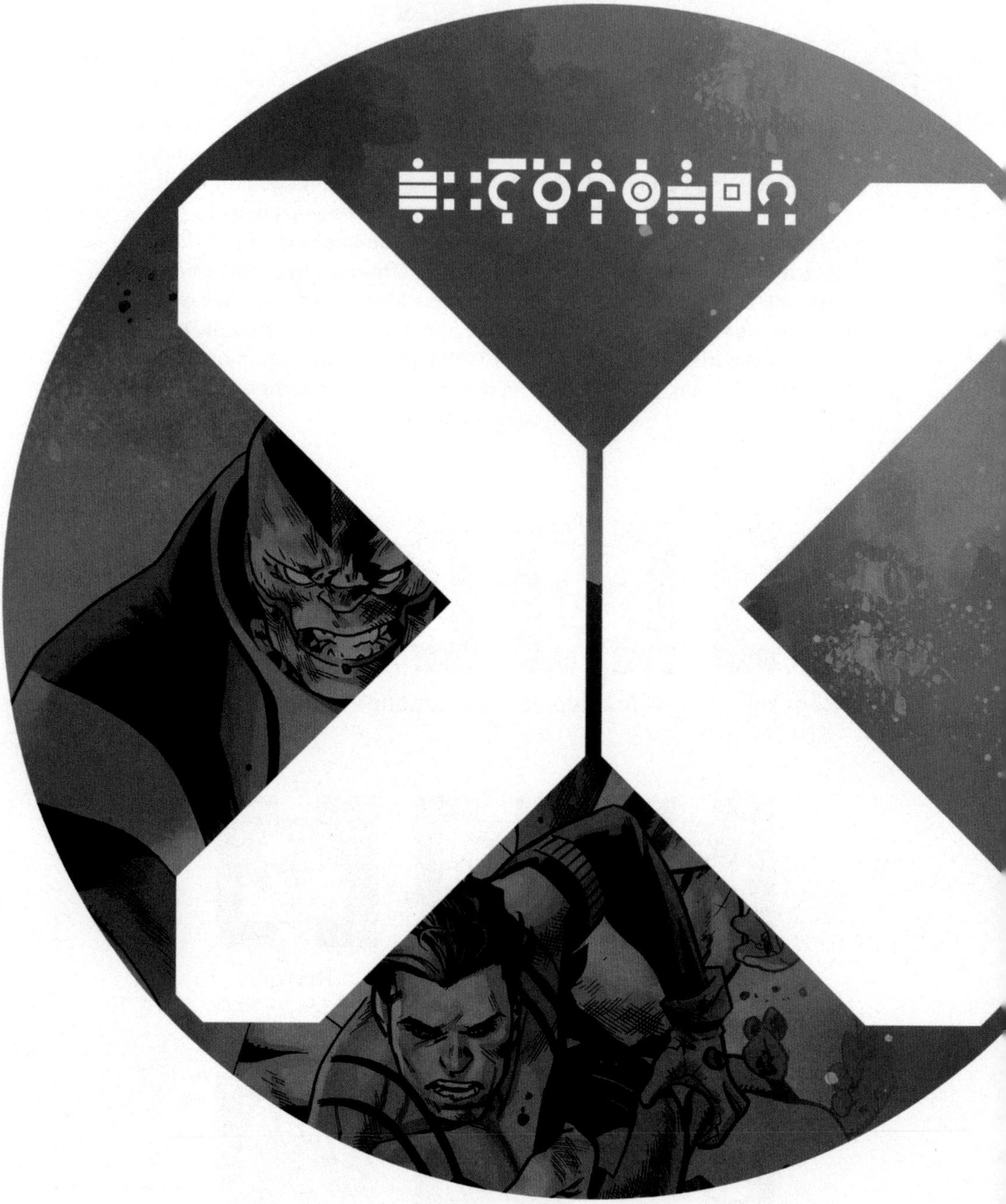

TINI HOWARD.....................................[WRITER]
MARCUS TO.......................................[ARTIST]
ERICK ARCINIEGA..........................[COLOR ARTIST]
VC's CORY PETIT............................[LETTERER]
TOM MULLER.....................................[DESIGN]

MAHMUD ASRAR & MATTHEW WILSON...........[COVER ARTISTS]

KOI PHAM & MORRY HOLLOWELL......[VARIANT COVER ARTISTS]

JAY BOWEN..................................[PRODUCTION]

JONATHAN HICKMAN...........................[HEAD OF X]
ANNALISE BISSA.......................[ASSISTANT EDITOR]
JORDAN D. WHITE................................[EDITOR]
C.B. CEBULSKI........................[EDITOR IN CHIEF]
JOE QUESADA...............[CHIEF CREATIVE OFFICER]
DAN BUCKLEY................................[PRESIDENT]
ALAN FINE........................[EXECUTIVE PRODUCER]

[03]EXCALIBUR

[ISSUE THREE]...........................
.............VERSE III: THREE COVENANTS

[00_so_below_X]
[X‾ɘʌoqɐ‾sɐ‾00]

[00_00.....0]
[00_00.....3]

[00_greater_]
[00_secrets_]

[00_____]

[00_exist___]

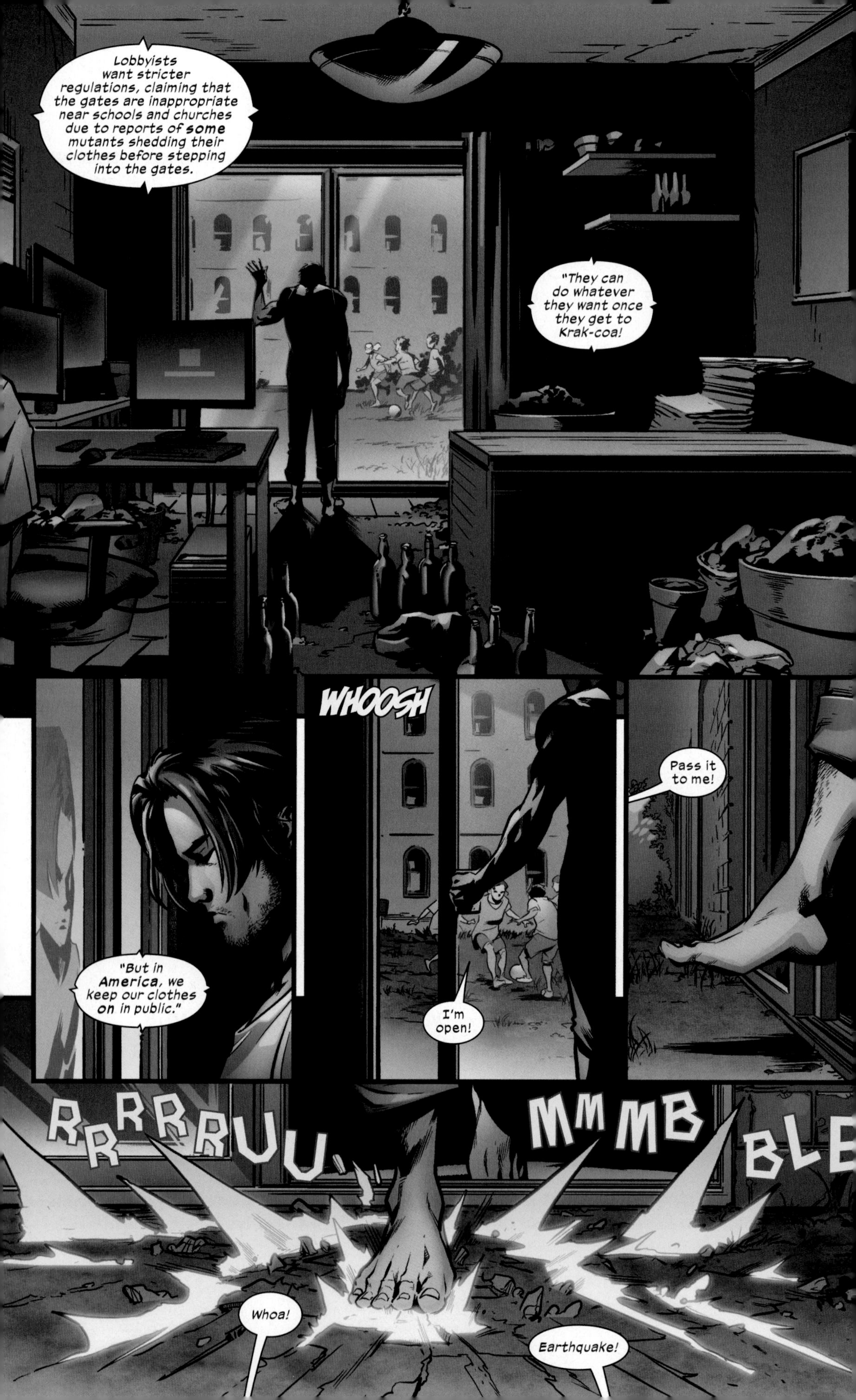
Lobbyists want stricter regulations, claiming that the gates are inappropriate near schools and churches due to reports of some mutants shedding their clothes before stepping into the gates.
"They can do whatever they want once they get to Krak-coa!
WHOOSH
"But in America, we keep our clothes on in public."
I'm open!
Pass it to me!
RRRRRUU
MMMB
BLE
Whoa!
Earthquake!

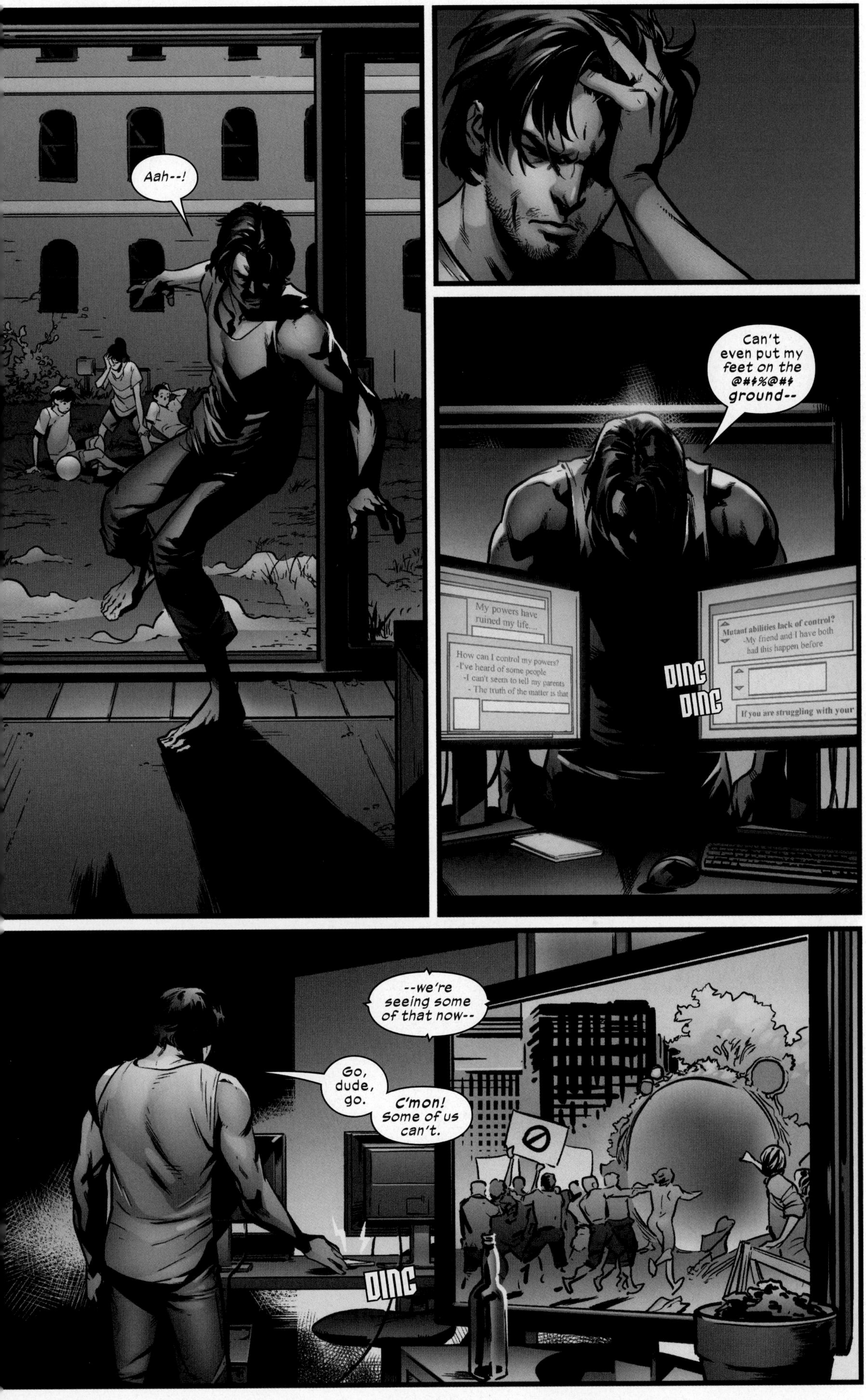
Aah--!
Can't even put my feet on the @#$%@#$ ground--
My powers have ruined my life...
How can I control my powers?
-I've heard of some people
-I can't seem to tell my parents
- The truth of the matter is that
Mutant abilities lack of control?
-My friend and I have both had this happen before
If you are struggling with your
DING
DING
--we're seeing some of that now--
Go, dude, go.
C'mon! Some of us can't.
DING

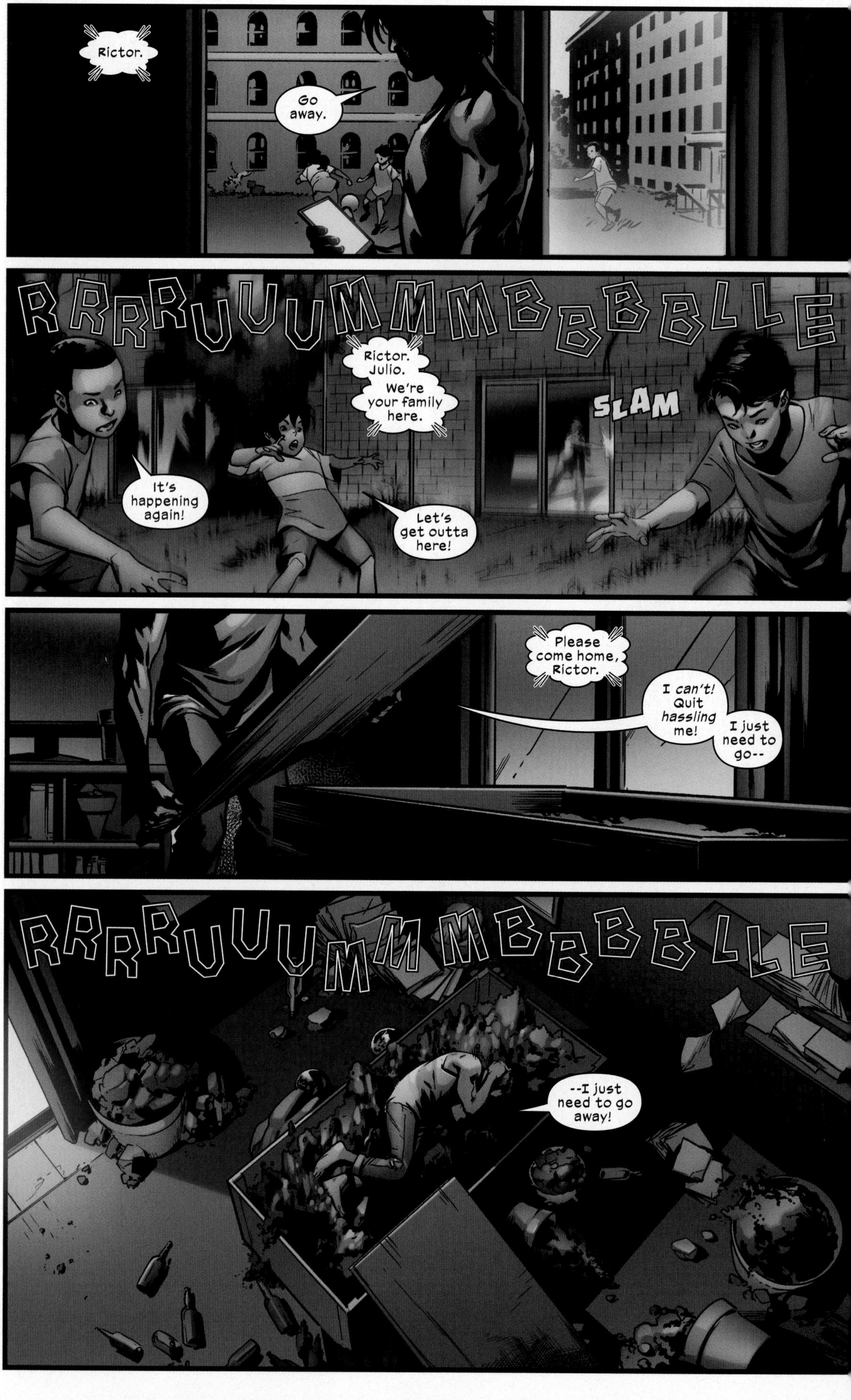
Rictor.
Go away.
RRRRUUUMMMMBBBLLE
Rictor. Julio.
We're your family here.
SLAM
It's happening again!
Let's get outta here!
Please come home, Rictor.
I can't! Quit hassling me!
I just need to go--
RRRRUUUMMMMBBBLLE
--I just need to go away!

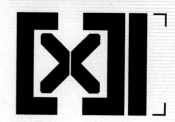

mutantsunmuted.com/q/krakoa

Looking for dogsitter for 1 week for Krakoa trip. (NYC)

Has anyone been and can confirm if phones charge TIA

TAMPONS on the ISLAND????

Serious question about childcare.

28/M, looking for another pea for my pod ;)

Power amplification/dulling on the island?

Is there a soccer team on the island?
Anyone wanna start one?

Going to Krakoa this weekend via ATLANTA GATE -
meetup details

Island-related relationship advice needed, yes,
another of these posts

POWER AMPLIFICATION/DULLING ON THE ISLAND?

> Hey, throwaway account here. Don't know where else to ask.

Has anyone had any problems with controlling their powers
that got better when they went to the island? Or is the opposite
more likely? If I'm having trouble maintaining control of my
mutation, would going to Krakoa help or make it worse?

Thanks.

> Hey! This is pretty vague - can you clarify what sort
of mutation you have? I'm not really sure why this would
be a concern.

> I'd rather not.

> Okay...Is there someone you could take
with you your first time, to hold your hand,
just in case something bad happens?

> No. Thanks anyway.

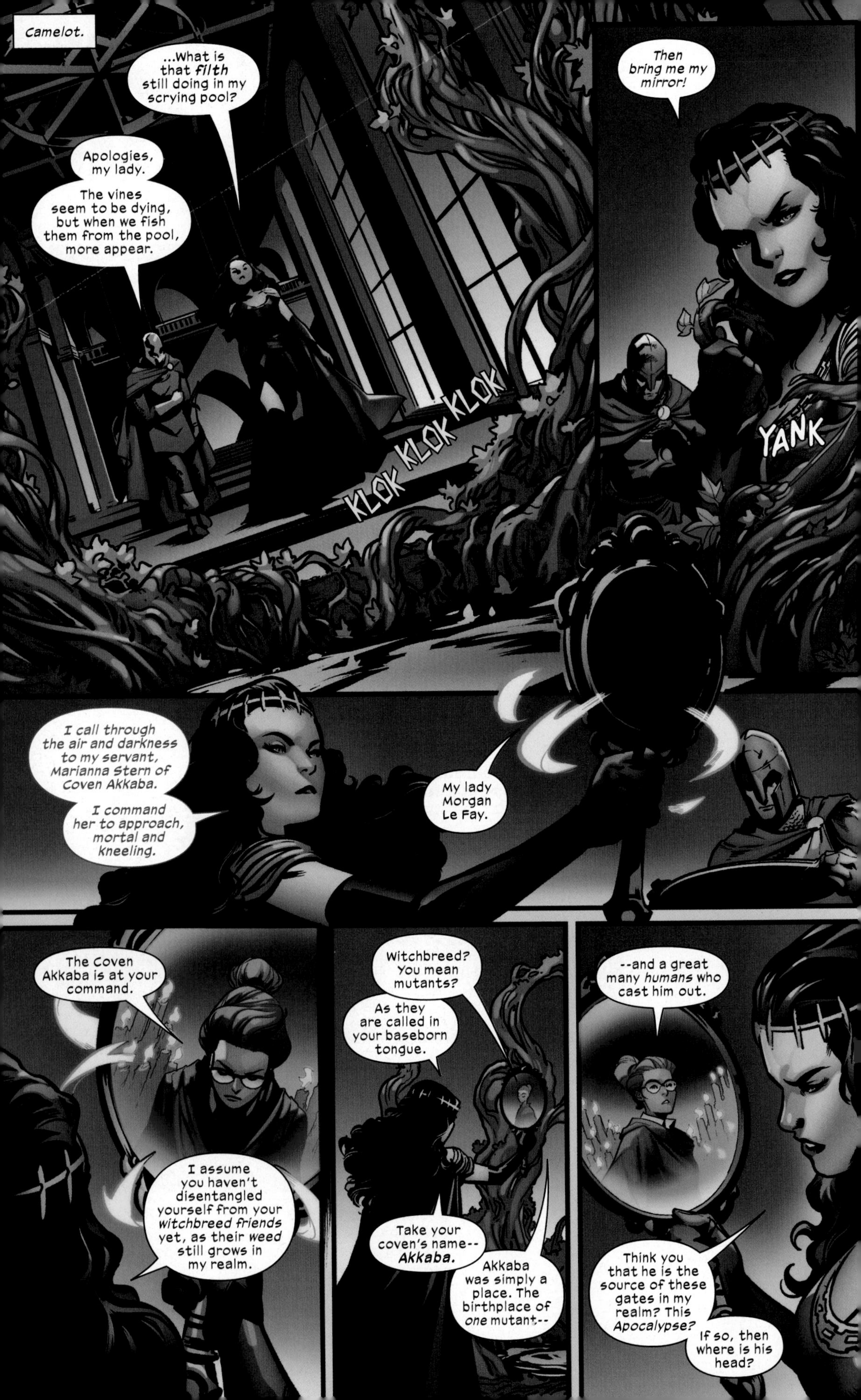
Camelot.
...What is that *filth* still doing in my scrying pool?
Apologies, my lady.
The vines seem to be dying, but when we fish them from the pool, more appear.
KLOK KLOK KLOK
Then bring me my mirror!
YANK
I call through the air and darkness to my servant, Marianna Stern of Coven Akkaba.
I command her to approach, mortal and kneeling.
My lady Morgan Le Fay.
The Coven Akkaba is at your command.
I assume you haven't disentangled yourself from your *witchbreed friends* yet, as their *weed* still grows in my realm.
Witchbreed? You mean mutants?
As they are called in your baseborn tongue.
Take your coven's name-- **Akkaba.**
Akkaba was simply a place. The birthplace of *one* mutant--
--and a great many *humans* who cast him out.
Think you that he is the source of these gates in my realm? This *Apocalypse?*
If so, then where is his head?

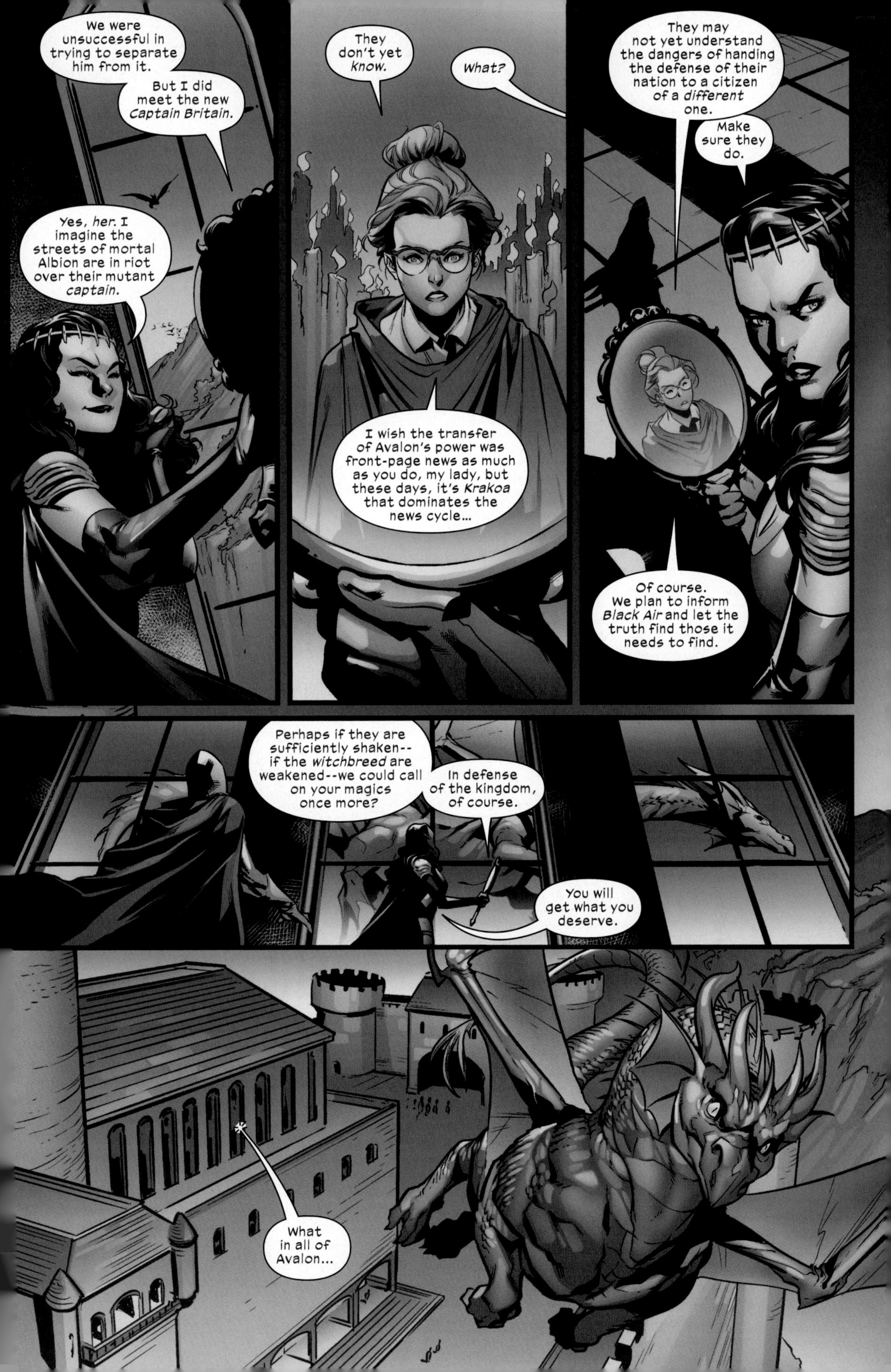
We were unsuccessful in trying to separate him from it.
But I did meet the new *Captain Britain.*
Yes, *her.* I imagine the streets of mortal Albion are in riot over their mutant *captain.*
They don't yet *know.*
What?
I wish the transfer of Avalon's power was front-page news as much as you do, my lady, but these days, it's *Krakoa* that dominates the news cycle...
They may not yet understand the dangers of handing the defense of their nation to a citizen of a *different* one.
Make sure they do.
Of course. We plan to inform *Black Air* and let the truth find those it needs to find.
Perhaps if they are sufficiently shaken-- if the *witchbreed* are weakened--we could call on your magics once more?
In defense of the kingdom, of course.
You will get what you deserve.
What in all of Avalon...

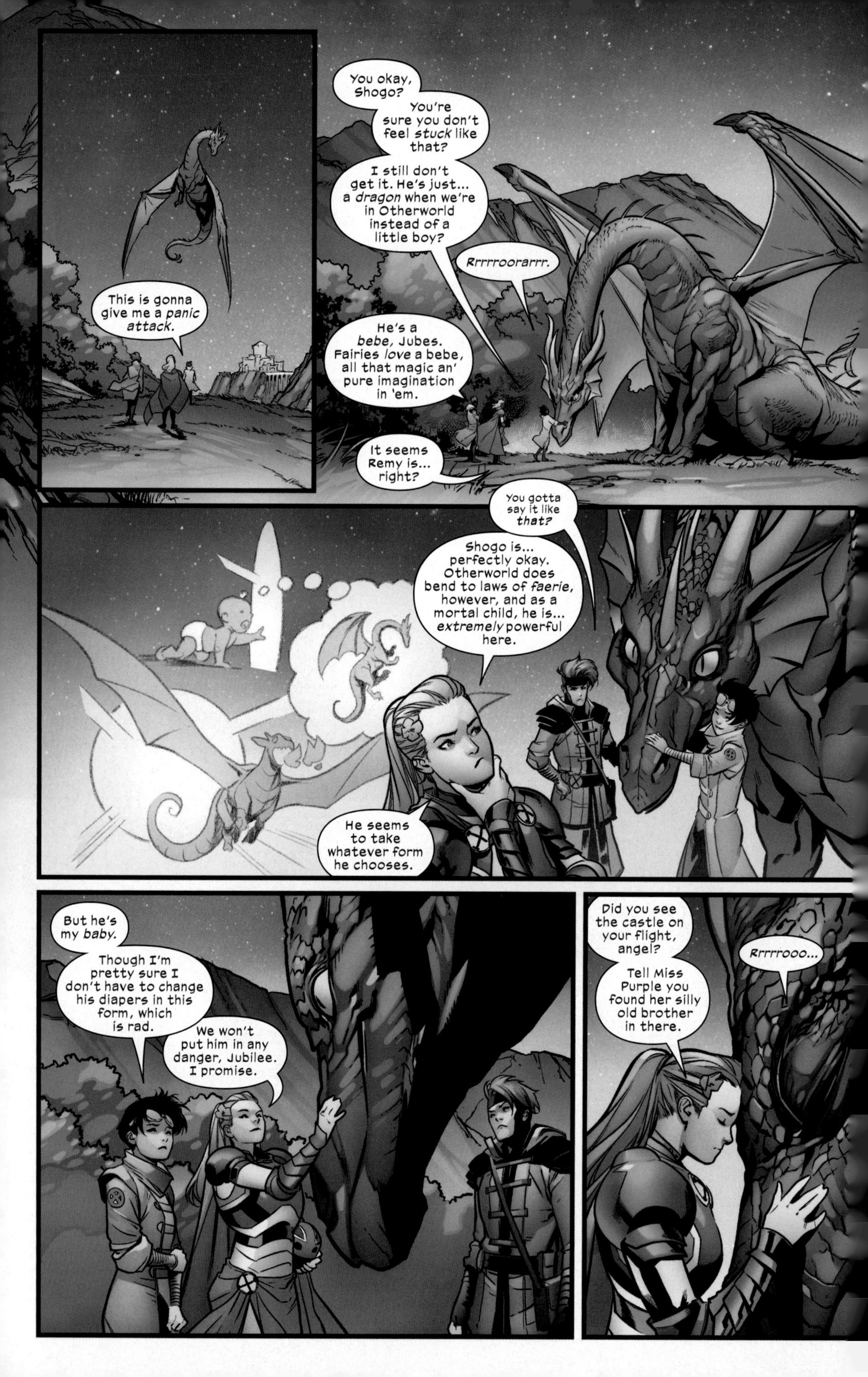
This is gonna give me a *panic attack.*
You okay, Shogo?
You're sure you don't feel *stuck* like that?
I still don't get it. He's just... a *dragon* when we're in Otherworld instead of a little boy?
Rrrrroorarrr.
He's a *bebe,* Jubes. Fairies *love* a bebe, all that magic an' pure imagination in 'em.
It seems Remy is... right?
You gotta say it like *that?*
Shogo is... perfectly okay. Otherworld does bend to laws of *faerie,* however, and as a mortal child, he is... *extremely* powerful here.
He seems to take whatever form he chooses.
But he's my *baby.*
Though I'm pretty sure I don't have to change his diapers in this form, which is rad.
We won't put him in any danger, Jubilee. I promise.
Did you see the castle on your flight, angel?
Tell Miss Purple you found her silly old brother in there.
Rrrrrooo...

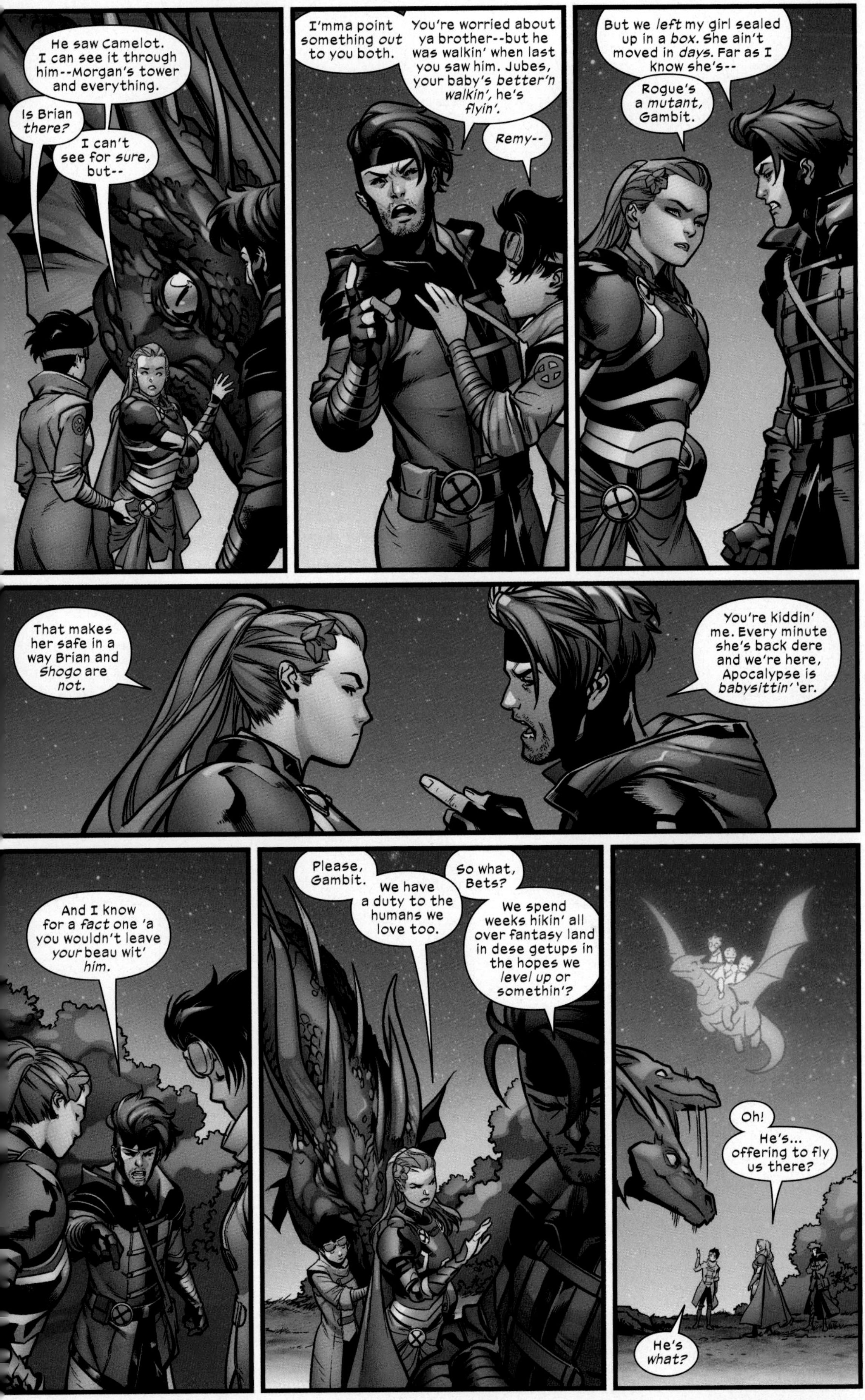
He saw Camelot. I can see it through him--Morgan's tower and everything.
Is Brian there?
I can't see for sure, but--
I'mma point something out to you both.
You're worried about ya brother--but he was walkin' when last you saw him. Jubes, your baby's better'n walkin', he's flyin'.
Remy--
But we left my girl sealed up in a box. She ain't moved in days. Far as I know she's--
Rogue's a mutant, Gambit.
That makes her safe in a way Brian and Shogo are not.
You're kiddin' me. Every minute she's back dere and we're here, Apocalypse is babysittin' 'er.
And I know for a fact one 'a you wouldn't leave your beau wit' him.
Please, Gambit.
We have a duty to the humans we love too.
So what, Bets?
We spend weeks hikin' all over fantasy land in dese getups in the hopes we level up or somethin'?
Oh! He's... offering to fly us there?
He's what?

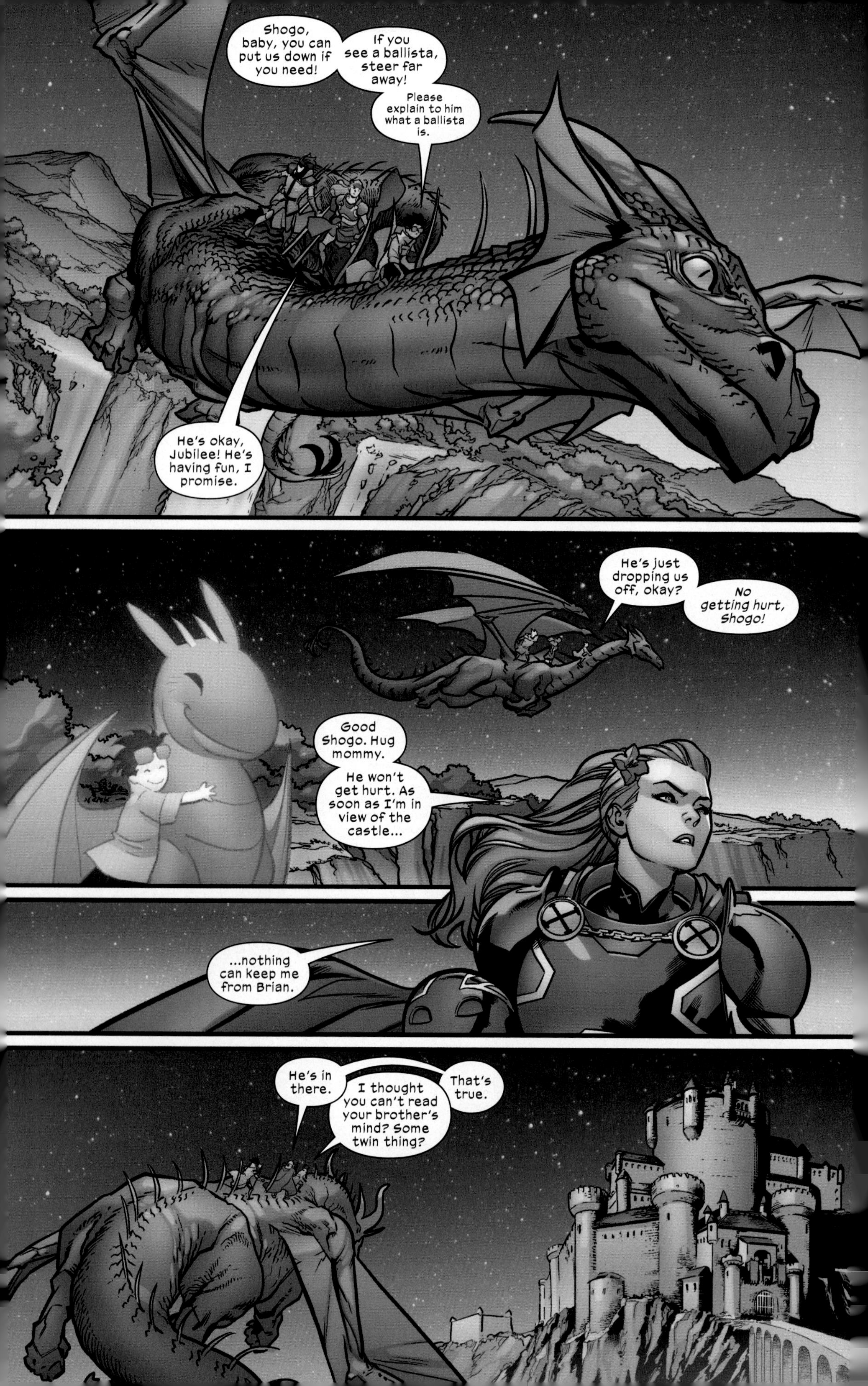
Shogo, baby, you can put us down if you need!
If you see a ballista, steer far away!
Please explain to him what a ballista is.
He's okay, Jubilee! He's having fun, I promise.
He's just dropping us off, okay?
No getting hurt, Shogo!
Good Shogo. Hug mommy.
He won't get hurt. As soon as I'm in view of the castle...
...nothing can keep me from Brian.
He's in there.
That's true.
I thought you can't read your brother's mind? Some twin thing?

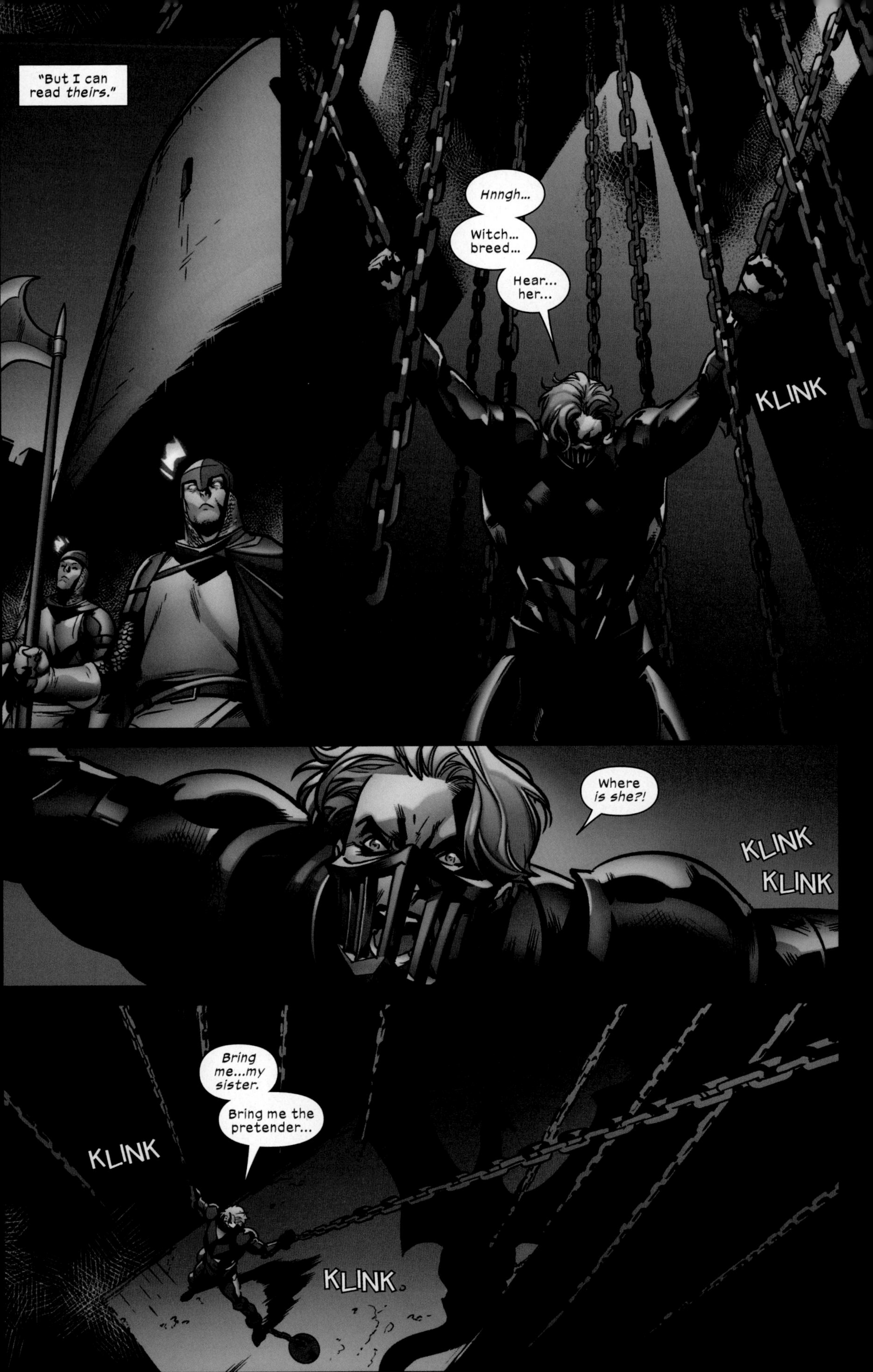
"But I can read *theirs.*"
Hnngh...
Witch... breed...
Hear... her...
KLINK
Where *is she?!*
KLINK
KLINK
Bring me...my sister.
Bring me the pretender...
KLINK
KLINK

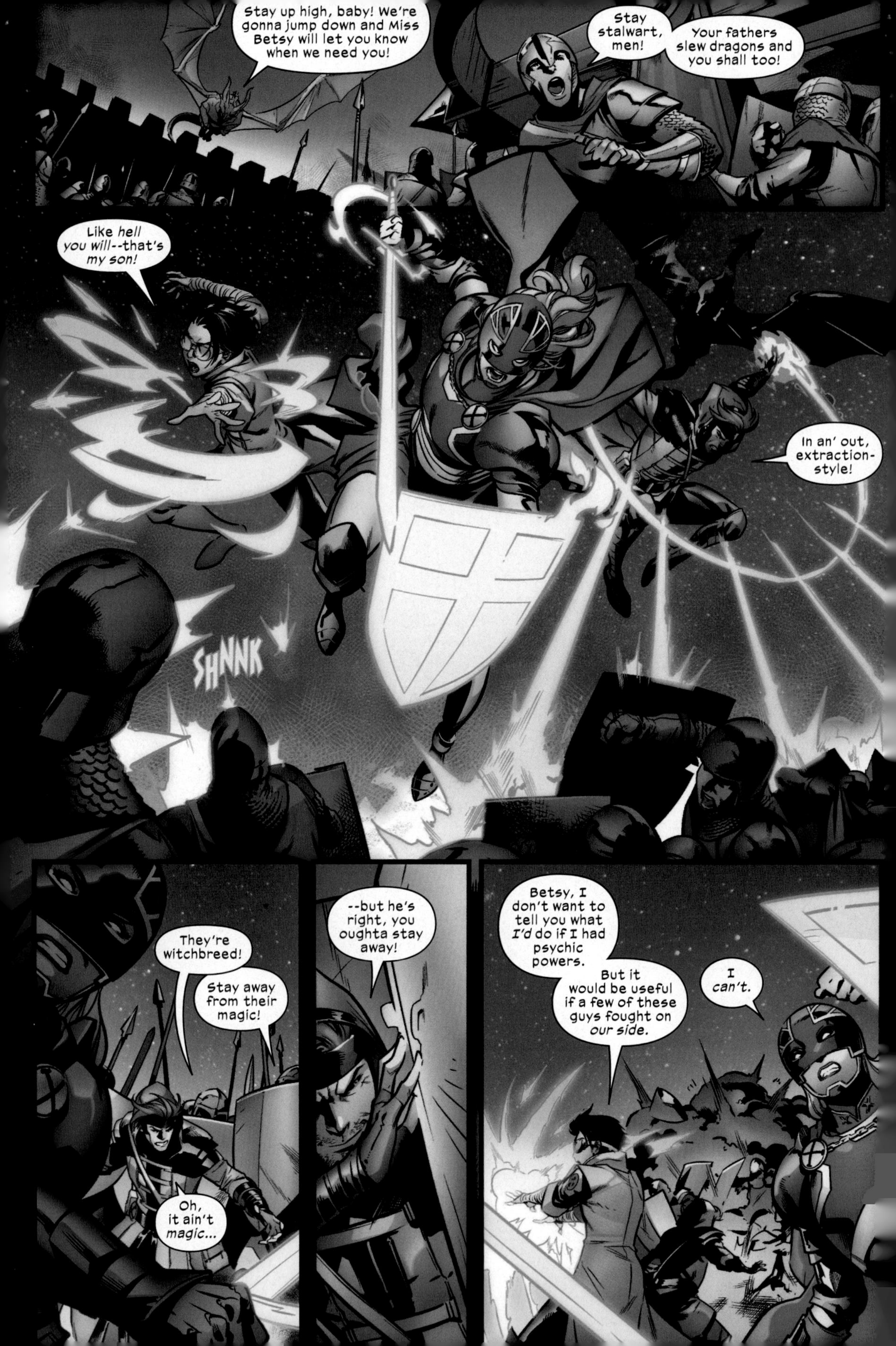

Stay up high, baby! We're gonna jump down and Miss Betsy will let you know when we need you!
Stay stalwart, men!
Your fathers slew dragons and you shall too!
Like *hell* you *will*--that's *my son!*
In an' out, extraction-style!
SHNNK
They're witchbreed!
Stay away from their magic!
Oh, it ain't *magic...*
--but he's right, you oughta stay away!
Betsy, I don't want to tell you what *I'd* do if I had psychic powers.
But it would be useful if a few of these guys fought on *our side.*
I *can't.*

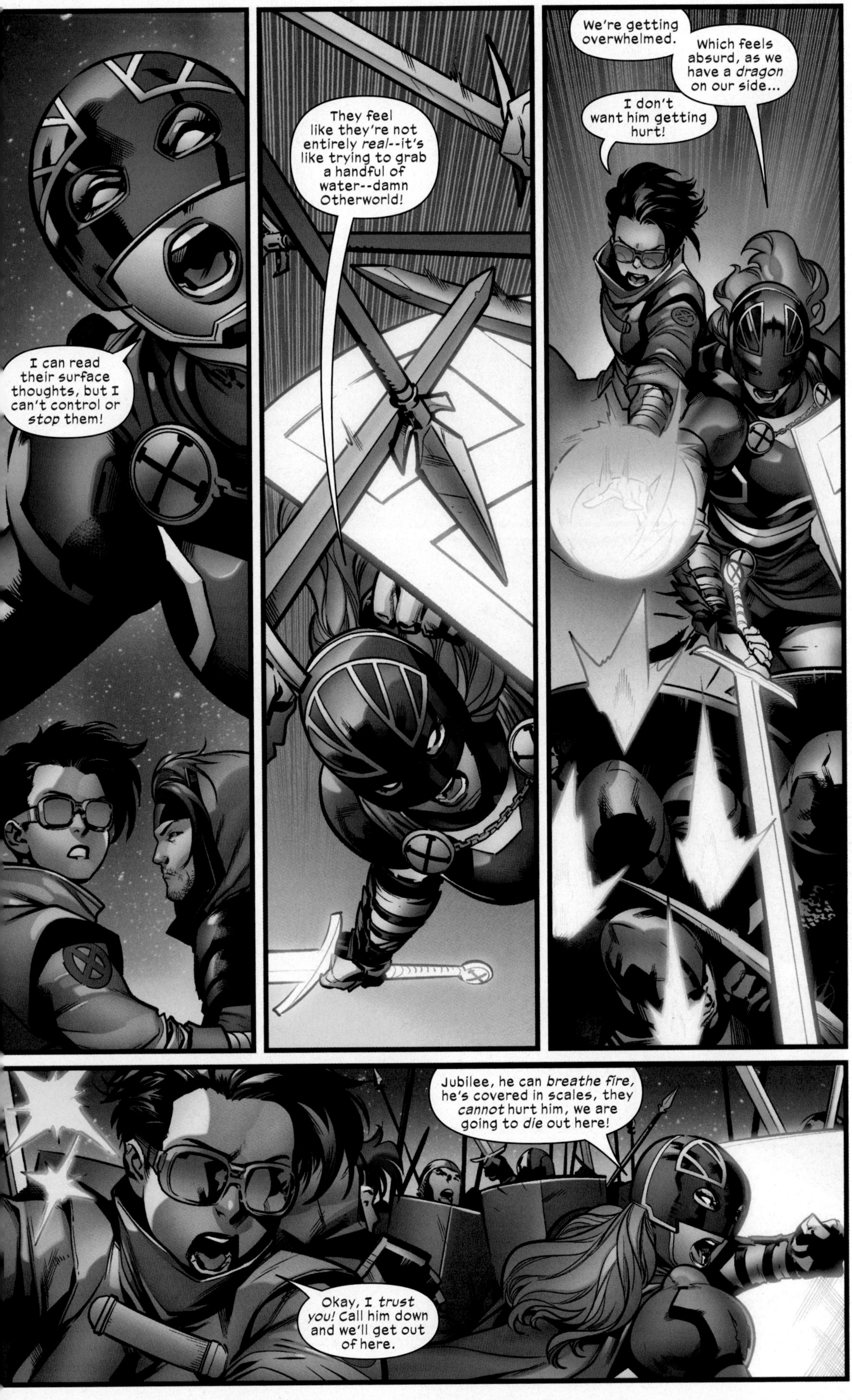

I can read their surface thoughts, but I can't control or *stop* them!
They feel like they're not entirely *real*--it's like trying to grab a handful of water--damn Otherworld!
We're getting overwhelmed.
Which feels absurd, as we have a *dragon* on our side...
I don't want him getting hurt!
Jubilee, he can *breathe fire,* he's covered in scales, they *cannot* hurt him, we are going to *die* out here!
Okay, I *trust you!* Call him down and we'll get out of here.

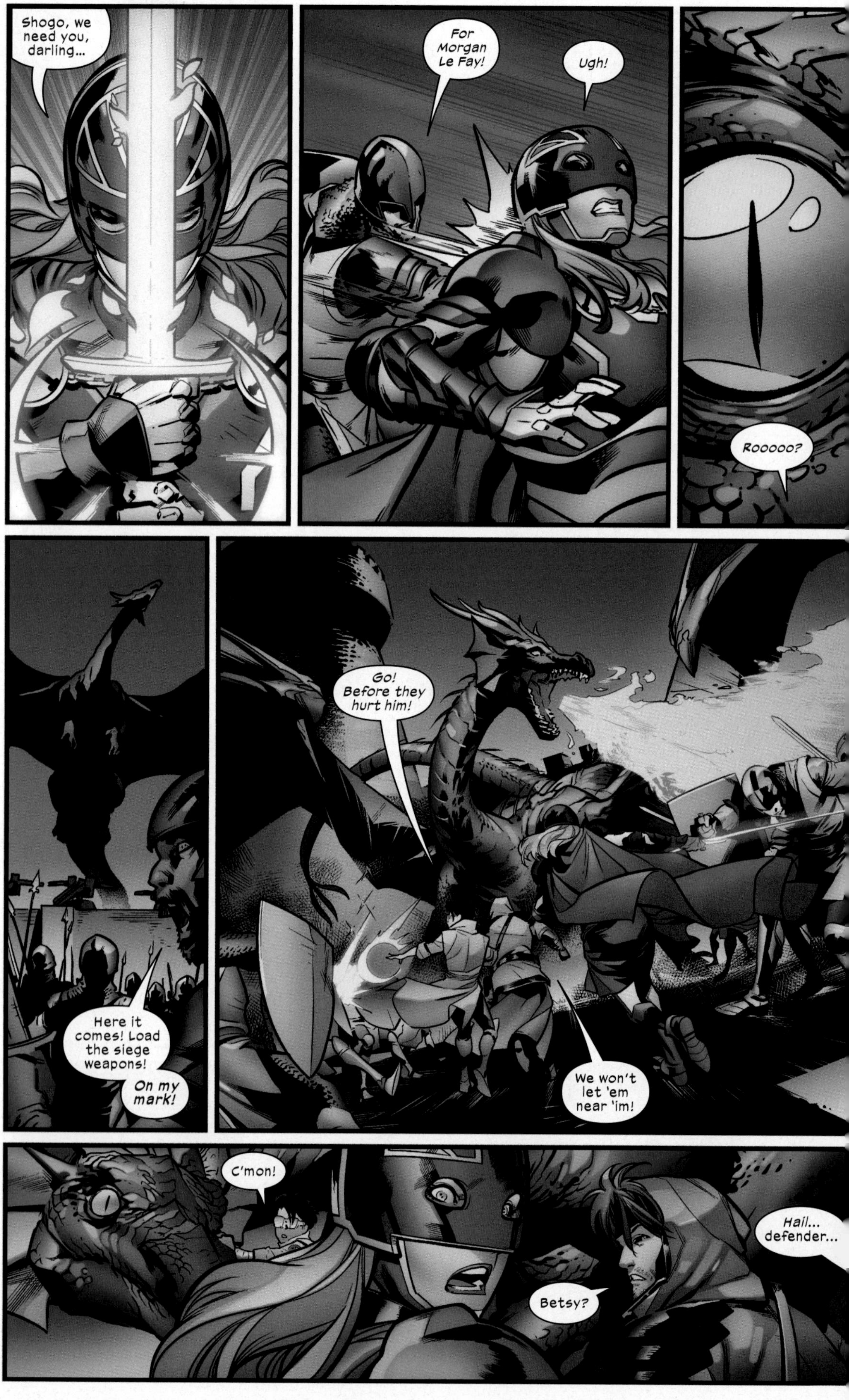
Shogo, we need you, darling...
For Morgan Le Fay!
Ugh!
Rooooo?
Here it comes! Load the siege weapons!
On my mark!
Go! Before they hurt him!
We won't let 'em near 'im!
C'mon!
Betsy?
Hail... defender...

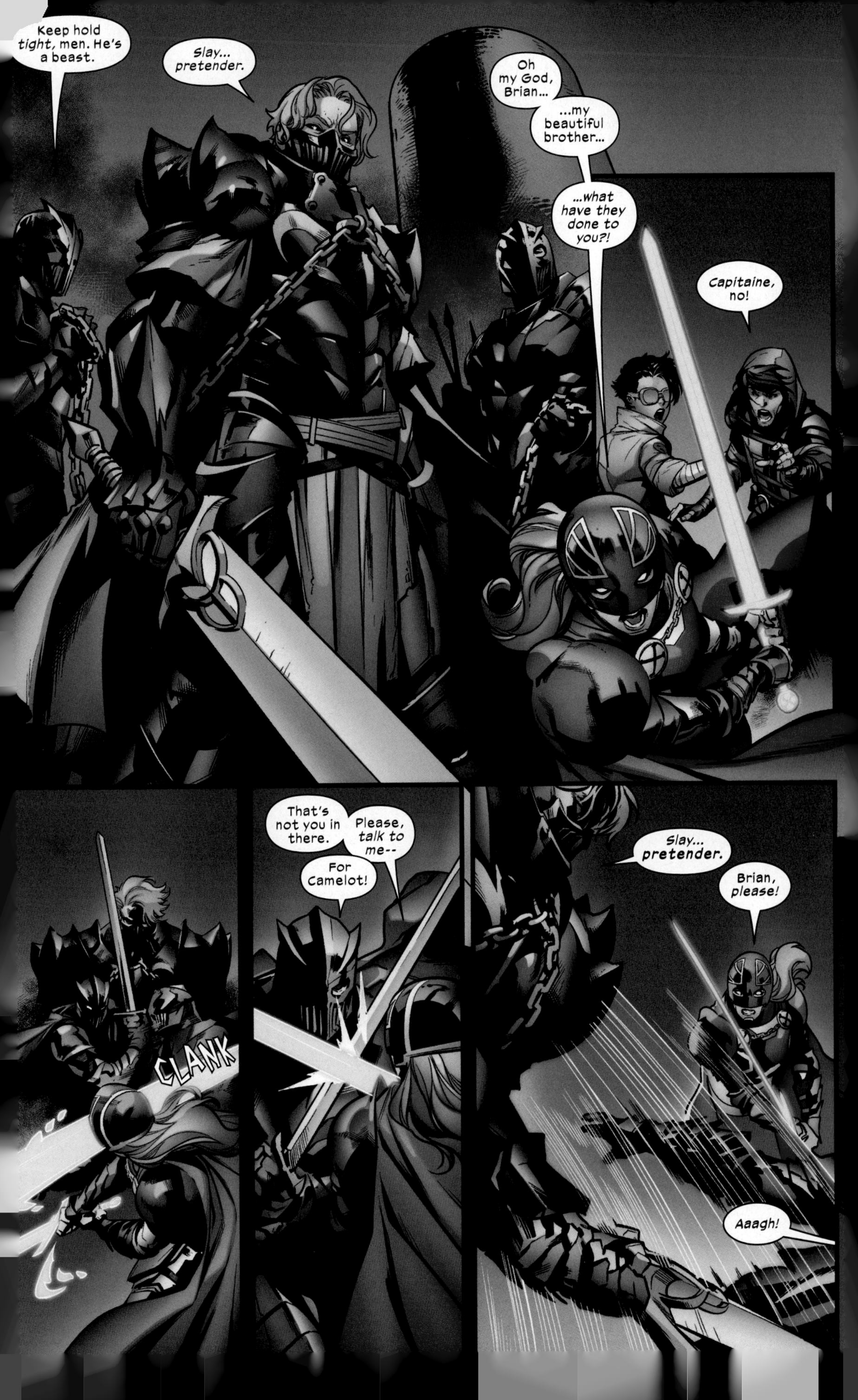

Keep hold tight, men. He's a beast.
Slay... pretender.
Oh my God, Brian...
...my beautiful brother...
...what have they done to you?!
Capitaine, no!
CLANK
That's not you in there.
Please, talk to me--
For Camelot!
Slay... pretender.
Brian, please!
Aaagh!

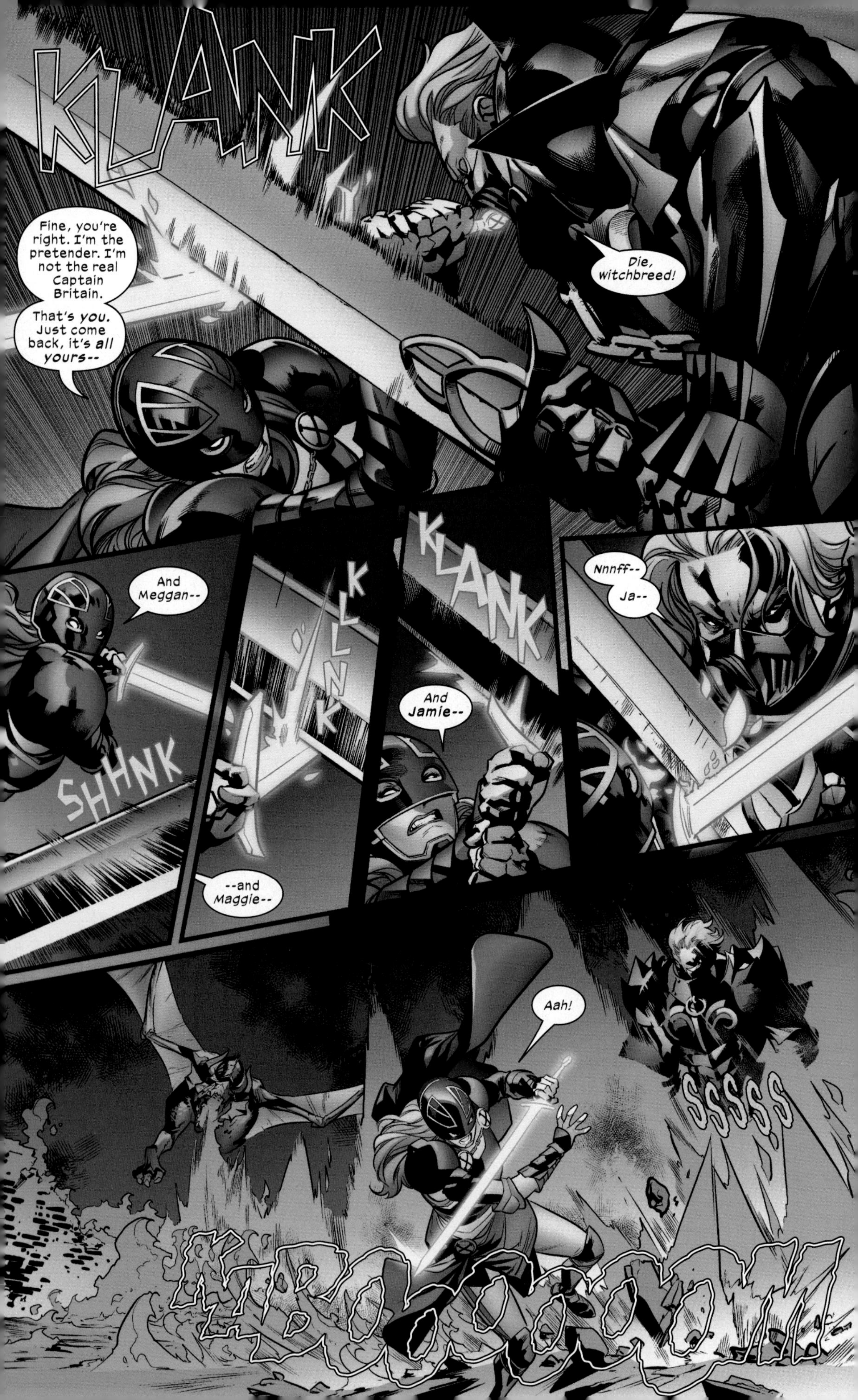
KLANK
Fine, you're right. I'm the pretender. I'm not the real Captain Britain.
That's *you.* Just come back, it's *all yours*--
Die, witchbreed!
And Meggan--
SHHNK
KLLNK
--and Maggie--
KLANK
And Jamie--
Nnnff--
Ja--
Aah!
SSSSS

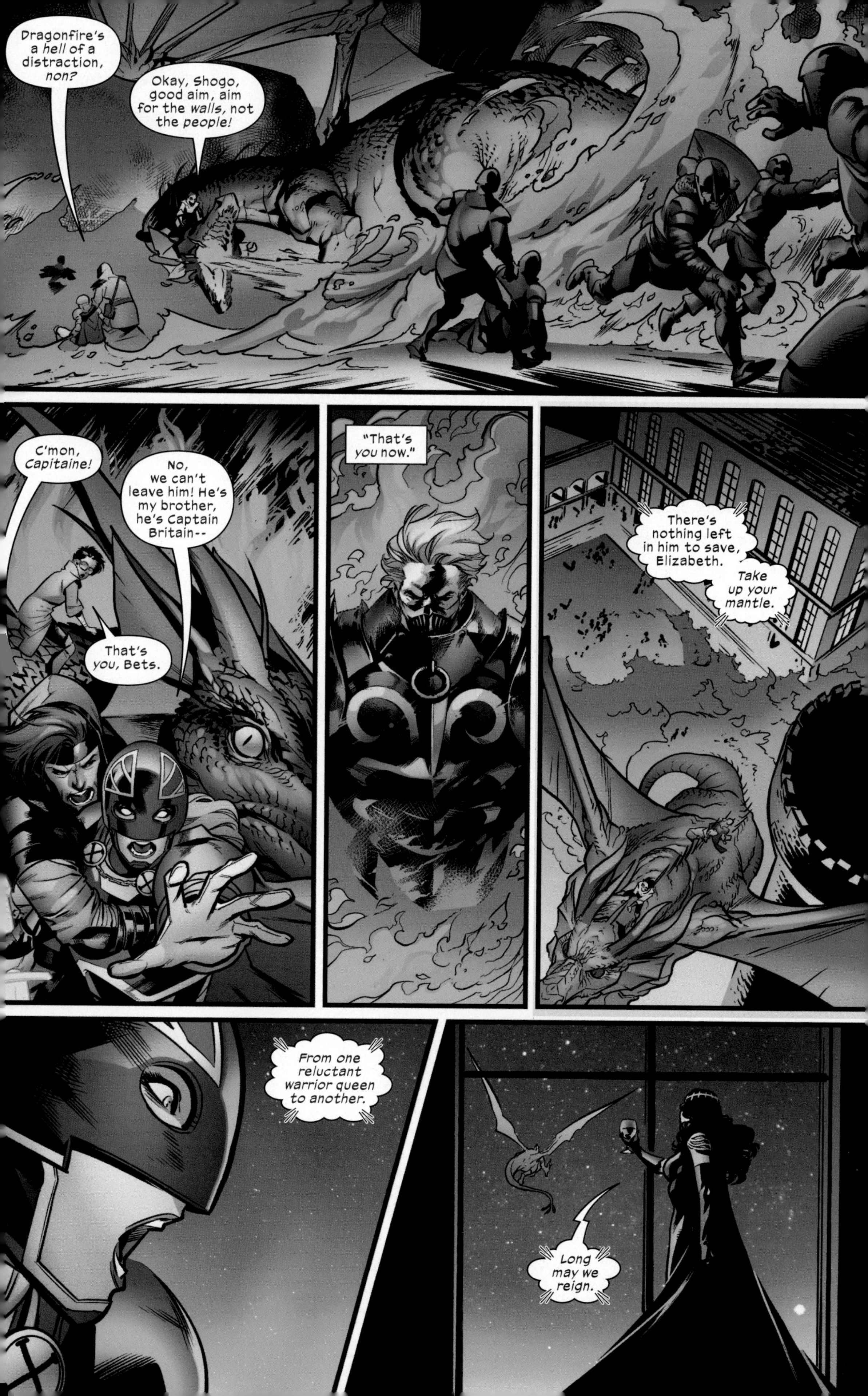

Dragonfire's a *hell* of a distraction, *non?*
Okay, Shogo, good aim, aim for the *walls,* not the *people!*
C'mon, *Capitaine!*
No, we can't leave him! He's my brother, he's Captain Britain--
That's *you,* Bets.
"That's *you* now."
There's nothing left in him to save, Elizabeth.
Take up your mantle.
From one reluctant warrior queen to another.
Long may we reign.

FOR IMMEDIATE AND OFFICIAL RELEASE TO MI-13 AND INTELLIGENCE PARTNERS (Project BLACK AIR, et al.):

Recent and routine intelligence monitoring suggests activity in the area of OTHERWORLD (Extradimensional zone *Alpha* including areas marked: Avalon, Camelot, etc.)

Flag and review surveillance of known Otherworld assets including:

- Braddock, Brian
- Braddock, Elizabeth
- Braddock, Jamie
- Braddock, Meggan *(née Puceanu)*
- Le Fay, Morgan
- Pryde, Katherine
- Ross, Courtney
- Summers, Rachel
- Wagner, Kurt

ENGAGE CAREFULLY.
Recent nation-building in the area of Krakoa necessitates extreme caution when engaging with mutants. Read and review all Agency Action Protocols prior to any engagement. **DO NOT ENGAGE MUTANTS ALONE.** Partnership is accountability.

— The Department

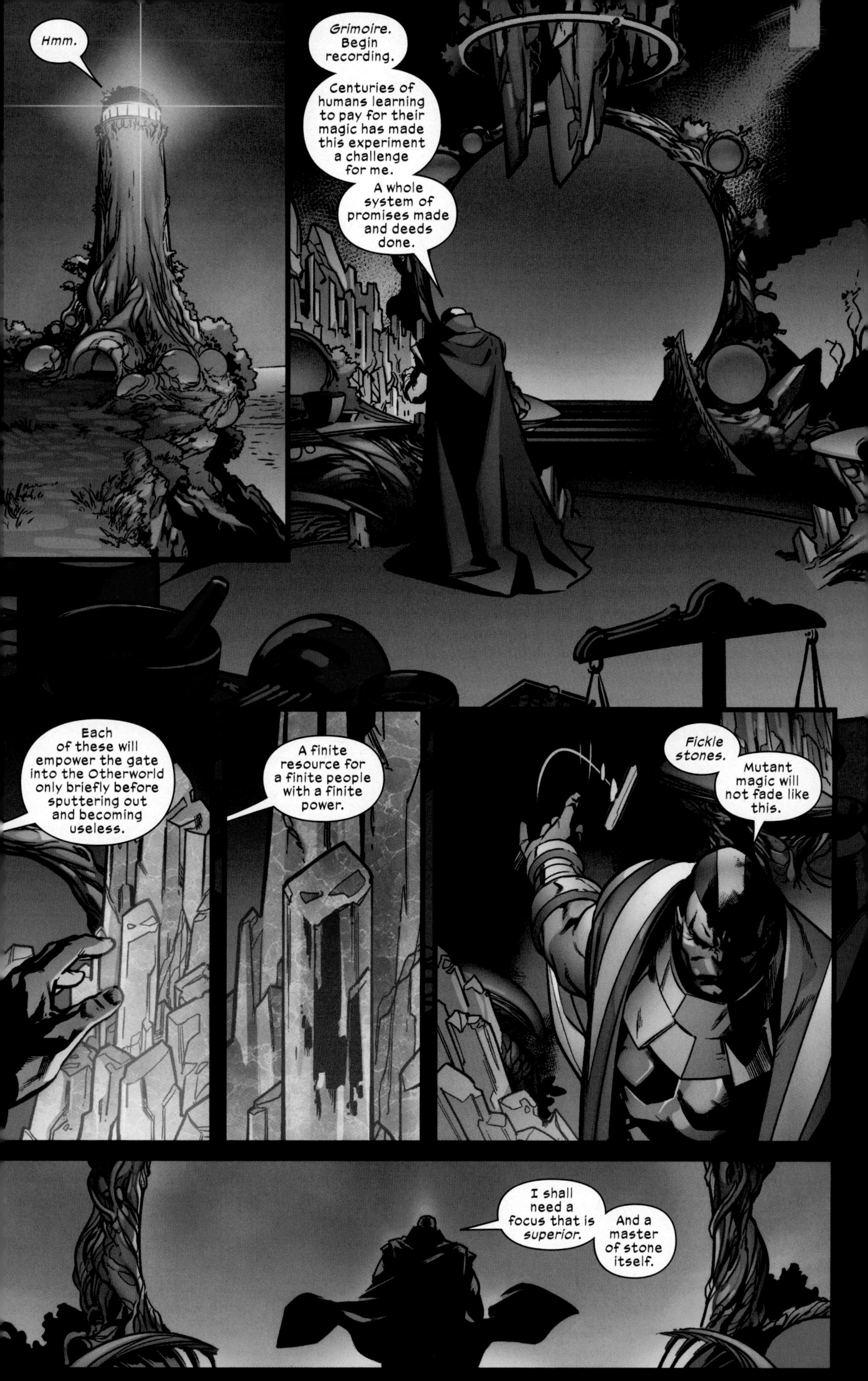

Hmm.
Grimoire. Begin recording.
Centuries of humans learning to pay for their magic has made this experiment a challenge for me.
A whole system of promises made and deeds done.
Each of these will empower the gate into the Otherworld only briefly before sputtering out and becoming useless.
A finite resource for a finite people with a finite power.
Fickle stones.
Mutant magic will not fade like this.
I shall need a focus that is *superior.*
And a master of stone itself.

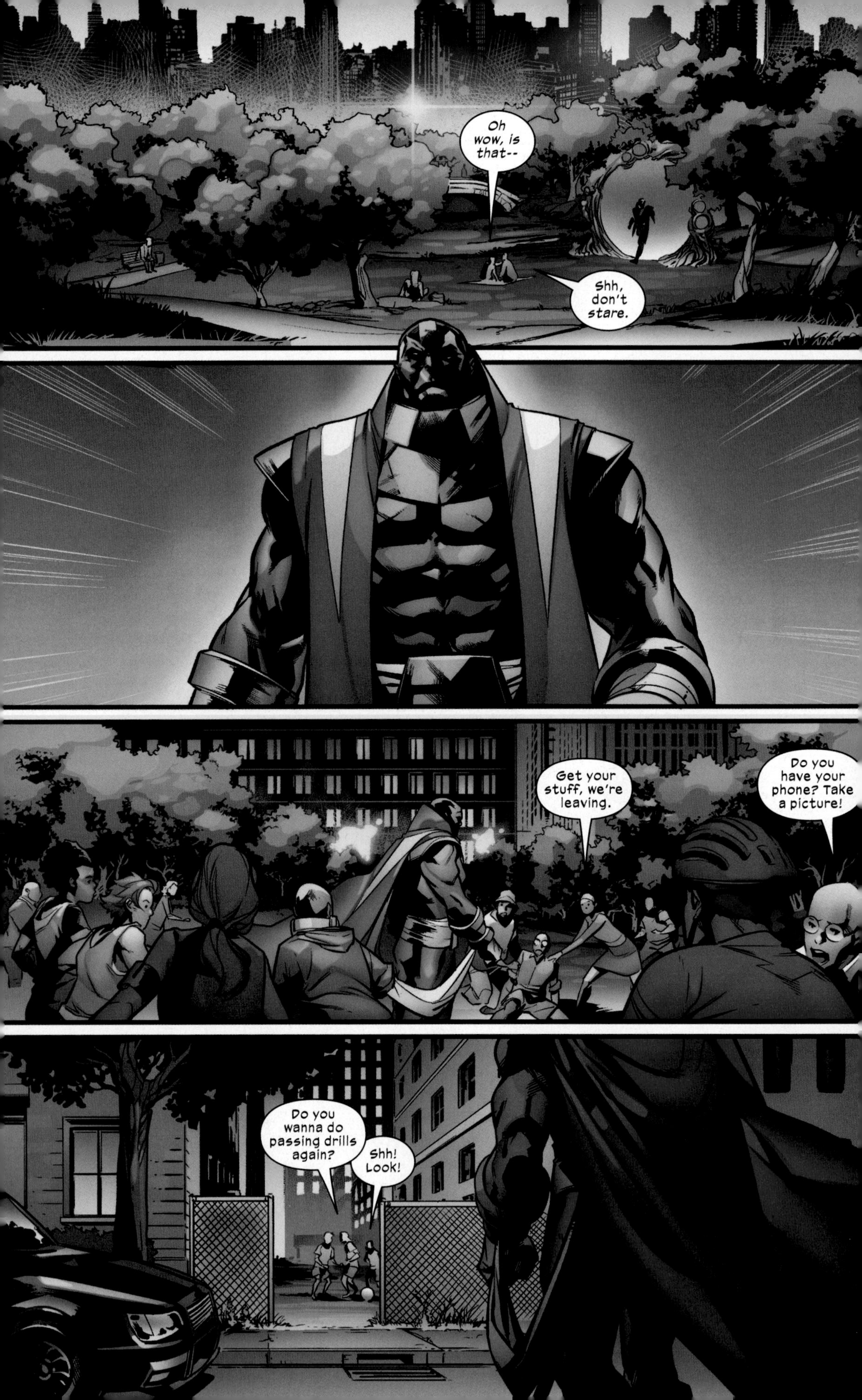

Oh wow, is that--
Shh, don't stare.
Get your stuff, we're leaving.
Do you have your phone? Take a picture!
Do you wanna do passing drills again?
Shh! Look!

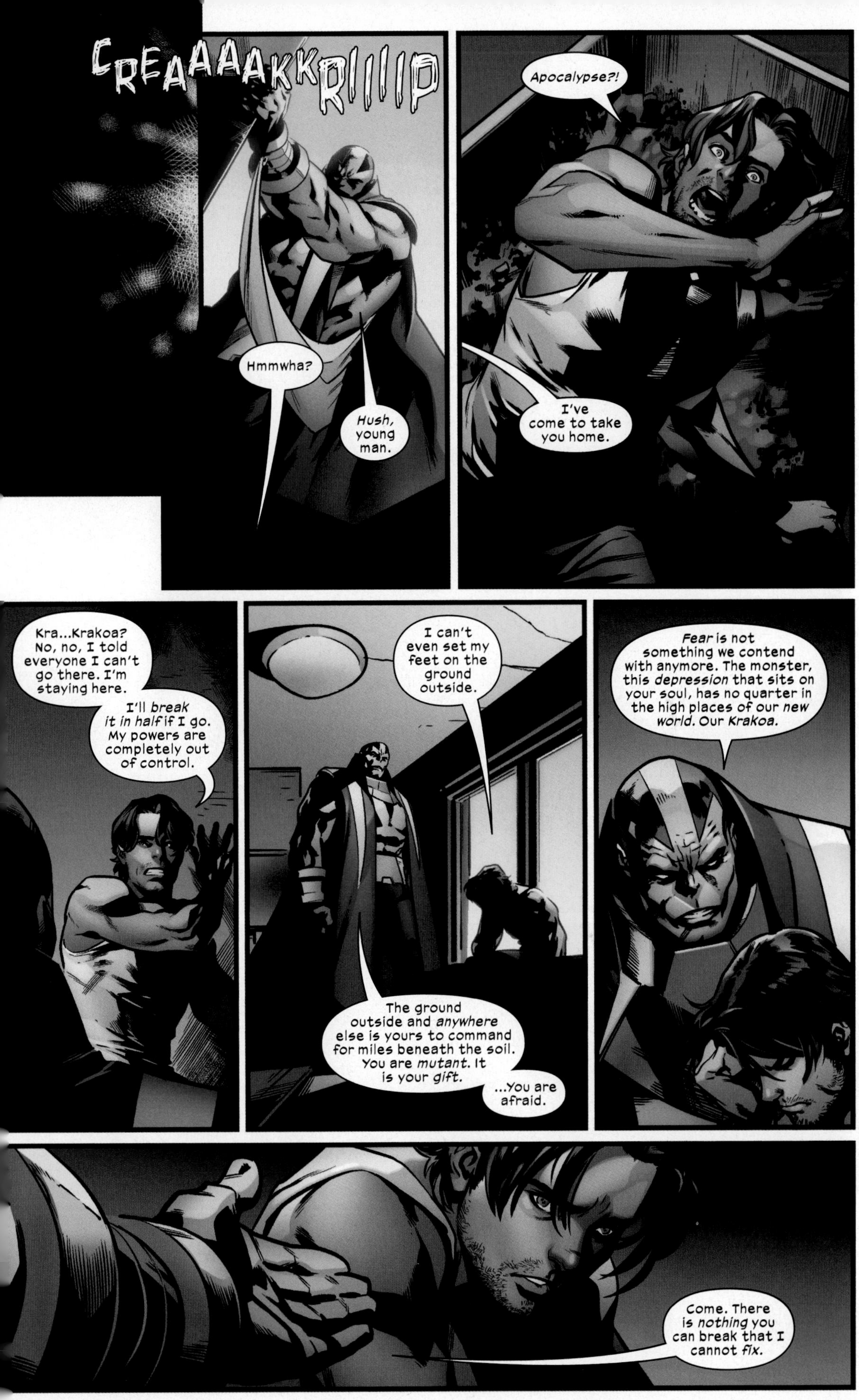
CREAAAAKKRIIIP
Hmmwha?
Hush, young man.
Apocalypse?!
I've come to take you home.
Kra...Krakoa? No, no, I told everyone I can't go there. I'm staying here.
I'll *break it in half* if I go. My powers are completely out of control.
I can't even set my feet on the ground outside.
The ground outside and *anywhere* else is yours to command for miles beneath the soil. You are *mutant*. It is your *gift*.
...You are afraid.
Fear is not something we contend with anymore. The monster, this *depression* that sits on your soul, has no quarter in the high places of our *new world*. Our *Krakoa*.
Come. There is *nothing* you can break that I cannot *fix*.

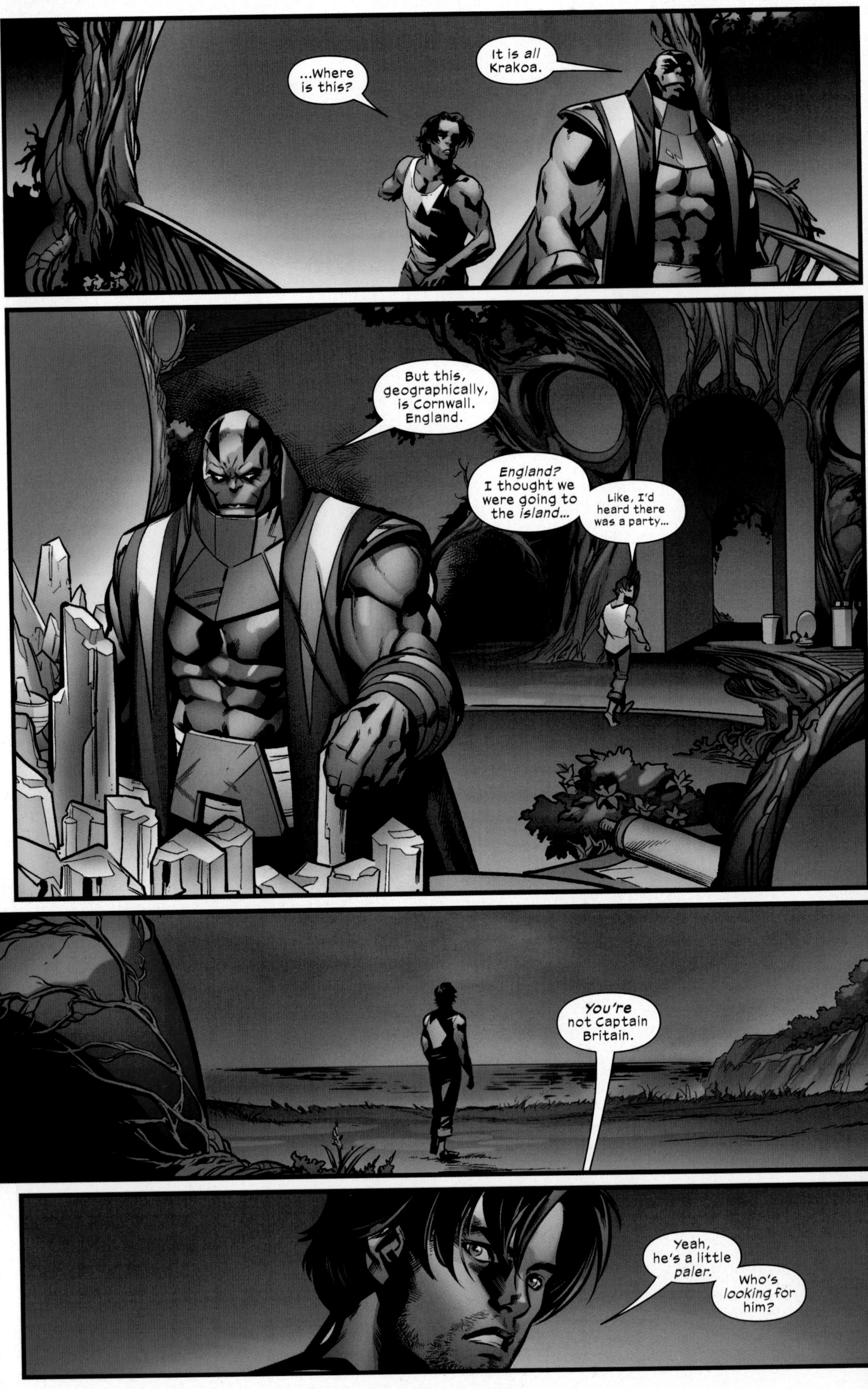
...Where is this?
It is *all* Krakoa.
But this, geographically, is Cornwall. England.
England? I thought we were going to the *island*...
Like, I'd heard there was a party...
You're not Captain Britain.
Yeah, he's a little *paler.*
Who's *looking* for him?

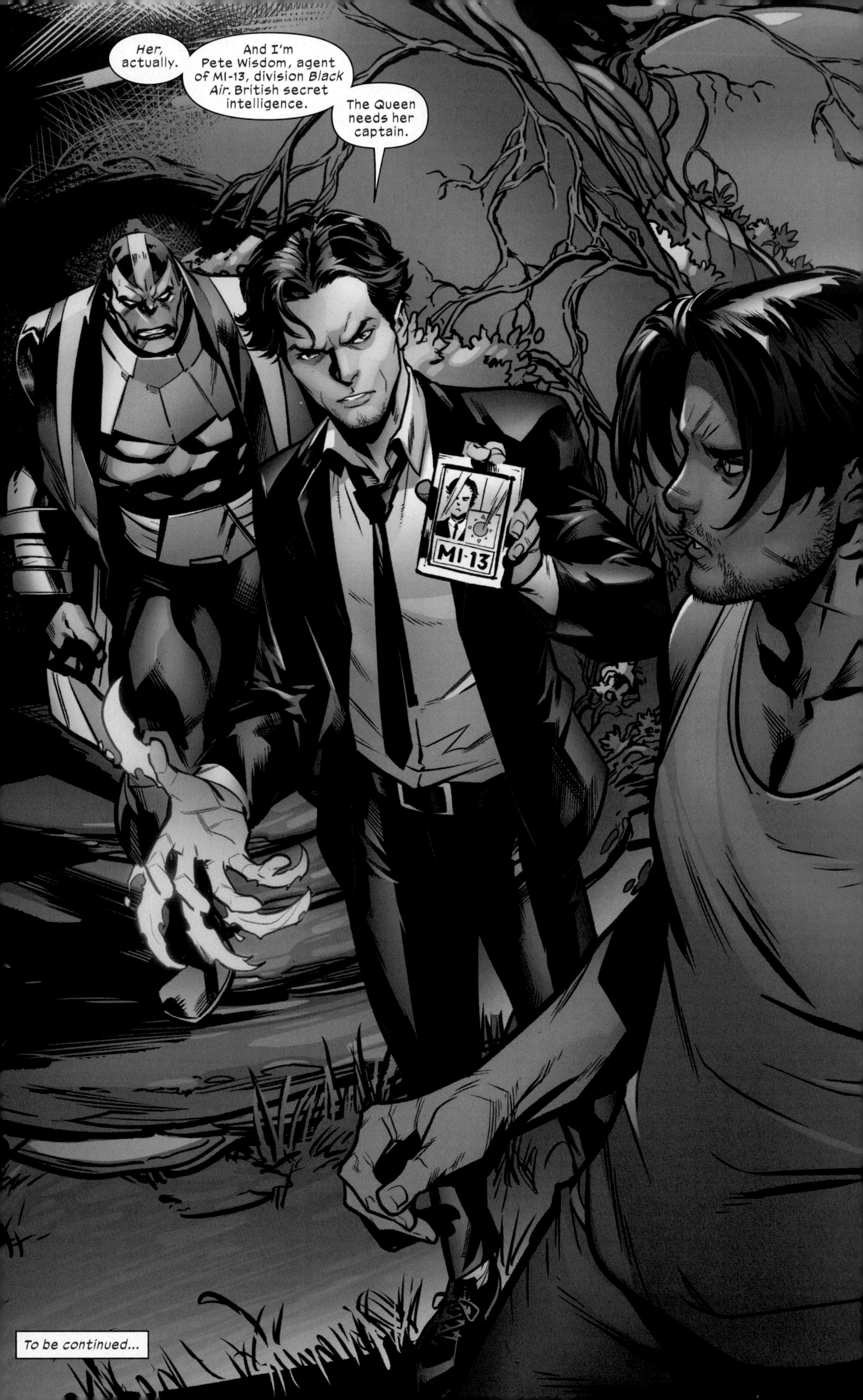
Her, actually.
And I'm Pete Wisdom, agent of MI-13, division *Black Air.* British secret intelligence.
The Queen needs her captain.
MI-13
To be continued...

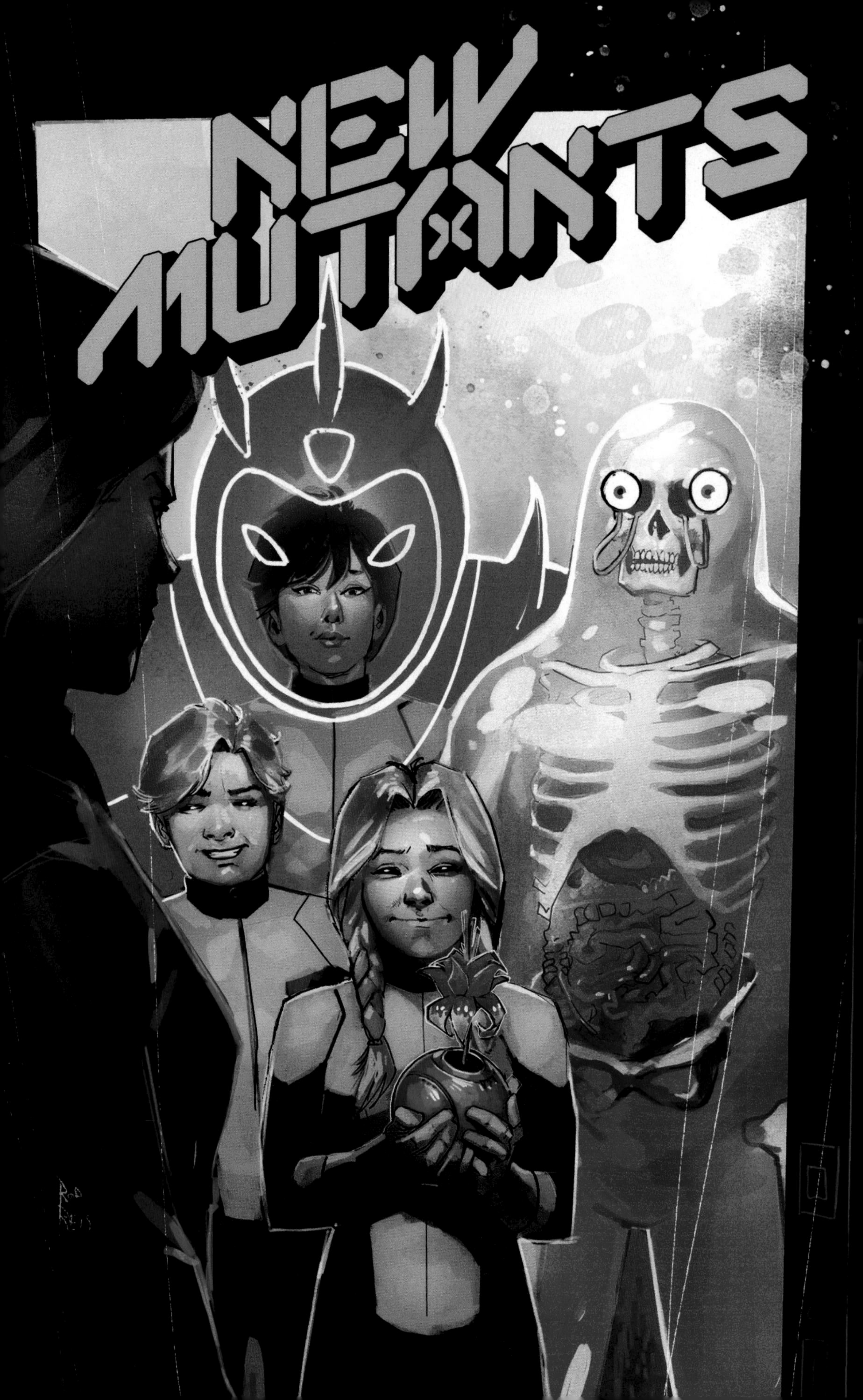
NEW
MUTANTS

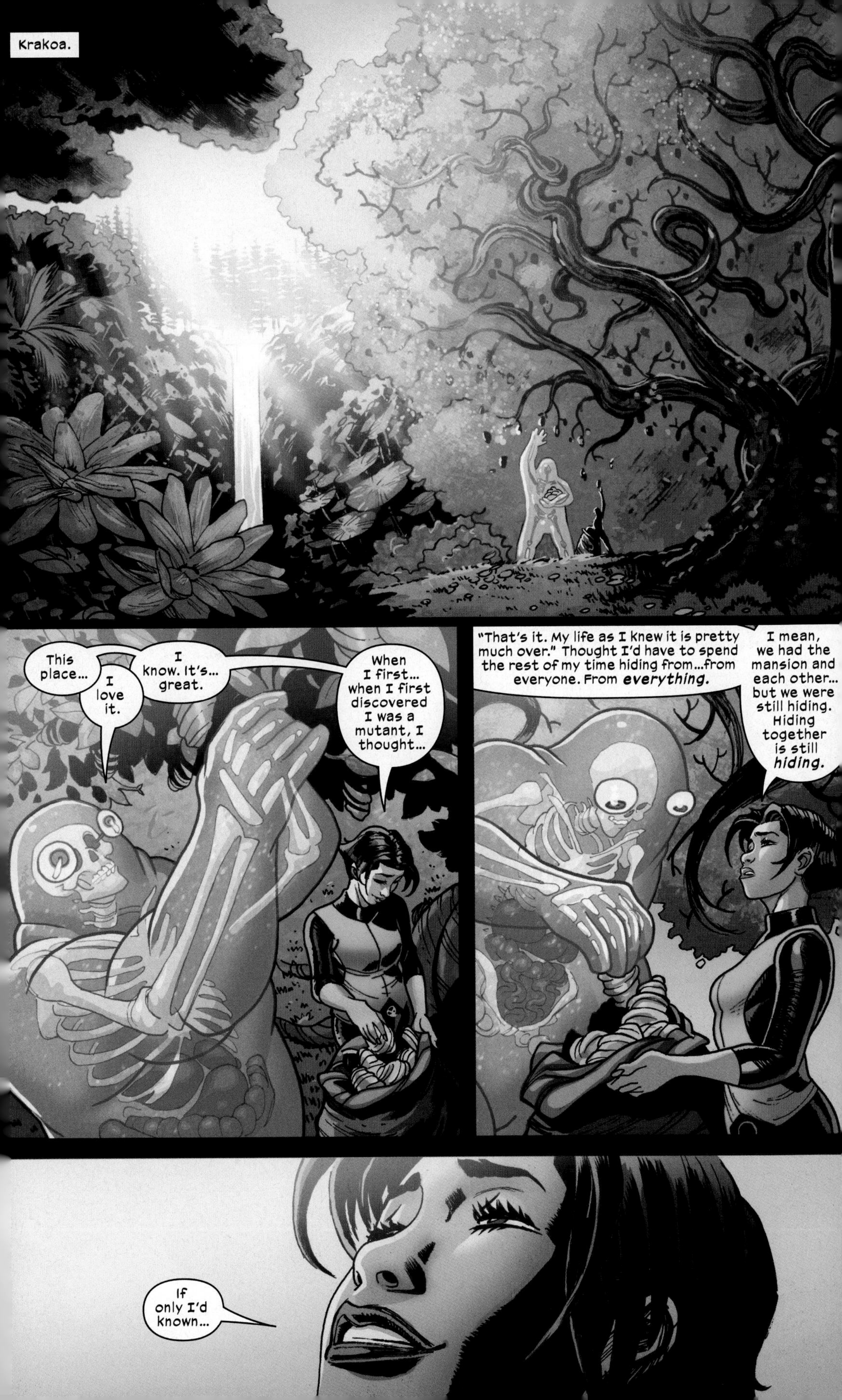
Krakoa.
This place...
I love it.
I know. It's... great.
When I first... when I first discovered I was a mutant, I thought...
"That's it. My life as I knew it is pretty much over." Thought I'd have to spend the rest of my time hiding from...from everyone. From *everything*.
I mean, we had the mansion and each other... but we were still hiding. Hiding together is still *hiding*.
If only I'd known...

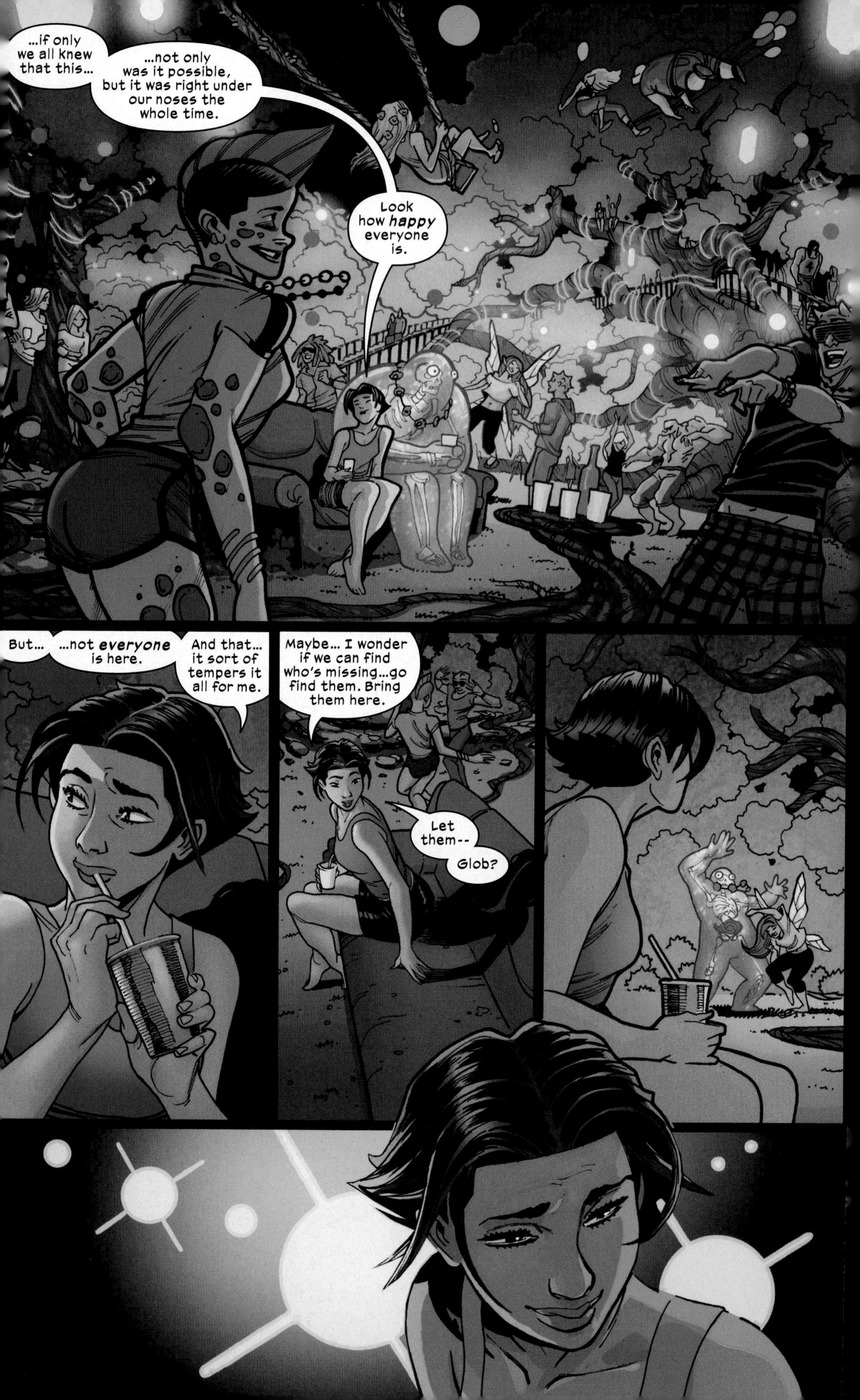

...if only we all knew that this...
...not only was it possible, but it was right under our noses the whole time.
Look how *happy* everyone is.
But...
...not *everyone* is here.
And that... it sort of tempers it all for me.
Maybe... I wonder if we can find who's missing...go find them. Bring them here.
Let them--
Glob?

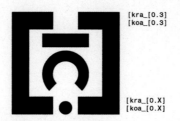

[kra_[0.3]
[koa_[0.3]

[kra_[0.X]
[koa_[0.X]

NO MUTANT IS AN ISLAND

The nation of Krakoa is a safe haven for mutantkind.

But there are still mutants who haven't come to the island -- and why would anyone want to miss out on paradise?

Armor

Glob

Sage

Boom-Boom

Maxime

Manon

[kra_[0.3]...]
[koa_[0.3]...]

[search..find]

[00_search____X]
[00_find______X]

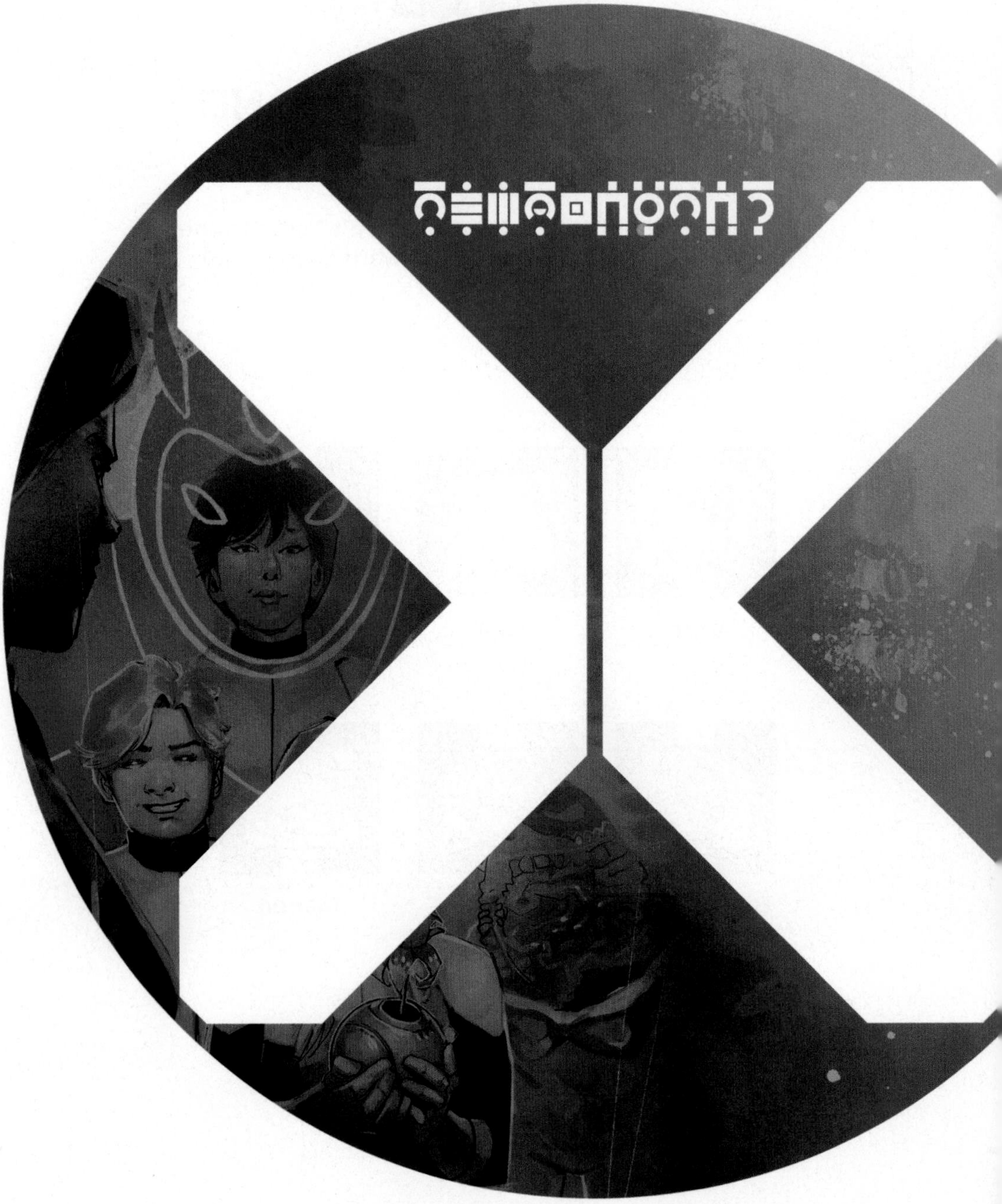

[00_search____X]
[00_find______X]

ED BRISSON....................................[WRITER]
FLAVIANO......................................[ARTIST]
CARLOS LOPEZ..............................[COLOR ARTIST]
VC's TRAVIS LANHAM...........................[LETTERER]
TOM MULLER....................................[DESIGN]

ROD REIS..................................[COVER ARTIST]

NICK RUSSELL................................[PRODUCTION]

JONATHAN HICKMAN............................[HEAD OF X]
ANNALISE BISSA........................[ASSISTANT EDITOR]
JORDAN D. WHITE...............................[EDITOR]
C.B. CEBULSKI.......................[EDITOR IN CHIEF]
JOE QUESADA.....................[CHIEF CREATIVE OFFICER]
DAN BUCKLEY.................................[PRESIDENT]
ALAN FINE.........................[EXECUTIVE PRODUCER]

[03] NEW MUTANTS

[ISSUE THREE]..............TO THE GRAVE

[00_search__X]
[00_find____X]

[00_00.....0]
[00_00.....3]

[00___krakoa]
[00_is______]

[00_calling_]

[00_answer?_]

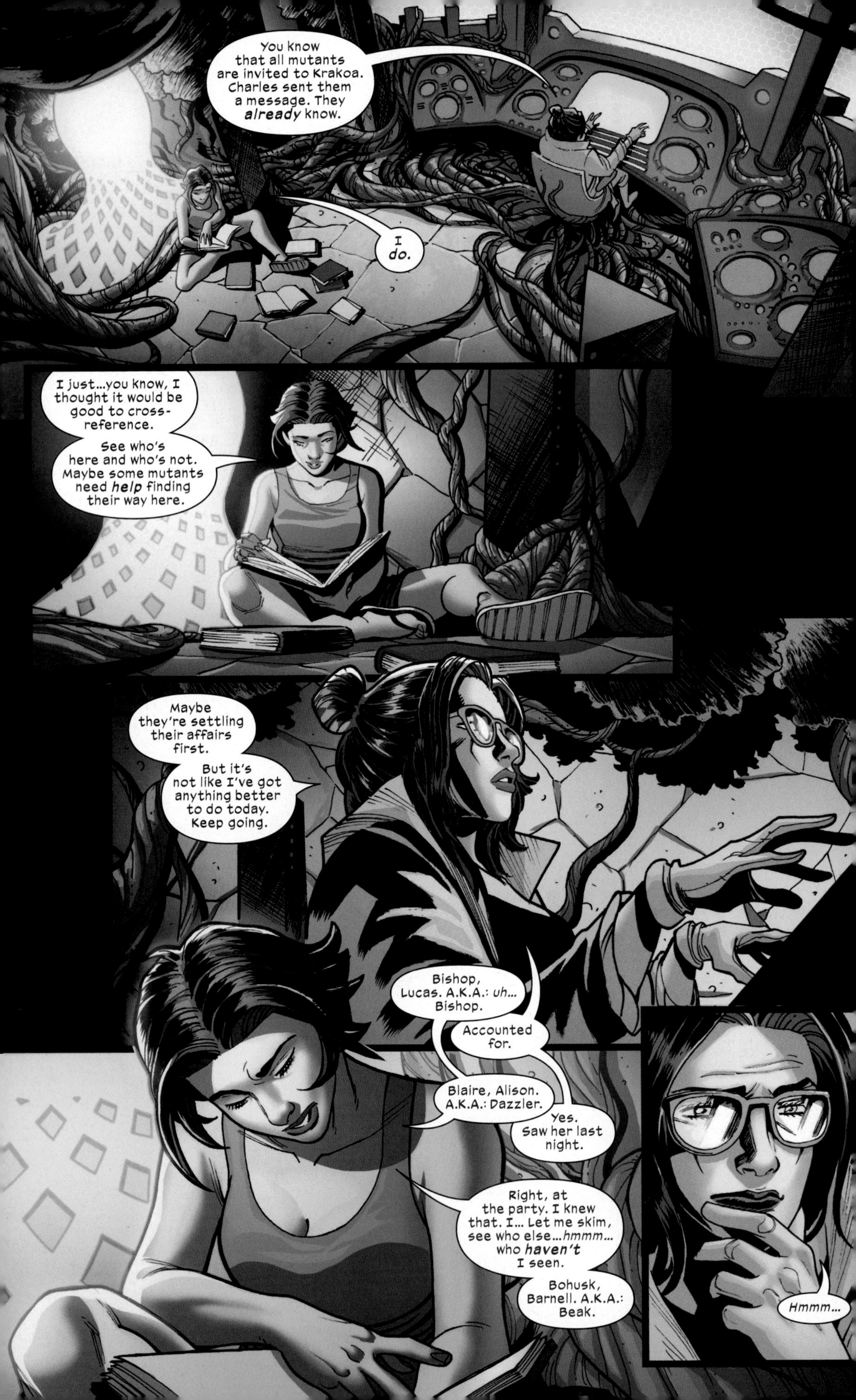
You know that all mutants are invited to Krakoa. Charles sent them a message. They *already* know.
I *do.*
I just...you know, I thought it would be good to cross-reference.
See who's here and who's not. Maybe some mutants need **help** finding their way here.
Maybe they're settling their affairs first.
But it's not like I've got anything better to do today. Keep going.
Bishop, Lucas. A.K.A.: *uh...* Bishop.
Accounted for.
Blaire, Alison. A.K.A.: Dazzler.
Yes. Saw her last night.
Right, at the party. I knew that. I... Let me skim, see who else...*hmmm...* who ***haven't*** I seen.
Bohusk, Barnell. A.K.A.: Beak.
Hmmm...

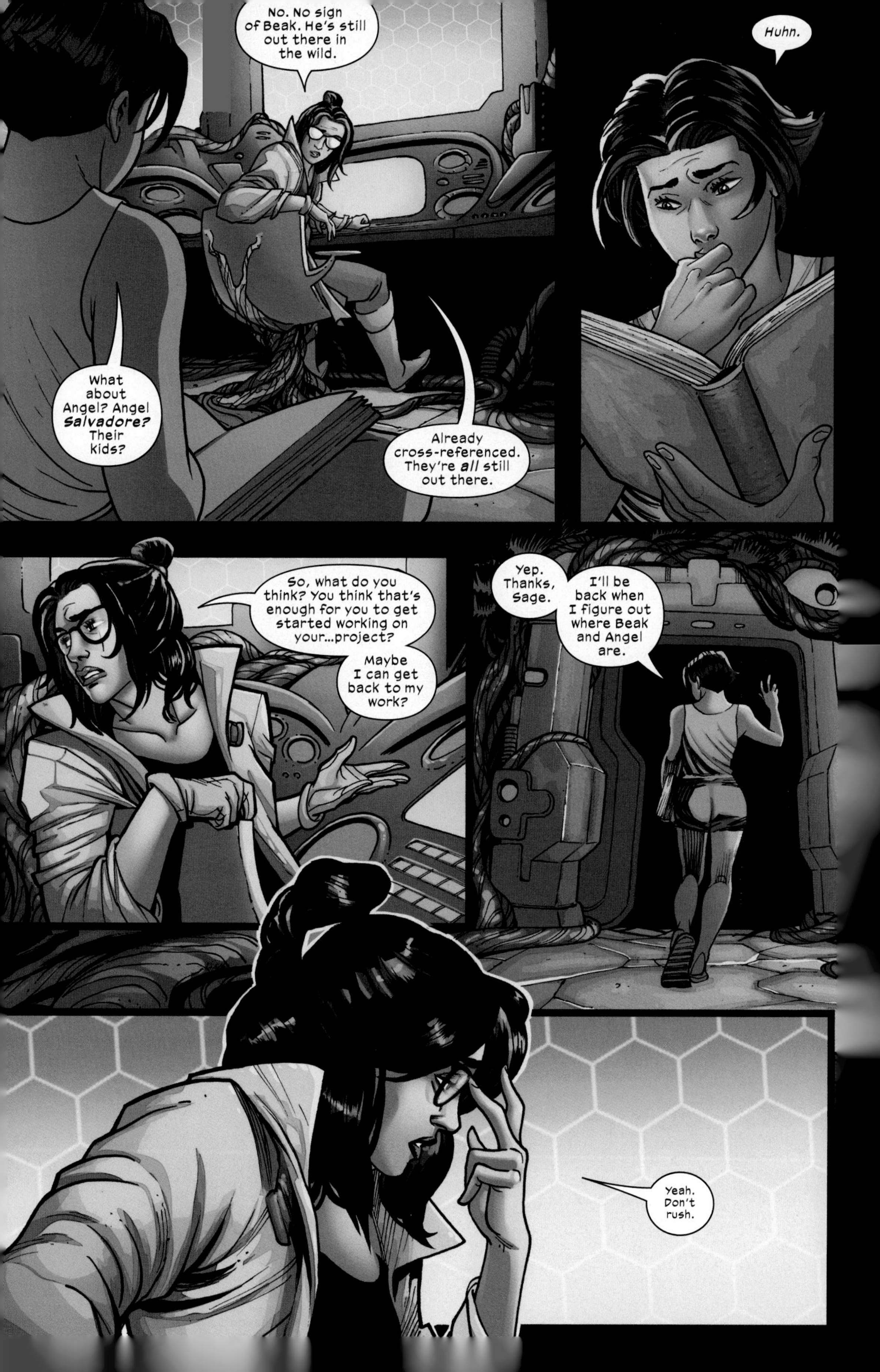

No. No sign of Beak. He's still out there in the wild.
What about Angel? Angel *Salvadore?* Their kids?
Already cross-referenced. They're *all* still out there.
Huhn.
So, what do you think? You think that's enough for you to get started working on your...project?
Maybe I can get back to my work?
Yep. Thanks, Sage.
I'll be back when I figure out where Beak and Angel are.
Yeah. Don't rush.

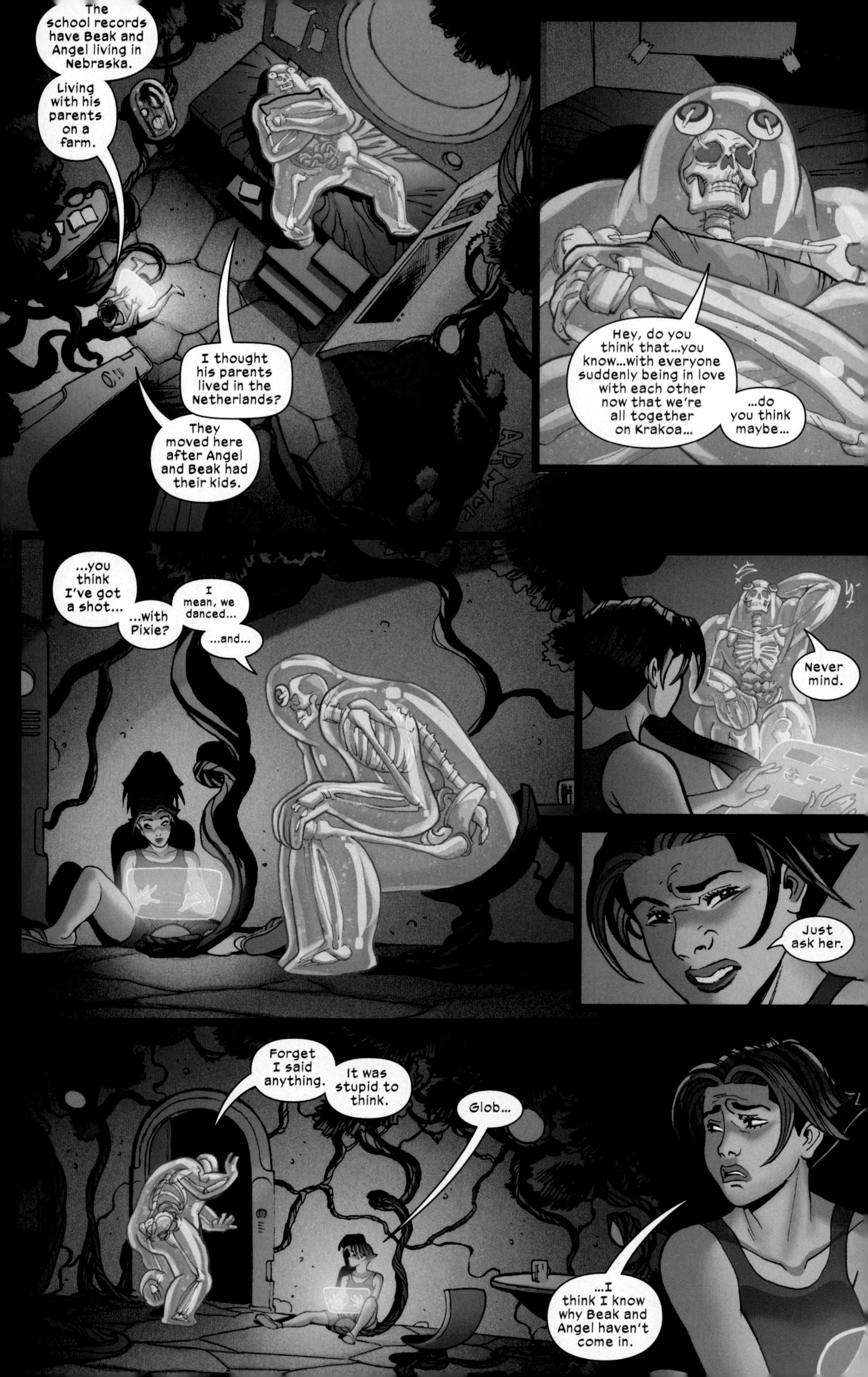
The school records have Beak and Angel living in Nebraska.
Living with his parents on a farm.
I thought his parents lived in the Netherlands?
They moved here after Angel and Beak had their kids.
Hey, do you think that...you know...with everyone suddenly being in love with each other now that we're all together on Krakoa...
...do you think maybe...
...you think I've got a shot...
...with Pixie?
I mean, we danced...
...and...
Never mind.
Just ask her.
Forget I said anything.
It was stupid to think.
Glob...
...I think I know why Beak and Angel haven't come in.

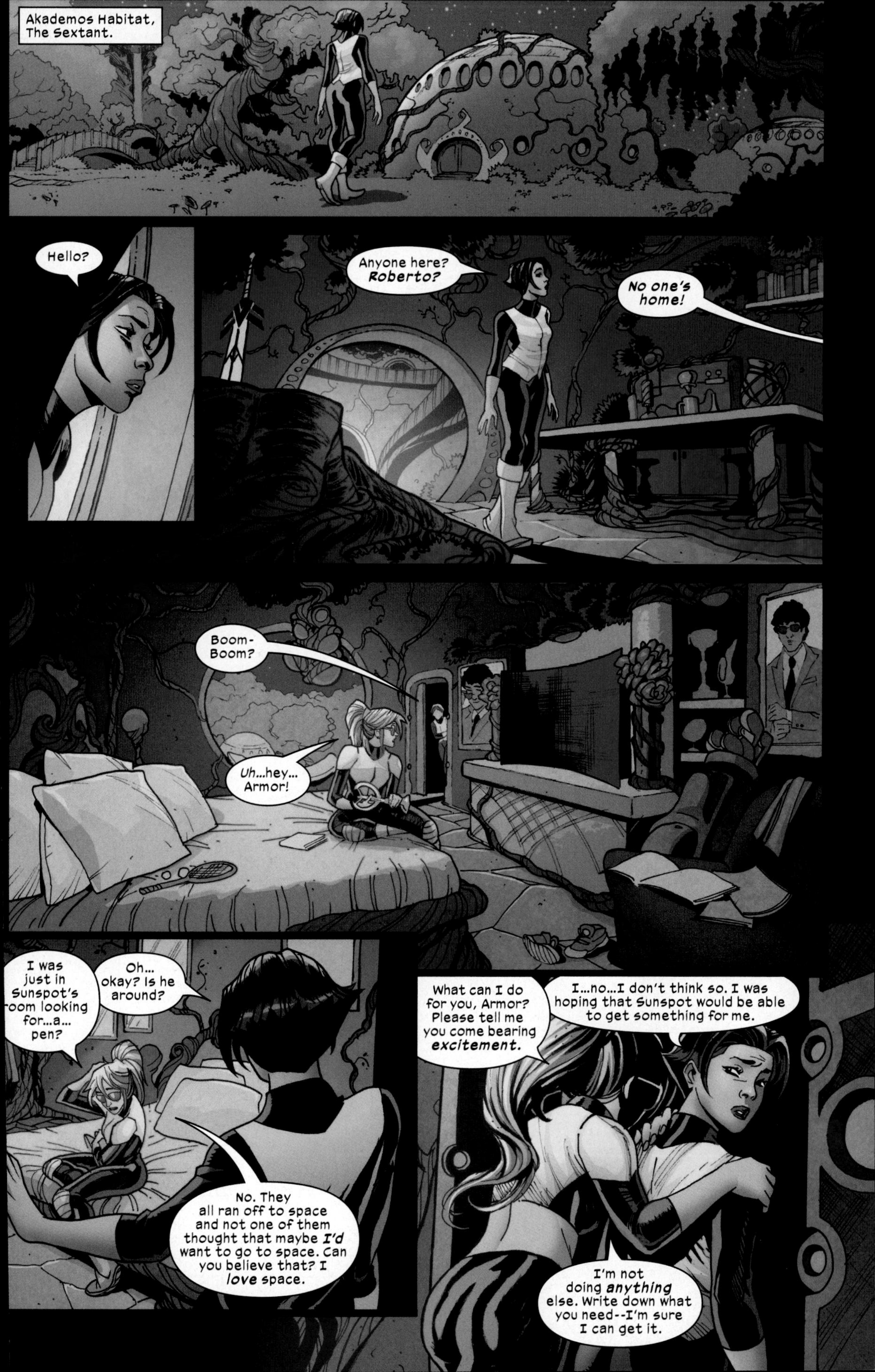
Akademos Habitat, The Sextant.
Hello?
Anyone here? *Roberto?*
No one's home!
Boom-Boom?
Uh...hey... Armor!
I was just in Sunspot's room looking for...a... pen?
Oh... okay? Is he around?
No. They all ran off to space and not one of them thought that maybe *I'd* want to go to space. Can you believe that? I *love* space.
What can I do for you, Armor? Please tell me you come bearing *excitement.*
I...no...I don't think so. I was hoping that Sunspot would be able to get something for me.
I'm not doing *anything* else. Write down what you need--I'm sure I can get it.

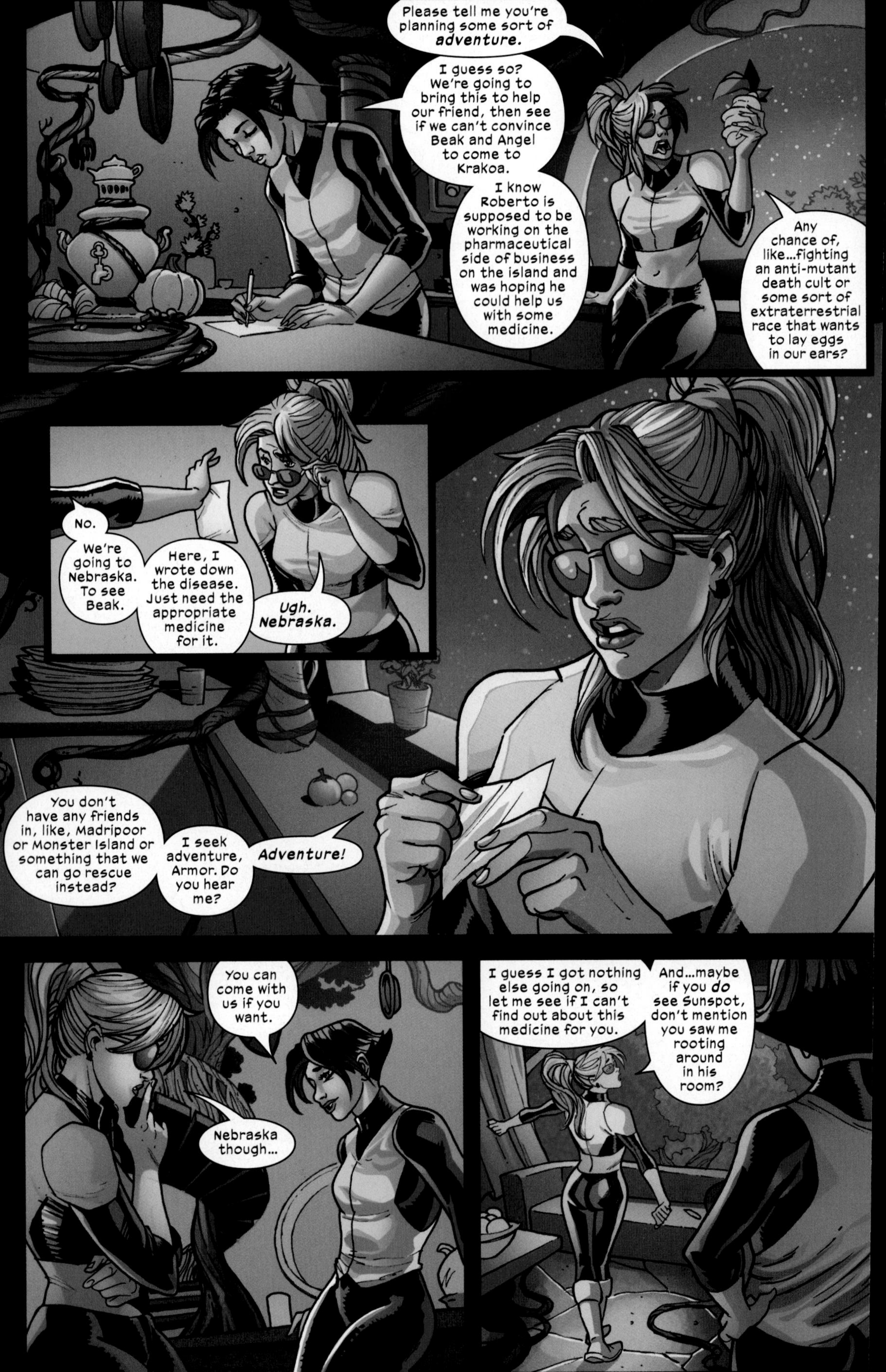
Please tell me you're planning some sort of *adventure.*
I guess so? We're going to bring this to help our friend, then see if we can't convince Beak and Angel to come to Krakoa.
I know Roberto is supposed to be working on the pharmaceutical side of business on the island and was hoping he could help us with some medicine.
Any chance of, like...fighting an anti-mutant death cult or some sort of extraterrestrial race that wants to lay eggs in our ears?
No.
We're going to Nebraska. To see Beak.
Here, I wrote down the disease. Just need the appropriate medicine for it.
Ugh. Nebraska.
You don't have any friends in, like, Madripoor or Monster Island or something that we can go rescue instead?
I seek adventure, Armor. Do you hear me?
Adventure!
You can come with us if you want.
Nebraska though...
I guess I got nothing else going on, so let me see if I can't find out about this medicine for you.
And...maybe if you *do* see Sunspot, don't mention you saw me rooting around in his room?

THE AKADEMOS HABITAT (THE SEXTANT)

The Akademos Habitat, also referred to as the Sextant, is a collection of biomes that serves as the home to younger generations of mutants. The Akademos also serves as an education center and training facility, where the young mutants exchange ideas and learn from one another, forgoing formal classroom studies and student/teacher relationships. All are students. All are teachers.

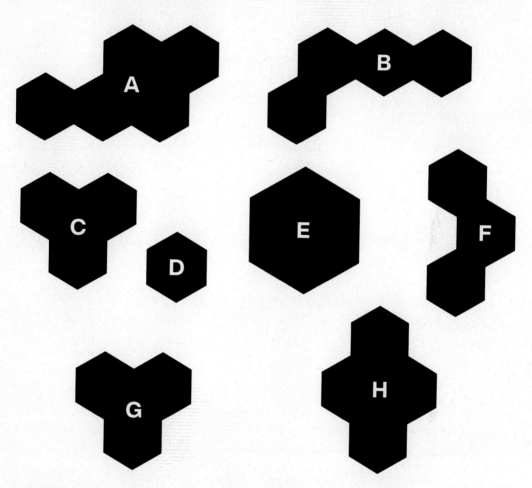

LEGEND:

A.	DELTA House	[Generation X]
B.	ZETA House	[The New X-Men]
C.	BETA House	[The Frost Academy]
D.	The Pod	[The Five]
E.	Lifedeath	[Communal]
F.	SIGMA House	[The Jean Grey School]
G.	OMEGA House	[REDACTED]
H.	ALPHA House	[The New Mutants]

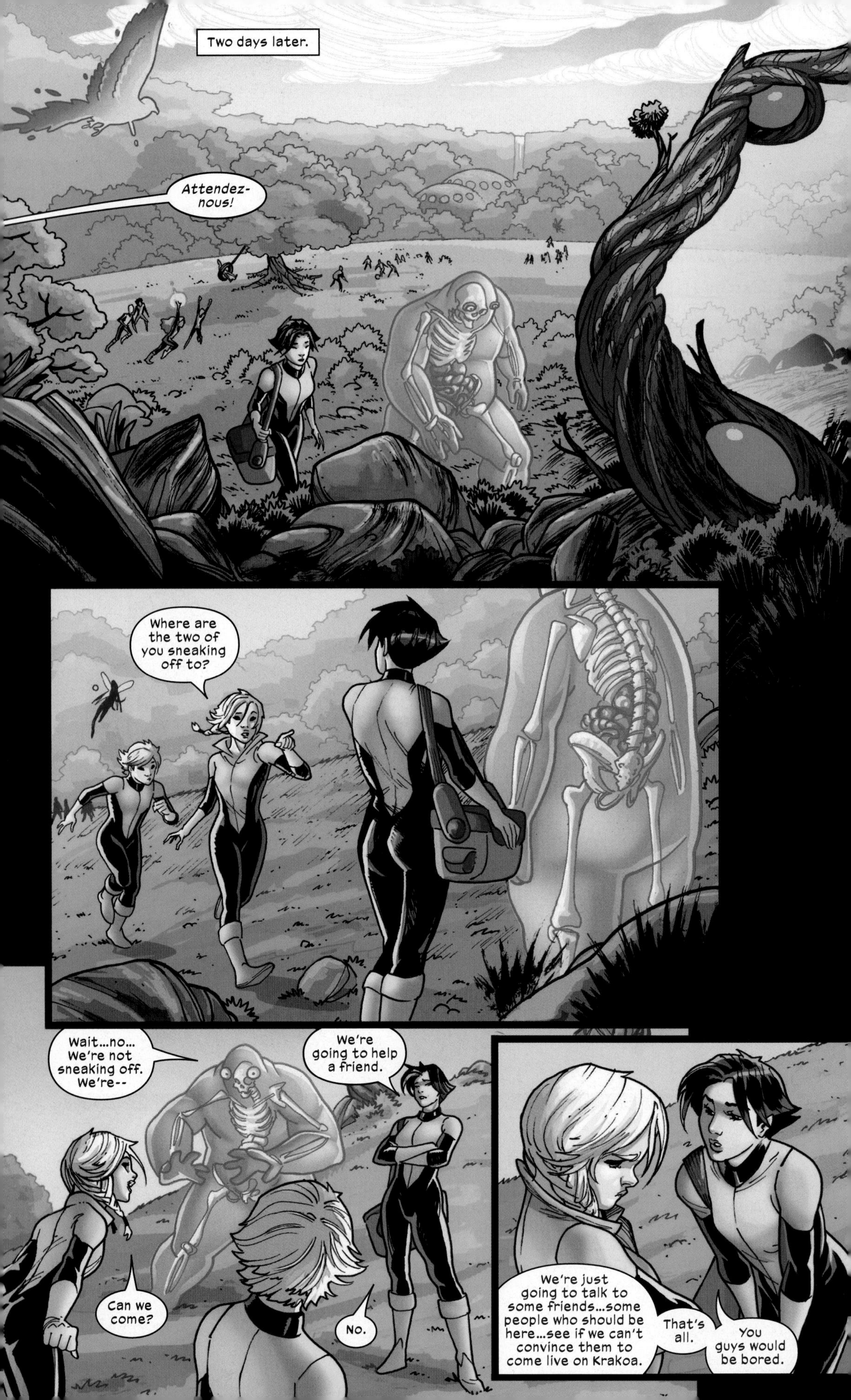
Two days later.
Attendez-nous!
Where are the two of you sneaking off to?
Wait...no... We're not sneaking off. We're--
We're going to help a friend.
Can we come?
No.
We're just going to talk to some friends...some people who should be here...see if we can't convince them to come live on Krakoa.
That's all.
You guys would be bored.

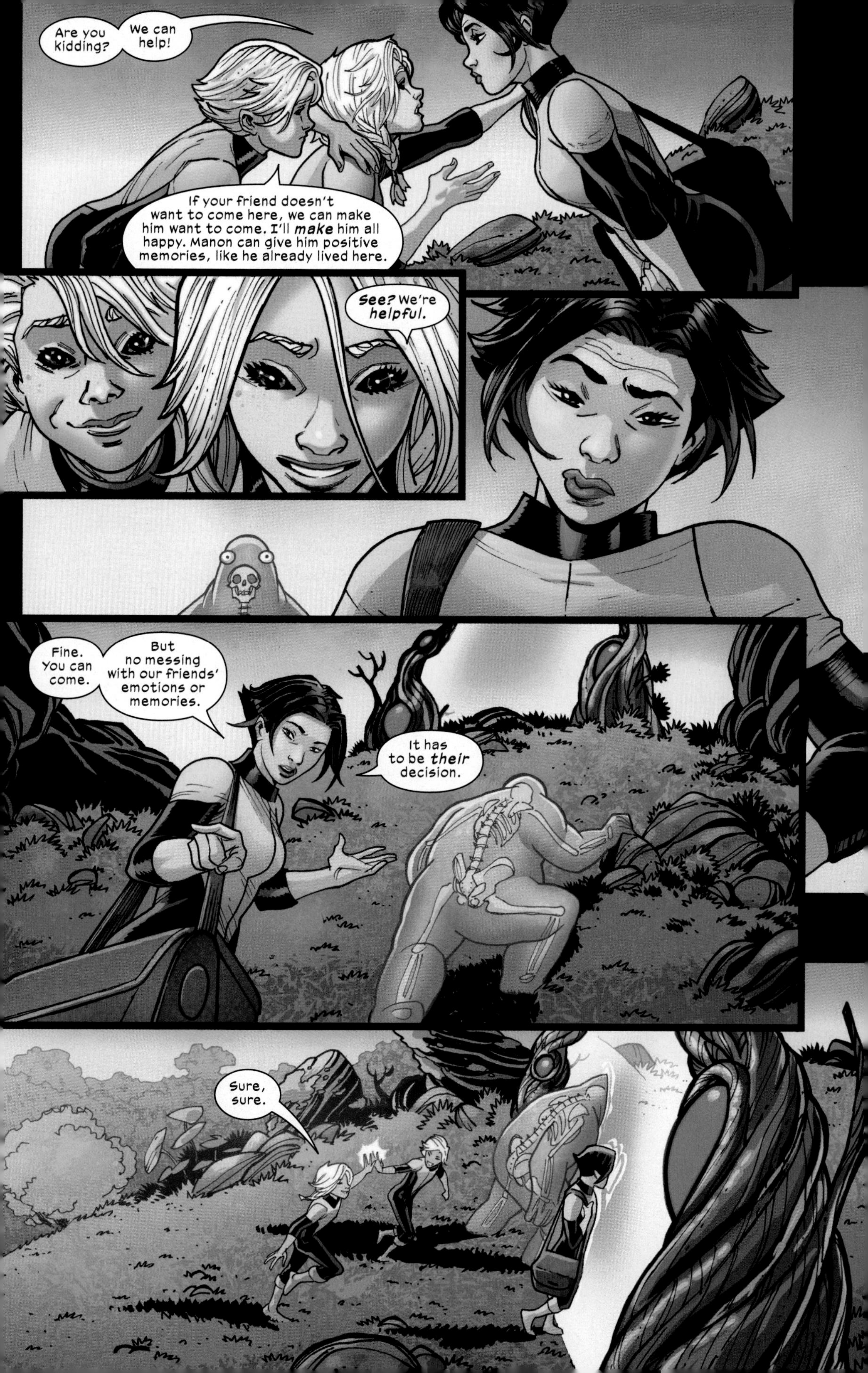
Are you kidding?
We can help!
If your friend doesn't want to come here, we can make him want to come. I'll *make* him all happy. Manon can give him positive memories, like he already lived here.
See? We're *helpful.*
Fine. You can come.
But no messing with our friends' emotions or memories.
It has to be *their* decision.
Sure, sure.

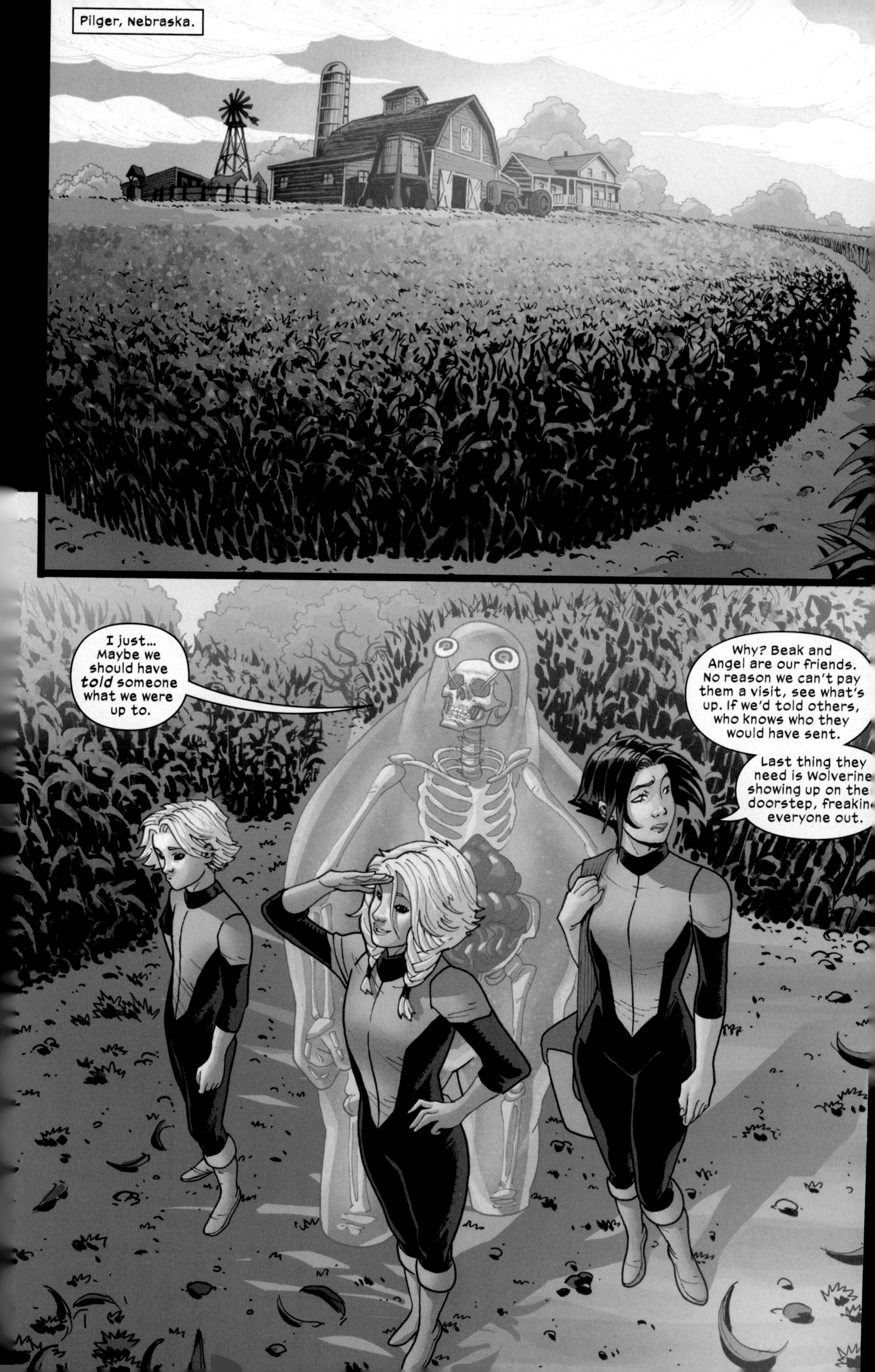
Pilger, Nebraska.
I just... Maybe we should have told someone what we were up to.
Why? Beak and Angel are our friends. No reason we can't pay them a visit, see what's up. If we'd told others, who knows who they would have sent.
Last thing they need is Wolverine showing up on the doorstep, freakin everyone out.

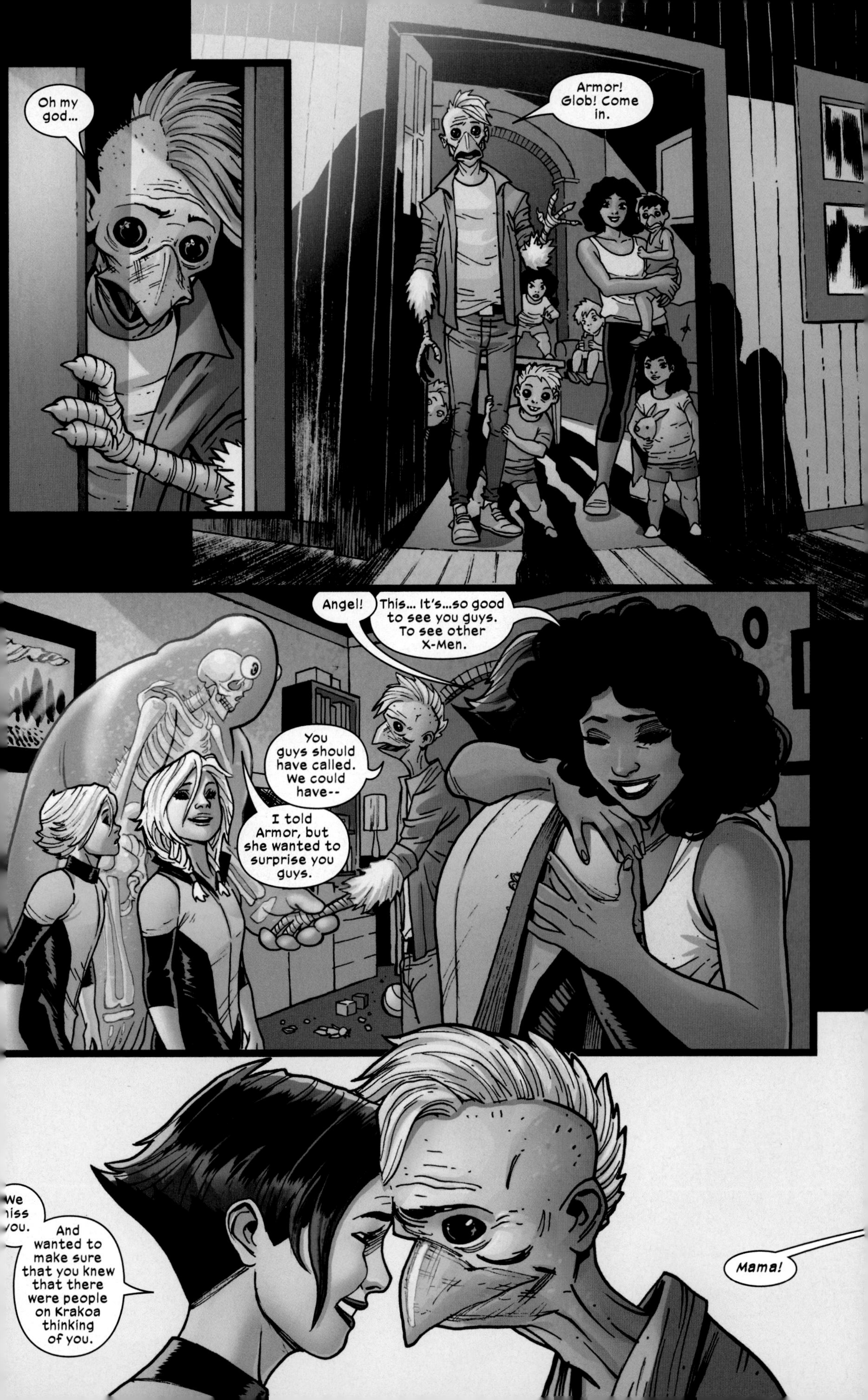
Oh my god...
Armor! Glob! Come in.
Angel!
This... It's...so good to see you guys. To see other X-Men.
You guys should have called. We could have--
I told Armor, but she wanted to surprise you guys.
And wanted to make sure that you knew that there were people on Krakoa thinking of you.
Mama!

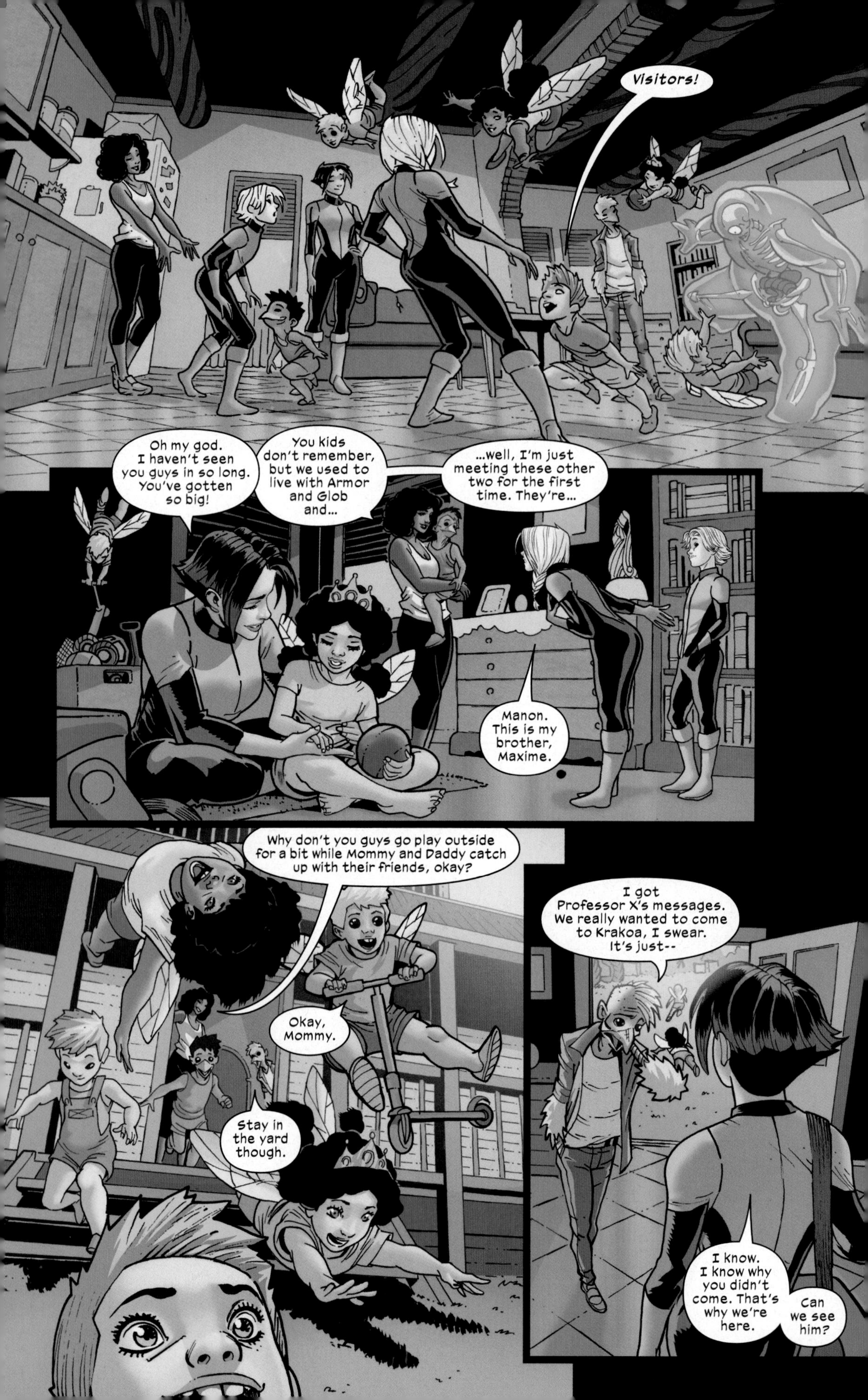
Visitors!
Oh my god. I haven't seen you guys in so long. You've gotten so big!
You kids don't remember, but we used to live with Armor and Glob and...
...well, I'm just meeting these other two for the first time. They're...
Manon. This is my brother, Maxime.
Why don't you guys go play outside for a bit while Mommy and Daddy catch up with their friends, okay?
Okay, Mommy.
Stay in the yard though.
I got Professor X's messages. We really wanted to come to Krakoa, I swear. It's just--
I know. I know why you didn't come. That's why we're here.
Can we see him?

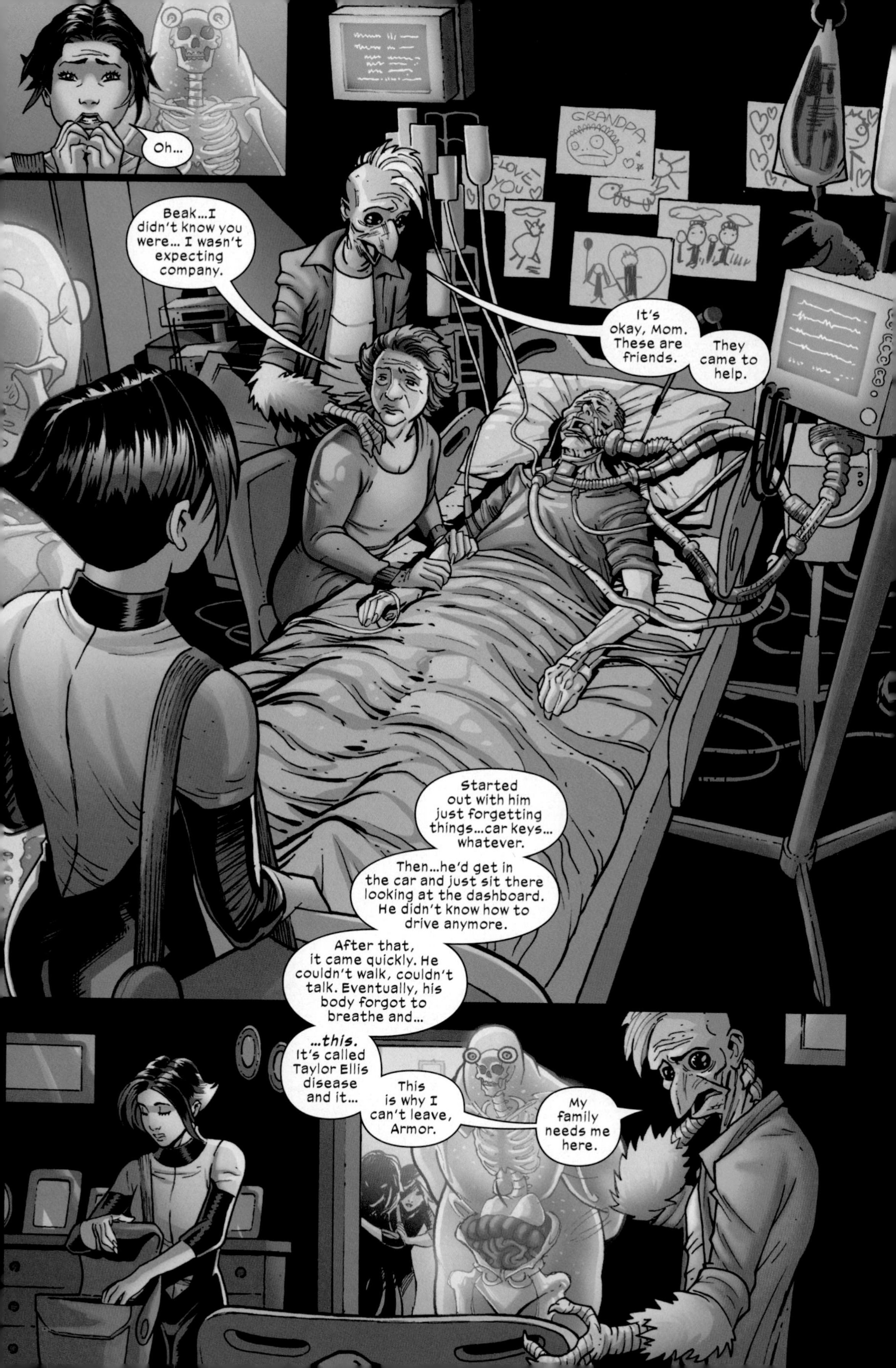
Oh...
Beak...I didn't know you were... I wasn't expecting company.
It's okay, Mom. These are friends.
They came to help.
GRANDPA
I LOVE YOU
Started out with him just forgetting things...car keys... whatever.
Then...he'd get in the car and just sit there looking at the dashboard. He didn't know how to drive anymore.
After that, it came quickly. He couldn't walk, couldn't talk. Eventually, his body forgot to breathe and...
...this. It's called Taylor Ellis disease and it...
This is why I can't leave, Armor.
My family needs me here.

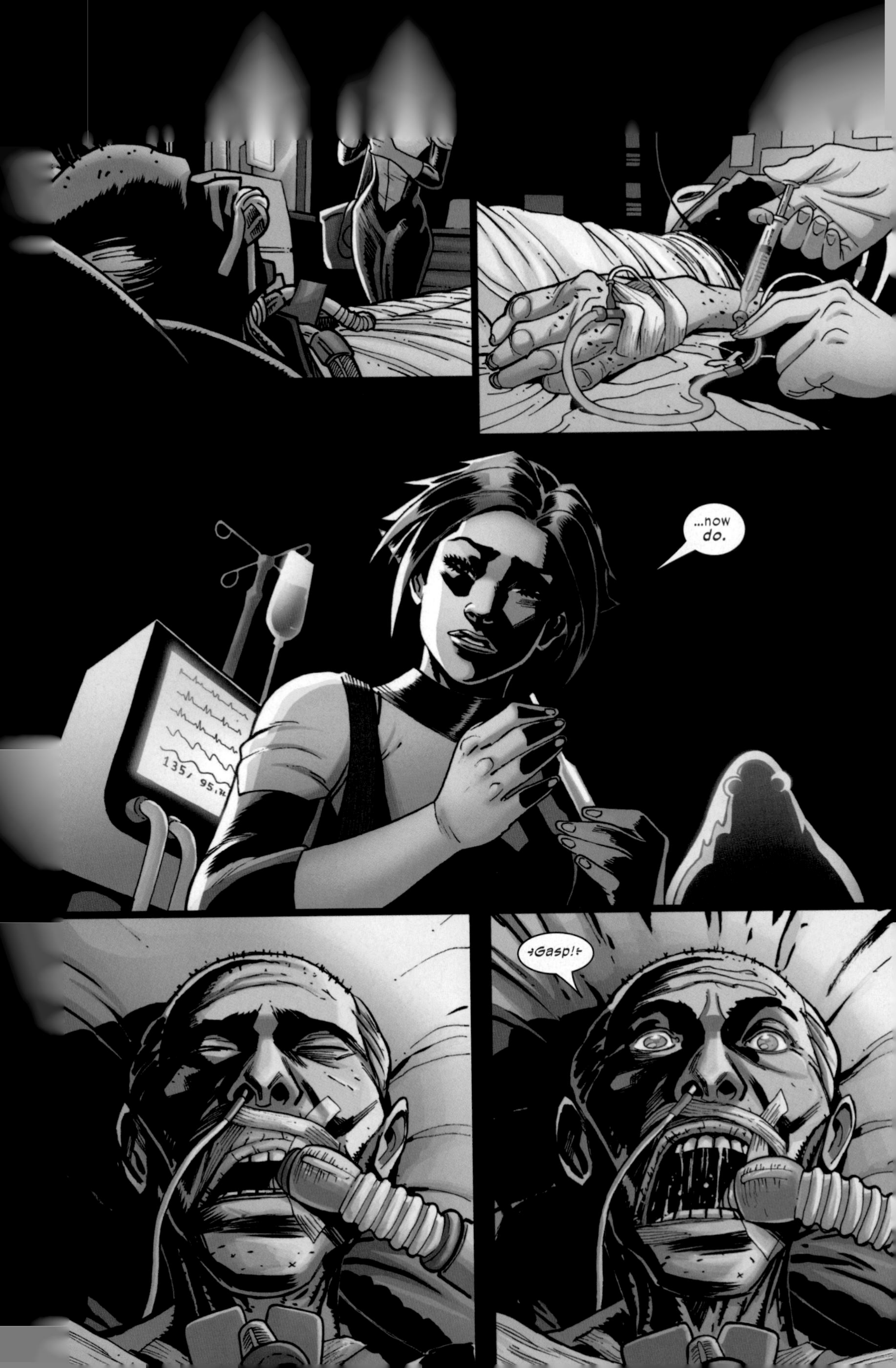
...now do.
135/ 95.
-Gasp!-

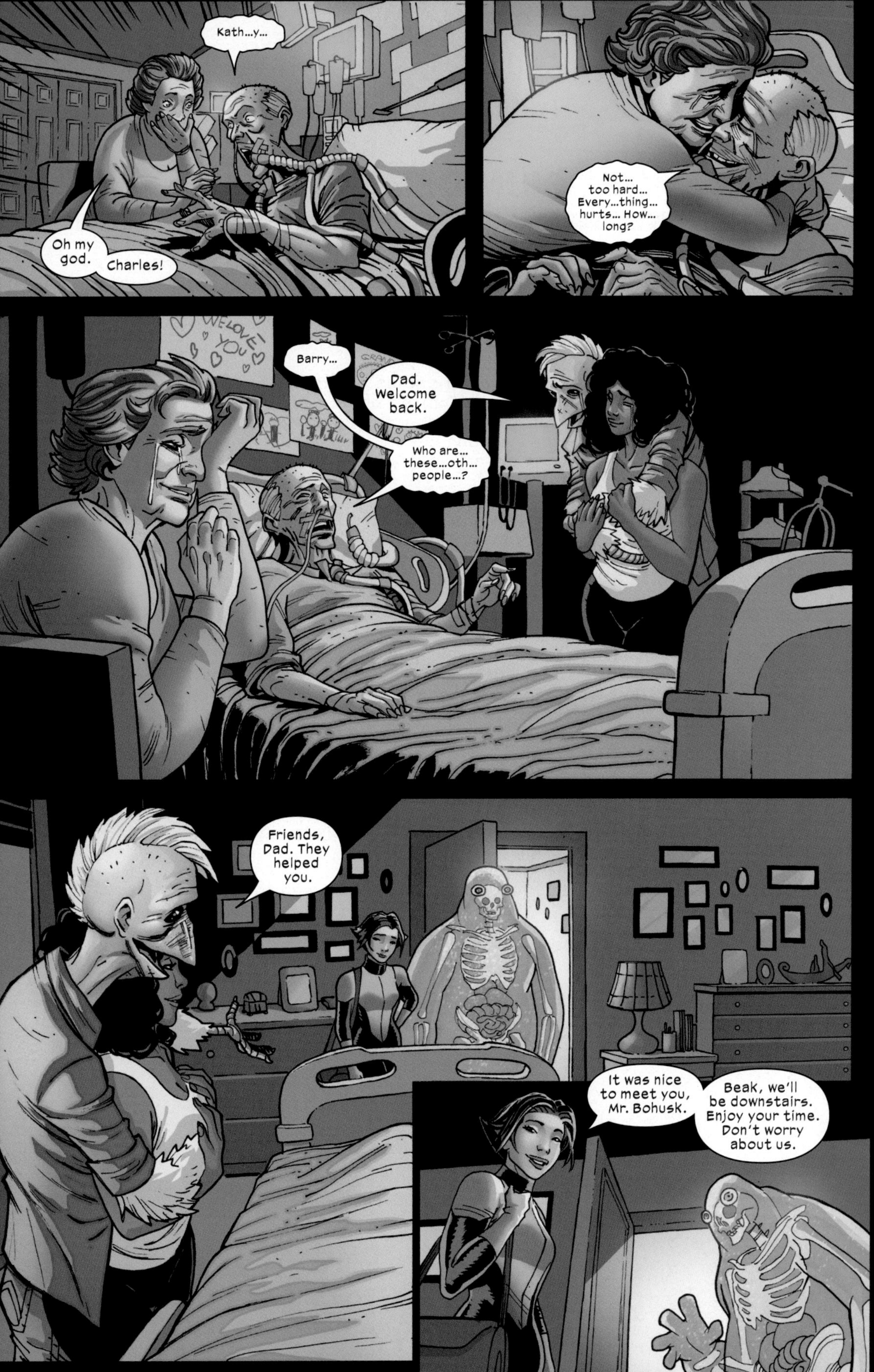

Kath...y...
Oh my god.
Charles!
Not... too hard... Every...thing... hurts... How... long?
Barry...
Dad. Welcome back.
Who are... these...oth... people...?
Friends, Dad. They helped you.
It was nice to meet you, Mr. Bohusk.
Beak, we'll be downstairs. Enjoy your time. Don't worry about us.

MUNUS MOTRICIUM DEMENTIA (MMD)

Munus Motricium Dementia is a rare form of dementia commonly referred to as "Taylor Ellis disease," named after the science fiction author Taylor Ellis, who brought the disease to the public spotlight after his own diagnosis in 1994. Ellis succumbed to the disease only four months after his diagnosis, at the age of 54.

While the cause of the disease largely remains a mystery to most scientists, it's believed that a mutation in red blood cells causes a build-up of plaque within the amygdala, hippocampus and prefrontal cortex. This plaque blocks pathways connected to cognitive memory, which results in an inability to carry out day-to-day functions, eventually resulting in a full system shut down.

Because of the rarity of the disease, there has been little research into the causes and potential cure. However, it has recently been reported that a cure will be made available to nations who've accepted the Krakoan Sovereignty Pact.

SYMPTOMS

People with MMD have trouble remembering how to carry out everyday tasks. Early signs include loss of ability to operate a phone or computer. In advanced cases, they will no longer recall how to walk and lack the ability to relearn forgotten tasks.

MMD STATISTICS

- There are an estimated 10,000 people with MMD globally.

- 90% of those diagnosed with MMD will die within six months. The mortality rate within a year of diagnosis is 100%.

- MMD is most commonly diagnosed in patients between the ages of 50-67.

—

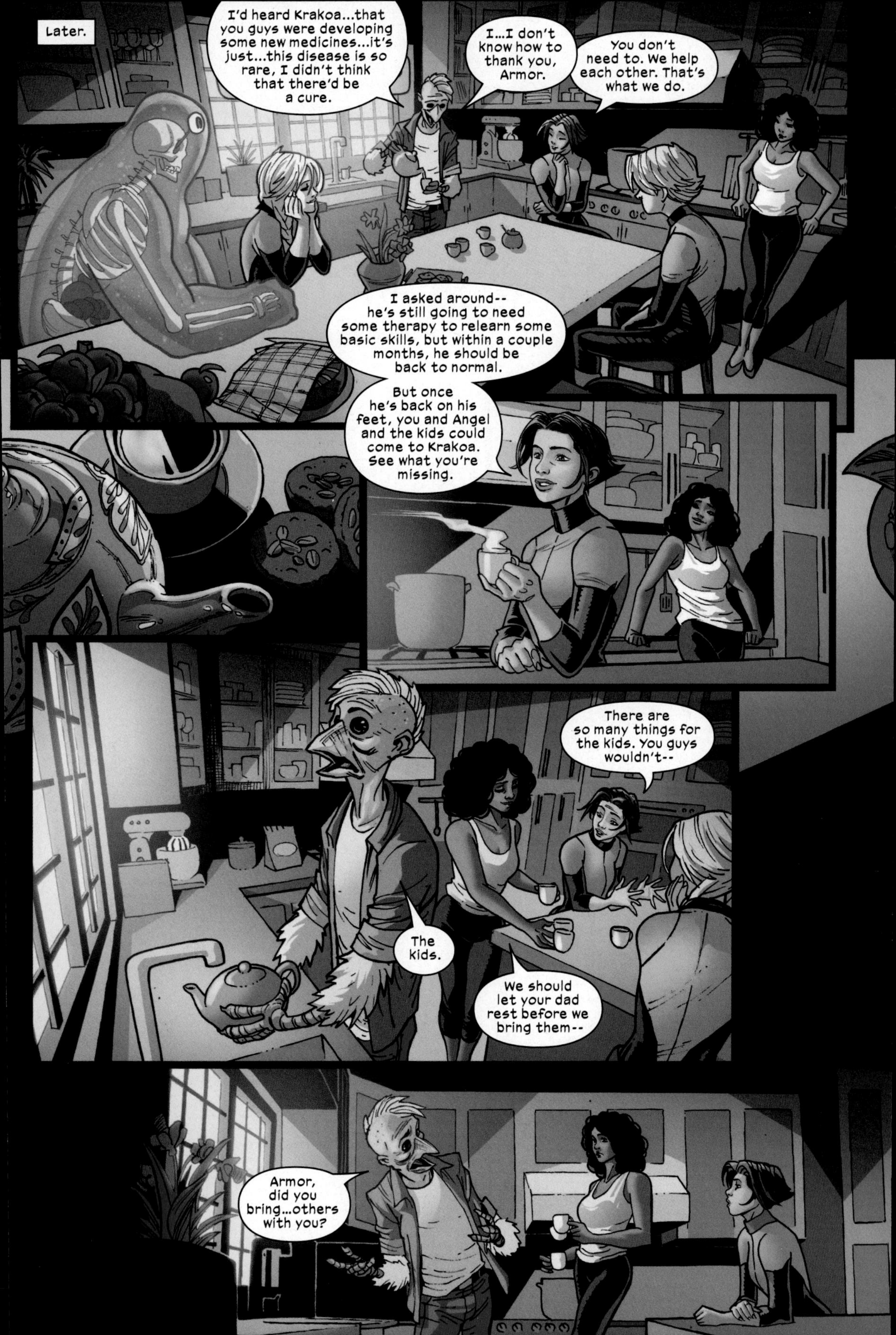
Later.
I'd heard Krakoa...that you guys were developing some new medicines...it's just...this disease is so rare, I didn't think that there'd be a cure.
I...I don't know how to thank you, Armor.
You don't need to. We help each other. That's what we do.
I asked around--he's still going to need some therapy to relearn some basic skills, but within a couple months, he should be back to normal.
But once he's back on his feet, you and Angel and the kids could come to Krakoa. See what you're missing.
There are so many things for the kids. You guys wouldn't--
The kids.
We should let your dad rest before we bring them--
Armor, did you bring...others with you?

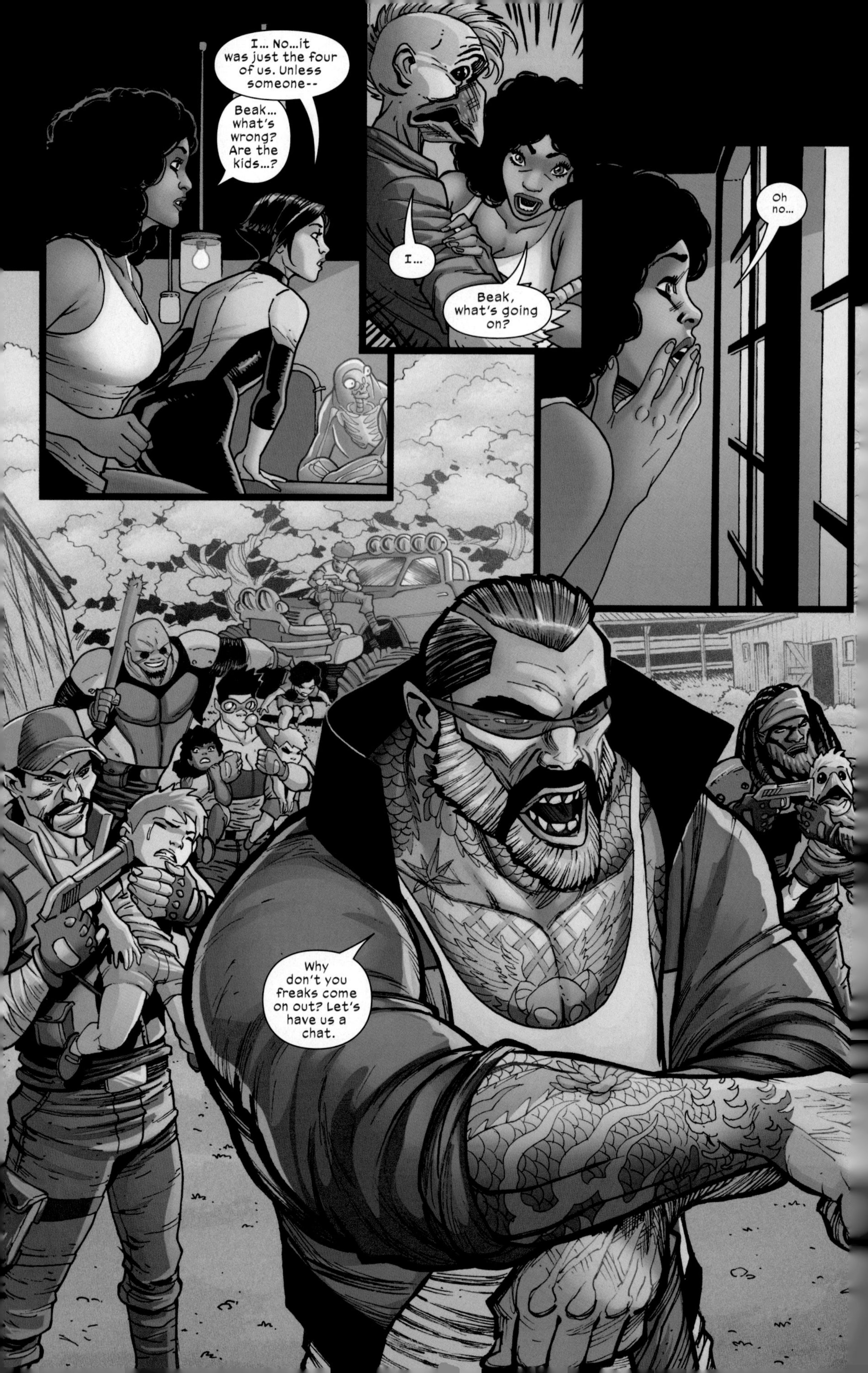
I... No...it was just the four of us. Unless someone--
Beak... what's wrong? Are the kids...?
I...
Beak, what's going on?
Oh no...
Why don't you freaks come on out? Let's have us a chat.

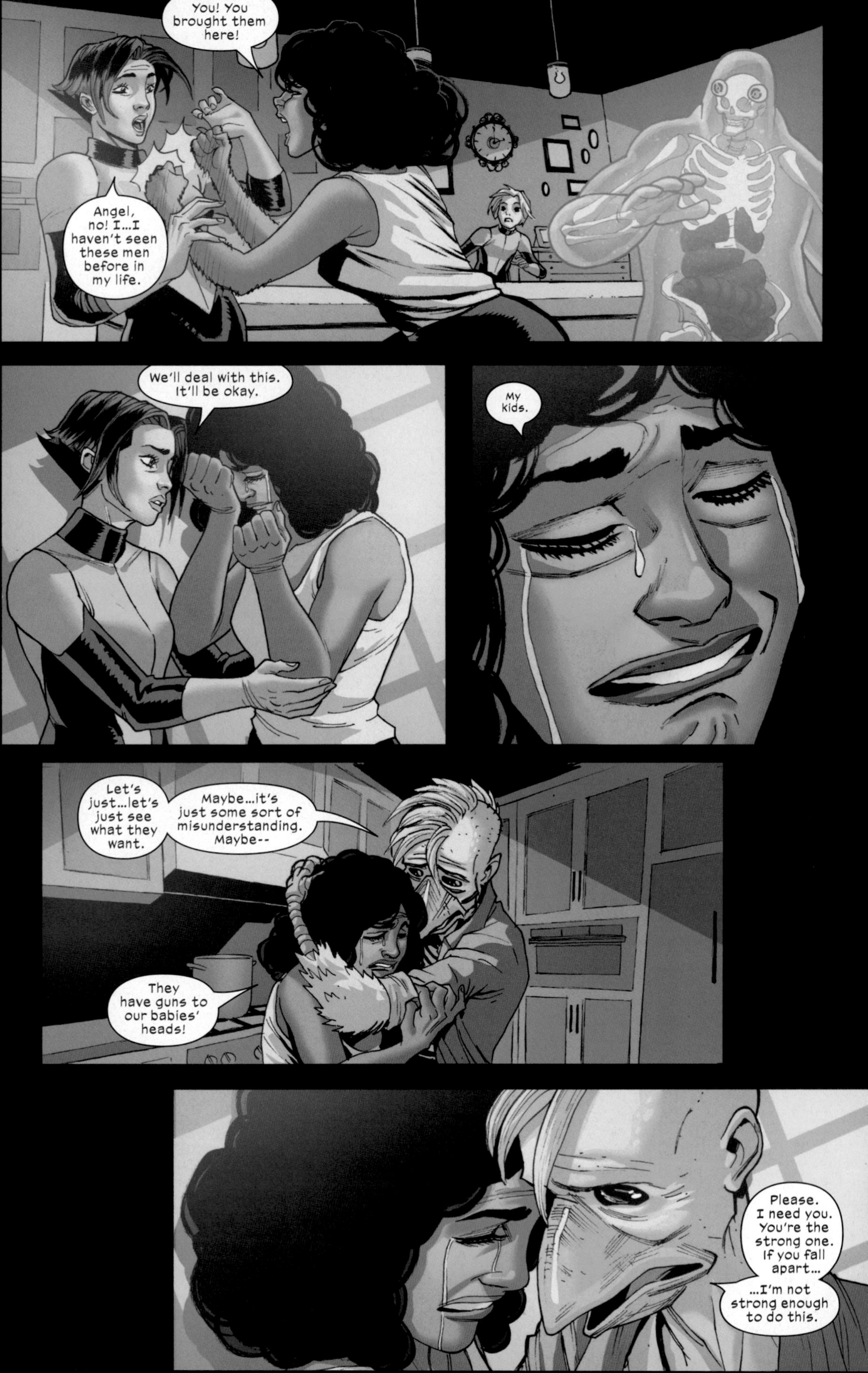

You! You brought them here!
Angel, no! I...I haven't seen these men before in my life.
We'll deal with this. It'll be okay.
My kids.
Let's just...let's just see what they want.
Maybe...it's just some sort of misunderstanding. Maybe--
They have guns to our babies' heads!
Please. I need you. You're the strong one. If you fall apart...
...I'm not strong enough to do this.

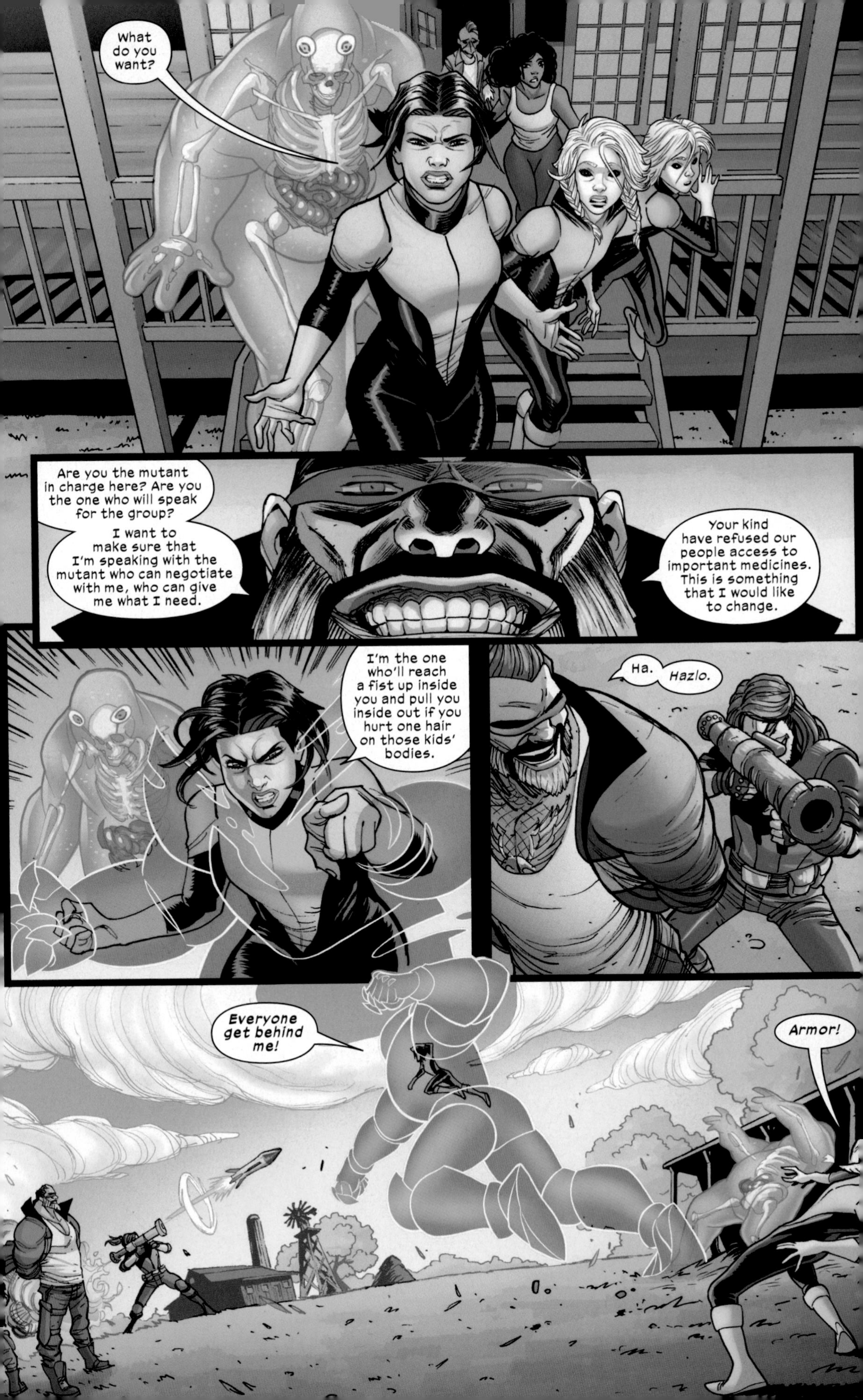
What do you want?
Are you the mutant in charge here? Are you the one who will speak for the group?
I want to make sure that I'm speaking with the mutant who can negotiate with me, who can give me what I need.
Your kind have refused our people access to important medicines. This is something that I would like to change.
I'm the one who'll reach a fist up inside you and pull you inside out if you hurt one hair on those kids' bodies.
Ha.
Hazlo.
Everyone get behind me!
Armor!

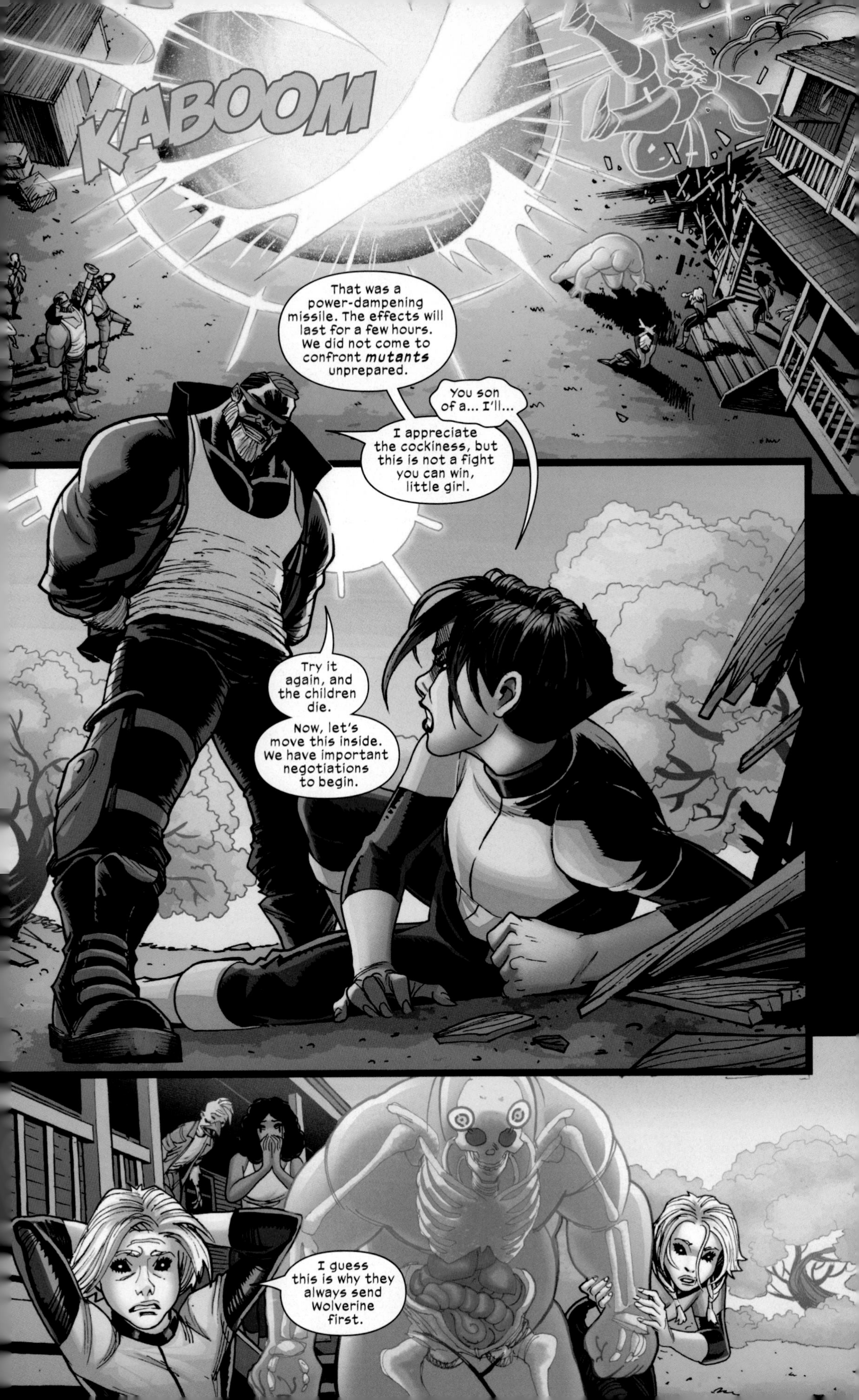
KABOOM
That was a power-dampening missile. The effects will last for a few hours. We did not come to confront *mutants* unprepared.
You son of a... I'll...
I appreciate the cockiness, but this is not a fight you can win, little girl.
Try it again, and the children die.
Now, let's move this inside. We have important negotiations to begin.
I guess this is why they always send Wolverine first.

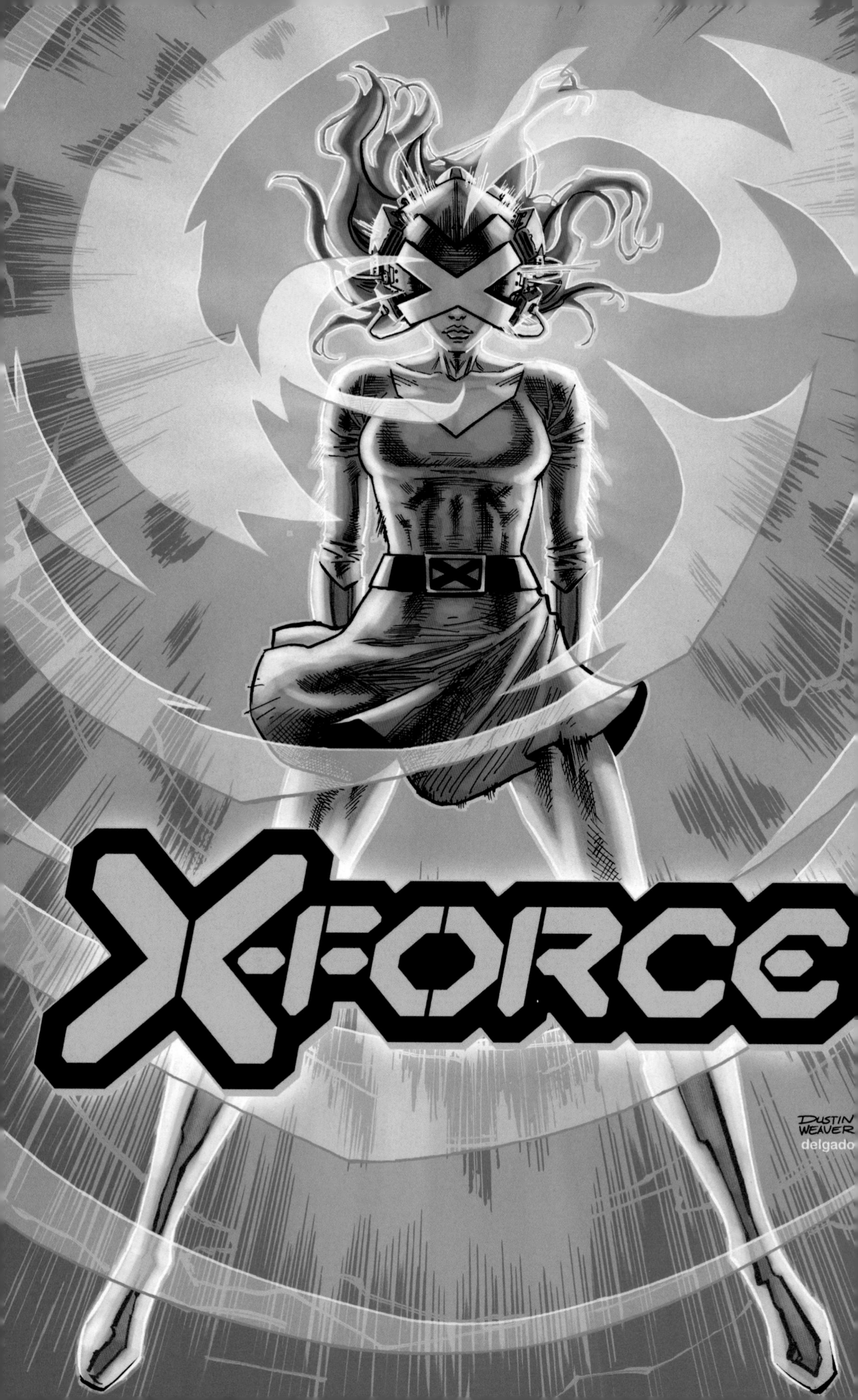
X-FORCE
DUSTIN WEAVER
delgado

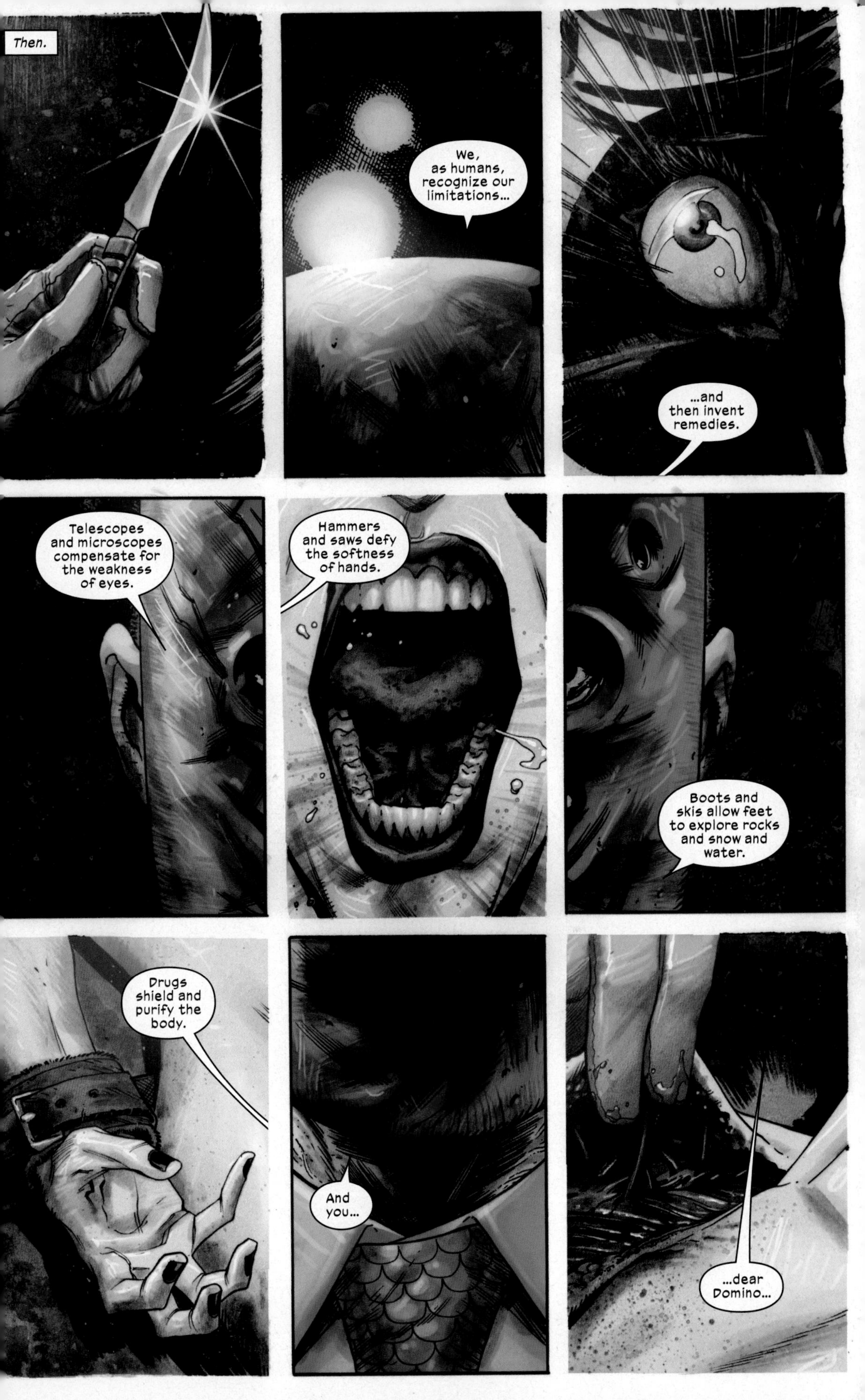
Then.
We, as humans, recognize our limitations...
...and then invent remedies.
Telescopes and microscopes compensate for the weakness of eyes.
Hammers and saws defy the softness of hands.
Boots and skis allow feet to explore rocks and snow and water.
Drugs shield and purify the body.
And you...
...dear Domino...

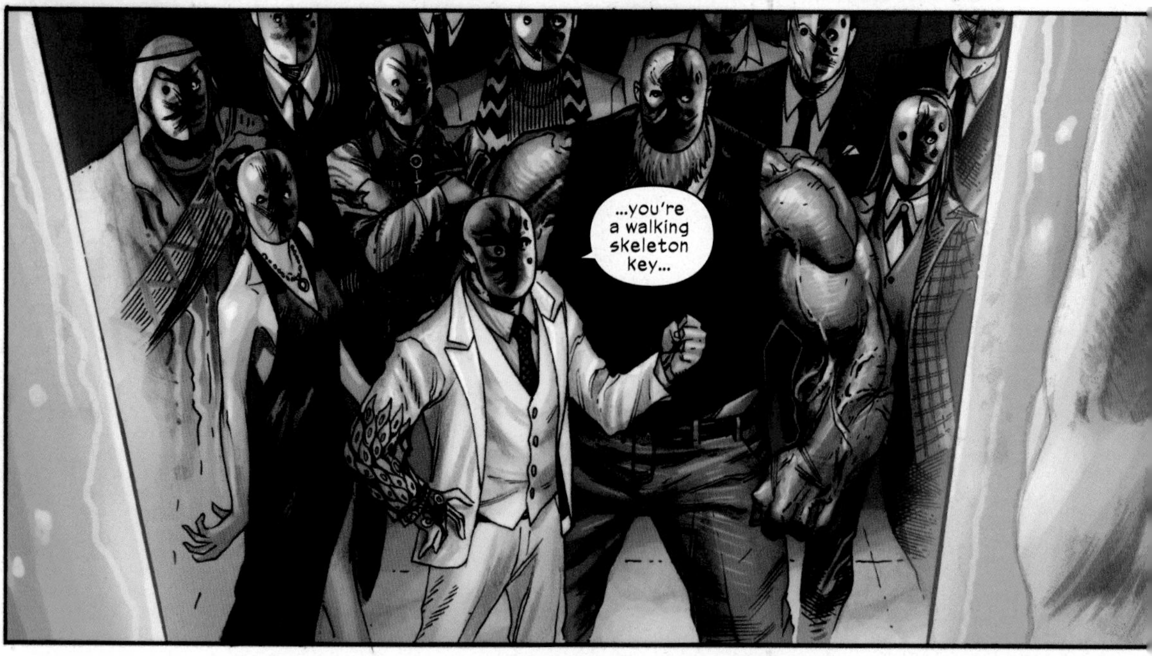
...you're a walking skeleton key...

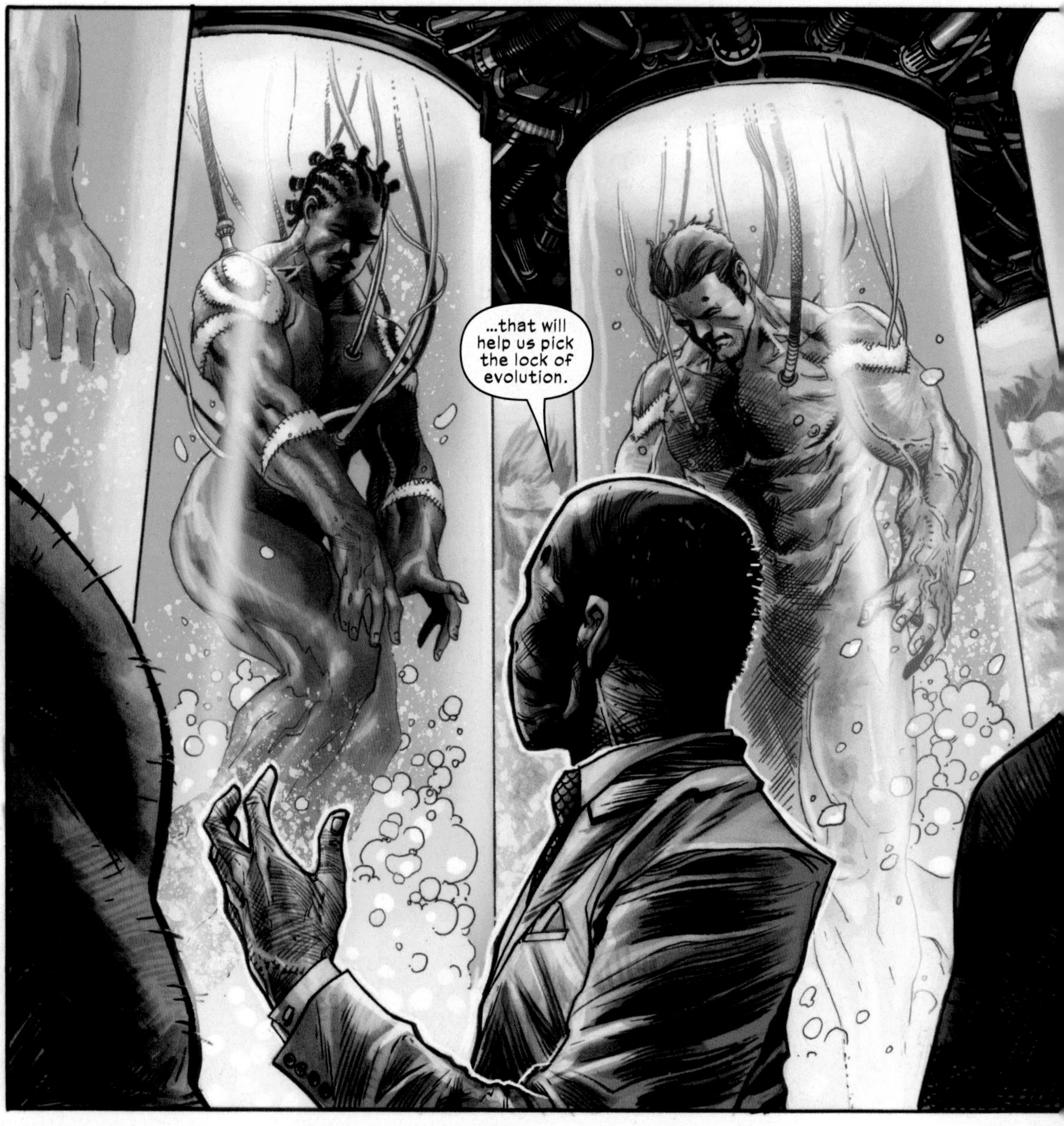
...that will help us pick the lock of evolution.

[kra_[0.3]
[koa_[0.3]

[kra_[0.X]
[koa_[0.X]

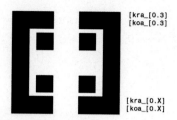

PAIN DON'T HURT

Mutants around the world are flocking to the island-nation of Krakoa for safety, security and to be part of the first mutant society.

Using skin grafts from Domino's body to fool Krakoa's defenses, a mercenary strike team infiltrated the island and assassinated Professor X, destroying his Cerebro helmet in the process. Jean Grey and Beast retrieved a backup Cerebro that the Professor had installed in the case of his demise. Meanwhile, Wolverine and Kid Omega followed the assassins' trail to South Korea, where they found a biomanufacturing plant full of half-grown killers and Domino half flayed and clinging to life!

Wolverine

Kid Omega

Domino

Beast

Jean Grey

Sage

Healer

Black Tom Cassidy

Magneto

Professor X

[kra_[0.3]...]
[koa_[0.3]...]

[00_mutant_espionage]
[00_law_order___X___]

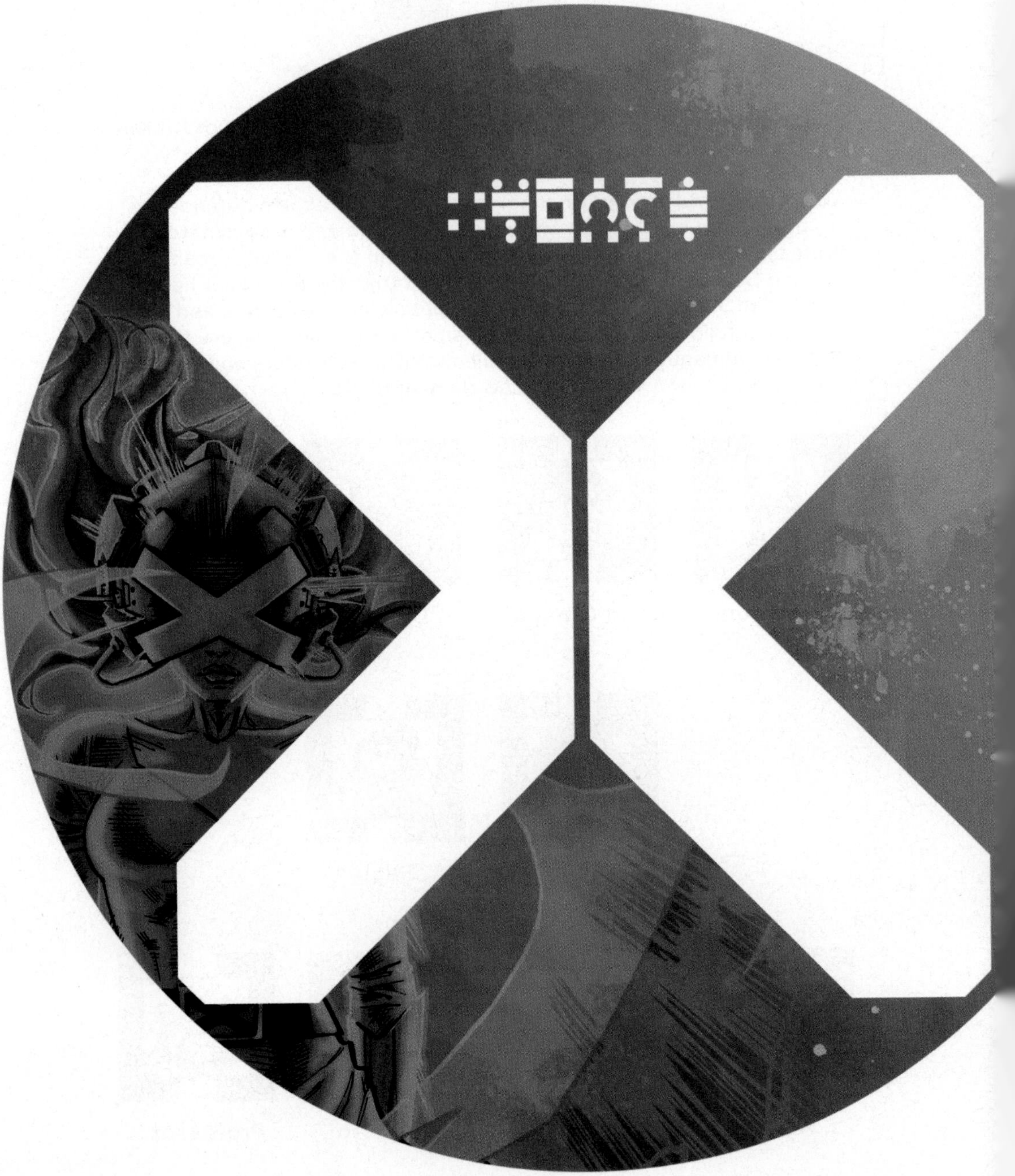

[00_mutant_espionage]
[00_law_order___X___]

BENJAMIN PERCY................................[WRITER]
JOSHUA CASSARA................................[ARTIST]
GURU-eFX................................[COLOR ARTIST]
VC's JOE CARAMAGNA............................[LETTERER]
TOM MULLER................................[DESIGN]

DUSTIN WEAVER & EDGAR DELGADO...........[COVER ARTISTS]

NICK RUSSELL..............................[PRODUCTION]

JONATHAN HICKMAN............................[HEAD OF X]
CHRIS ROBINSON.......................[ASSISTANT EDITOR]
JORDAN D. WHITE................................[EDITOR]
C.B. CEBULSKI..........................[EDITOR IN CHIEF]
JOE QUESADA....................[CHIEF CREATIVE OFFICER]
DAN BUCKLEY...............................[PRESIDENT]
ALAN FINE..........................[EXECUTIVE PRODUCER]

[03] X-FORCE

[ISSUE THREE].........THE SKELETON KEY

[00_mutant_espionage]
[00_law_order___X___]

[00_00...0]
[00_00...3]

[00_probe_]
[00______]

[00______]

[00______X]

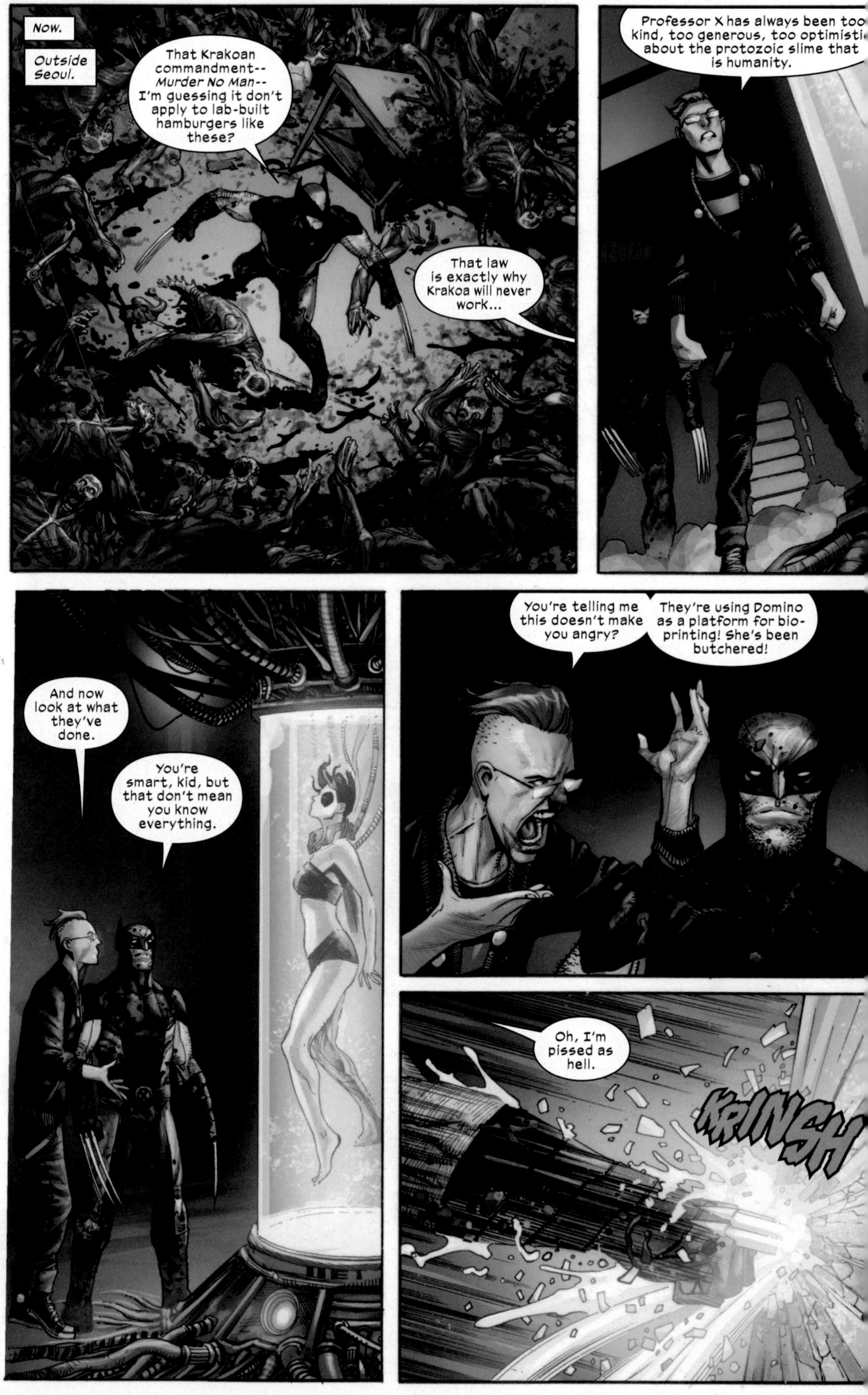

Now.
Outside Seoul.
That Krakoan commandment-- Murder No Man-- I'm guessing it don't apply to lab-built hamburgers like these?
That law is exactly why Krakoa will never work...
Professor X has always been too kind, too generous, too optimisti about the protozoic slime that is humanity.
And now look at what they've done.
You're smart, kid, but that don't mean you know everything.
You're telling me this doesn't make you angry?
They're using Domino as a platform for bio-printing! She's been butchered!
Oh, I'm pissed as hell.
KRINSH

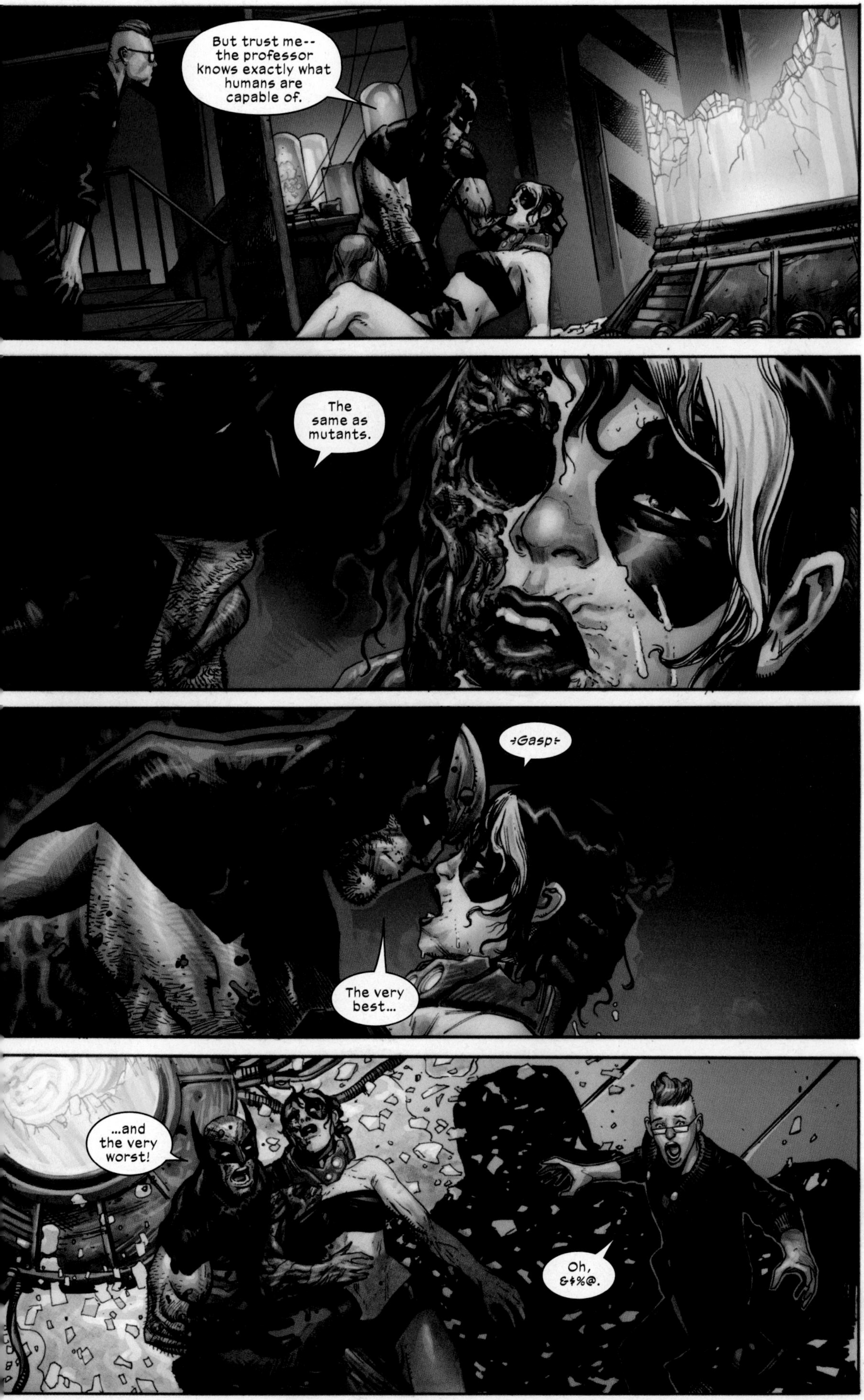
But trust me--
the professor
knows exactly what
humans are
capable of.
The
same as
mutants.
-Gasp-
The very
best...
...and
the very
worst!
Oh,
&$%@.

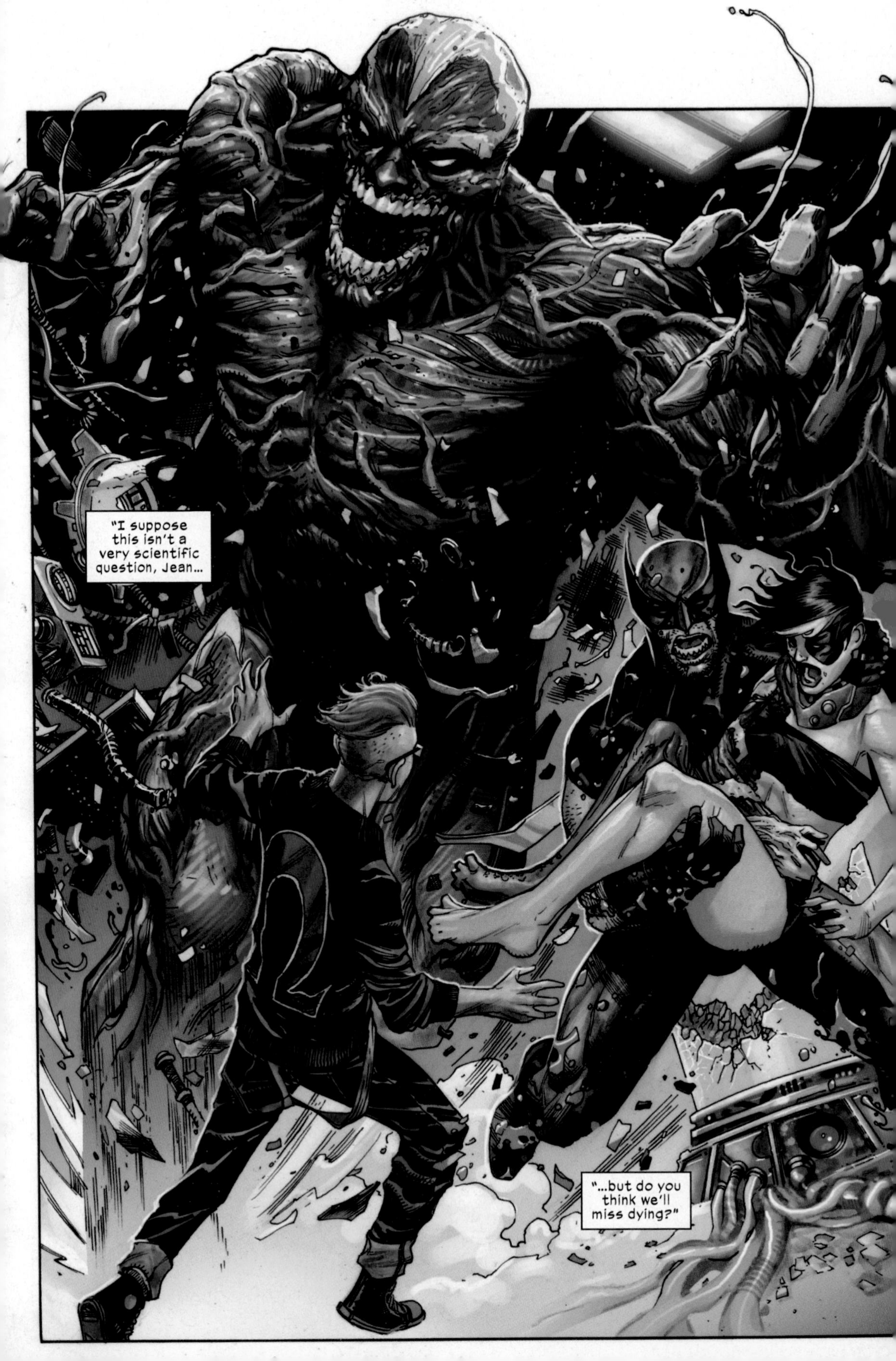
"I suppose this isn't a very scientific question, Jean...
"...but do you think we'll miss dying?"

Krakoa.

If your plan works...if we can bring Charles back... I'm trying to imagine what that means for mutantkind.

Because he's not one life...

He's all of our lives.

Will we become recklessly assured? Shouldn't we have a healthy fear of death?

No. Not at all. And here's why...

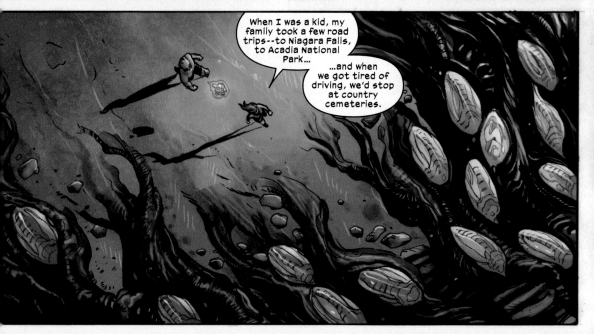

When I was a kid, my family took a few road trips--to Niagara Falls, to Acadia National Park...

...and when we got tired of driving, we'd stop at country cemeteries.

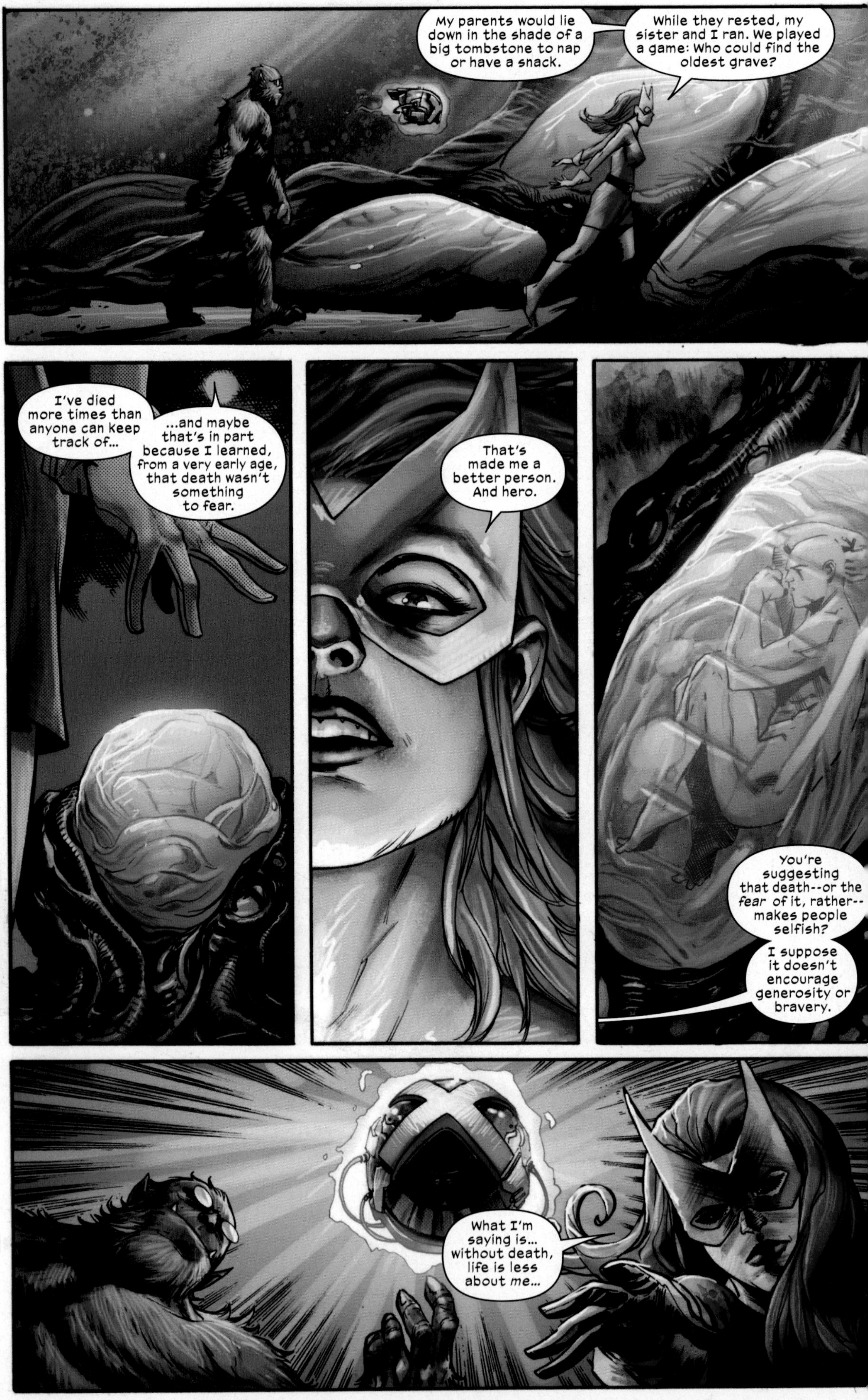
My parents would lie down in the shade of a big tombstone to nap or have a snack.
While they rested, my sister and I ran. We played a game: Who could find the oldest grave?
I've died more times than anyone can keep track of...
...and maybe that's in part because I learned, from a very early age, that death wasn't something to fear.
That's made me a better person. And hero.
You're suggesting that death--or the *fear* of it, rather--makes people selfish?
I suppose it doesn't encourage generosity or bravery.
What I'm saying is... without death, life is less about *me*...

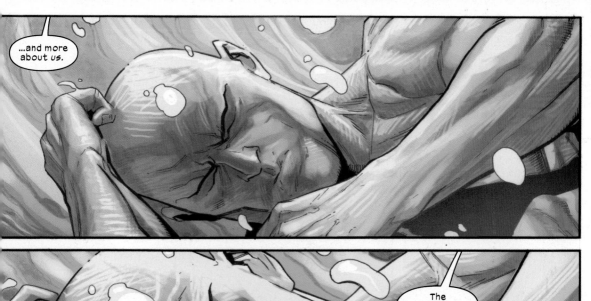

...and more about *us*.

The long game of mutantkind.

That's the dream of Krakoa.

SKLECH

And we're charged with protecting it.

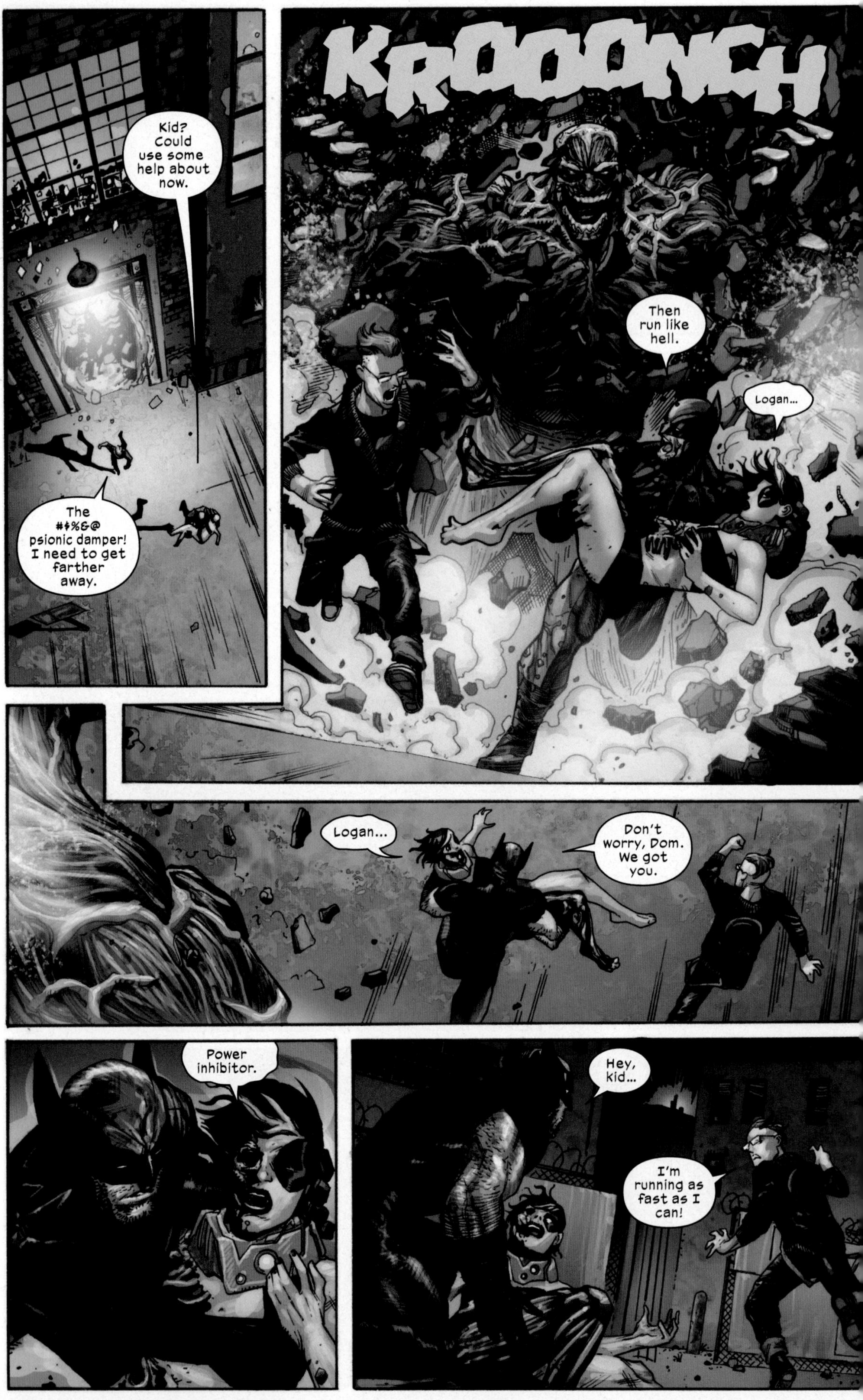
Kid? Could use some help about now.
The #$%&@ psionic damper! I need to get farther away.
KROOONCH
Then run like hell.
Logan...
Logan...
Don't worry, Dom. We got you.
Power inhibitor.
Hey, kid...
I'm running as fast as I can!

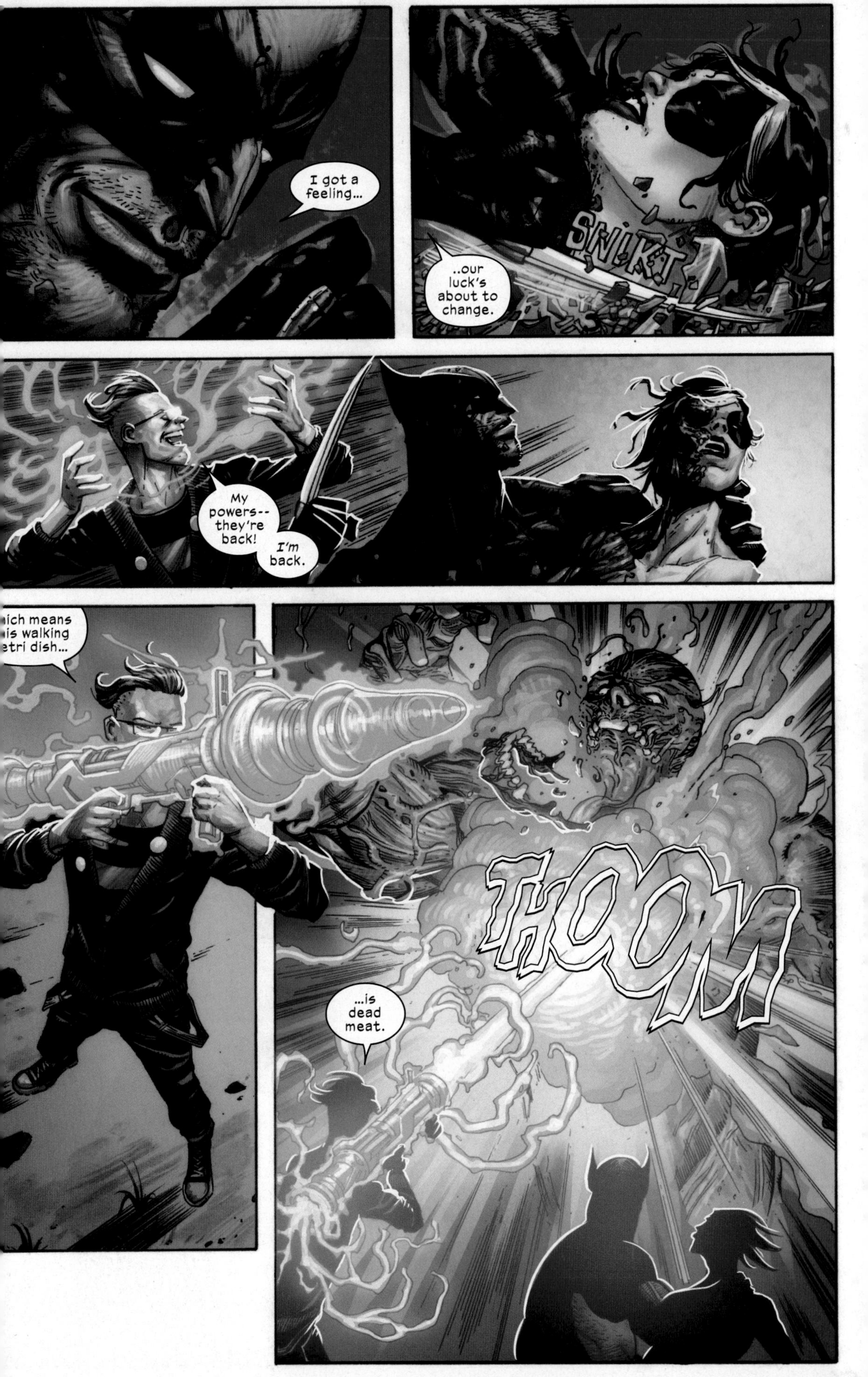
I got a feeling...
SNIKT
..our luck's about to change.
My powers--they're back!
I'm back.
ich means is walking etri dish...
THOOM
...is dead meat.

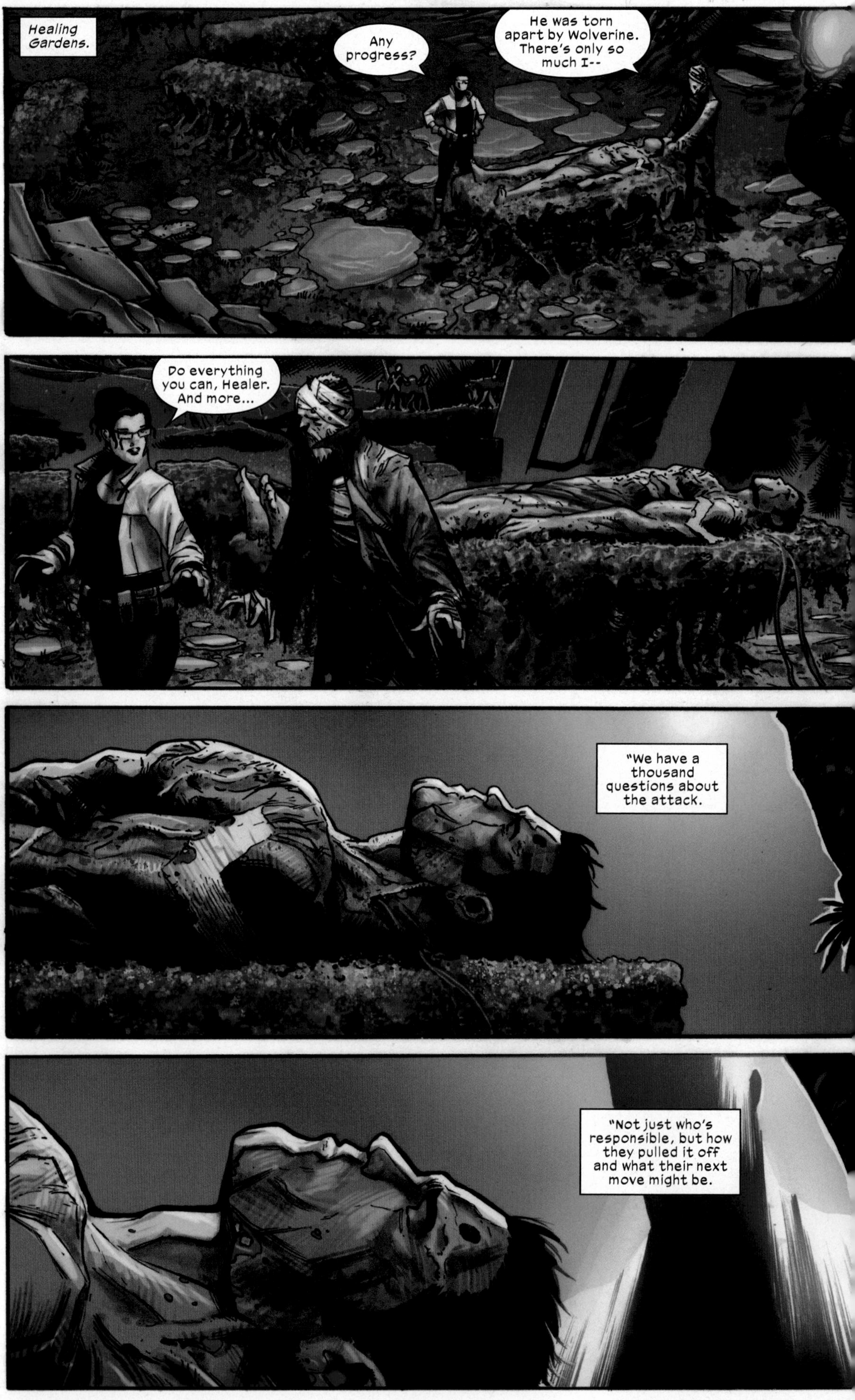
Healing Gardens.
Any progress?
He was torn apart by Wolverine. There's only so much I--
Do everything you can, Healer. And more...
"We have a thousand questions about the attack.
"Not just who's responsible, but how they pulled it off and what their next move might be.

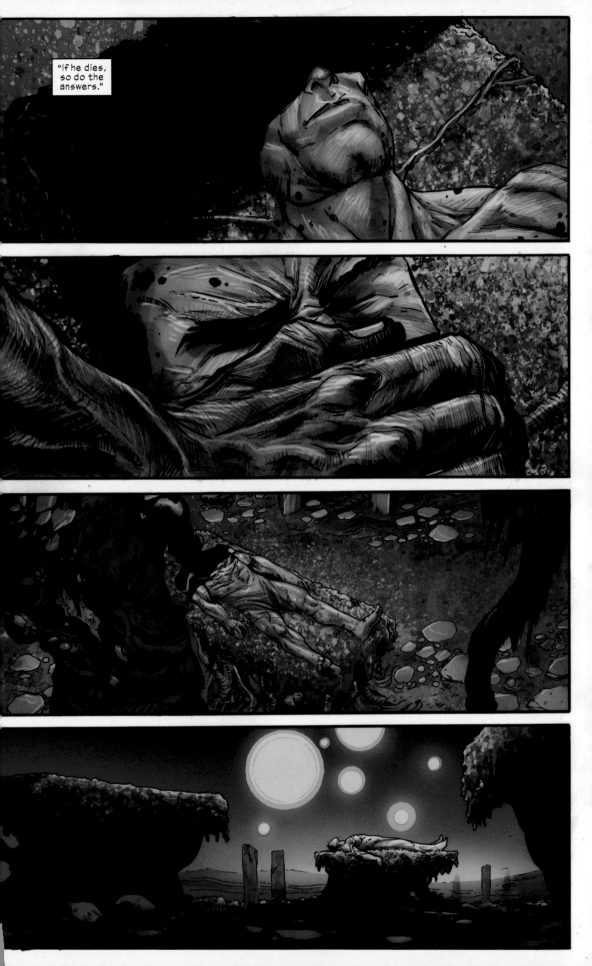

"If he dies,
so do the
answers."

THE FIFTH ASSASSIN

No one questioned the death of the fifth assassin. His condition was serious, and there is only so much that can be done when a body has been stabbed and shredded by Adamantium claws.

The plan was to strip down his remains — along with the remains of the other four — to the very marrow in the hopes of discovering some biometric identification.

These were not people after all; they were property. Valuable property. And valuable property is tagged and chipped for reclamation.

Perhaps Dr. Reyes or Healer would have found some signature trace, even on a cellular level. The bodies contained many secrets. Reinforced bones. An abundance of fast-twitch muscle fibers. Oversized adrenal glands. Hidden weapons in the form of explosive putty and garroting wire and calcium daggers nested in the forearm.

But this — a comprehensive autopsy — was not to be. Because like the South Korean lab, the bodies detonated. Their skeletons became shrapnel no different than screws and stainless steel stuffed into an IED. The blast tore Healer apart, and he has been fast-tracked for resurrection.

The brain and spinal cord of each body were believed to be the source of the explosion.

It is unclear whether the assassins were outfitted with a biological timer or if this was an ambush that presented itself in response to the deep anatomical query.

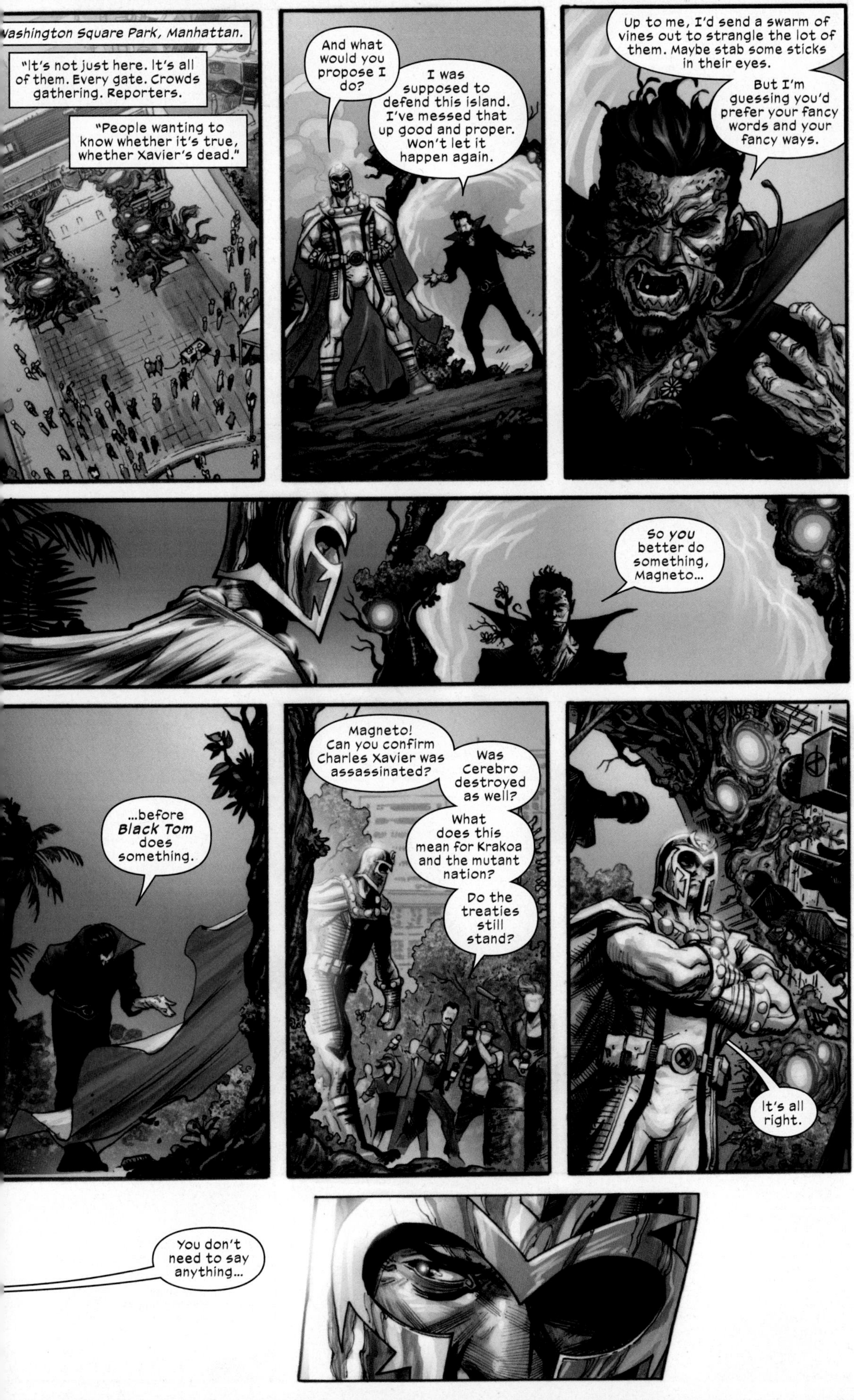

Washington Square Park, Manhattan.
"It's not just here. It's all of them. Every gate. Crowds gathering. Reporters.
"People wanting to know whether it's true, whether Xavier's dead."
And what would you propose I do?
I was supposed to defend this island. I've messed that up good and proper. Won't let it happen again.
Up to me, I'd send a swarm of vines out to strangle the lot of them. Maybe stab some sticks in their eyes.
But I'm guessing you'd prefer your fancy words and your fancy ways.
So you better do something, Magneto...
...before Black Tom does something.
Magneto! Can you confirm Charles Xavier was assassinated?
Was Cerebro destroyed as well?
What does this mean for Krakoa and the mutant nation?
Do the treaties still stand?
It's all right.
You don't need to say anything...

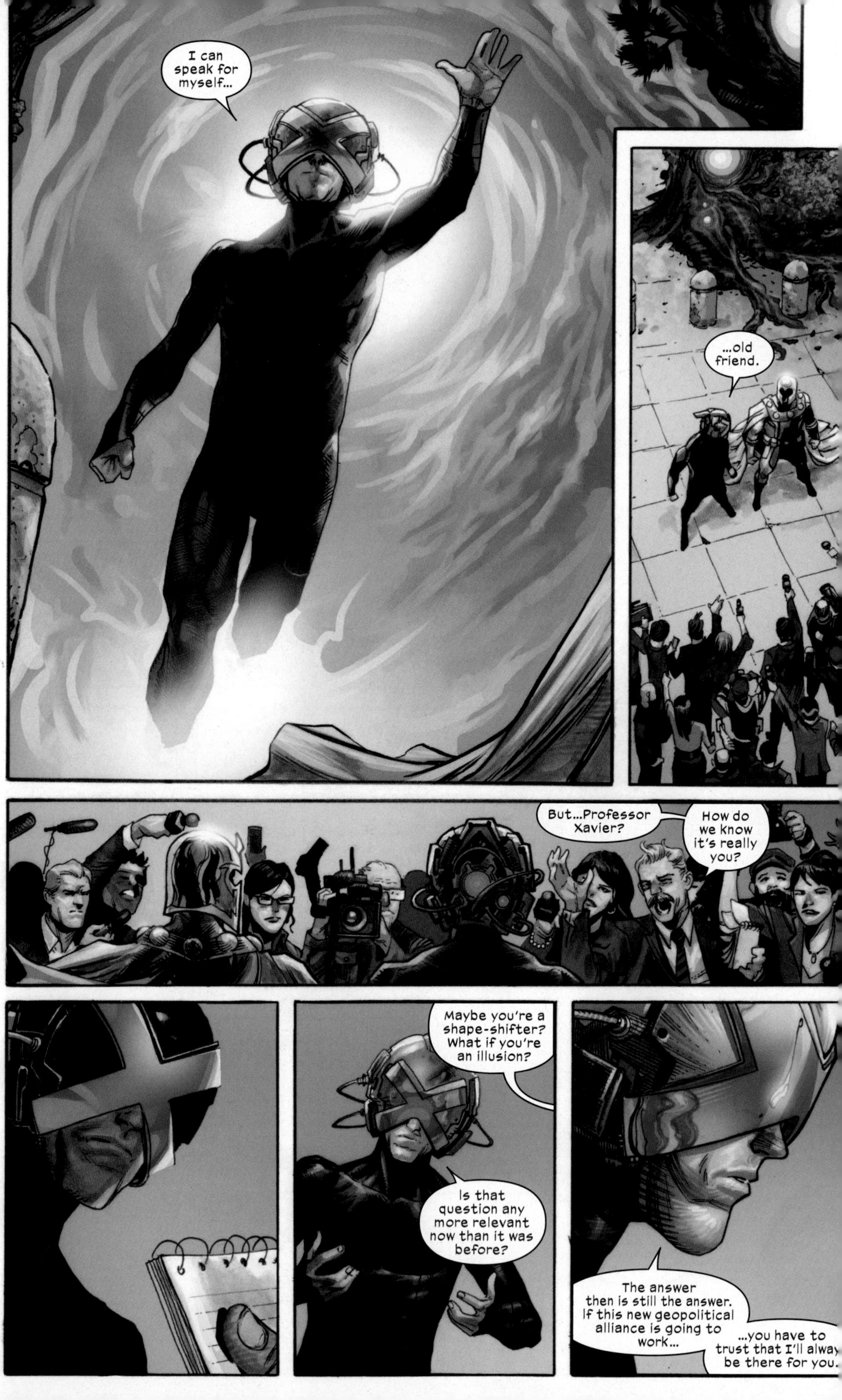
I can speak for myself...
...old friend.
But...Professor Xavier?
How do we know it's really you?
Maybe you're a shape-shifter? What if you're an illusion?
Is that question any more relevant now than it was before?
The answer then is still the answer. If this new geopolitical alliance is going to work...
...you have to trust that I'll alway be there for you.

THE CEREBRO SWORD

When Xavier once again walked among his people, some could not help but cheer and cry with gladness. Others embraced him. Others shook his hand. Others bowed or knelt on one knee.

Forge grabbed him by the shoulders and dragged him close and offered a big, hearty kiss on the mouth, startling a laugh out of the Professor.

When he and Magneto finally had a private moment, his old friend did not smile or clap him on the back. Instead he stared long and hard at Charles before offering a gift...

The shattered remains of Cerebro, which he had shaped into a sword.

"I suggest you keep this close," he said.

Xavier took it by the hilt and promised to do as Magneto advised.

In his living quarters, he hung the Cerebro Sword on the wall above his bed. As a totem and as a reminder. When he lay down, the point of it gleamed at him.

He had never been a sound sleeper, even less so now, and that was a good thing. A man at war cannot be a man at peace.

Every now and then the sword would wink and glimmer with light or hum with the data still coursing through it.

Cerebro was broken, but forged anew and refined, like Xavier's dream.

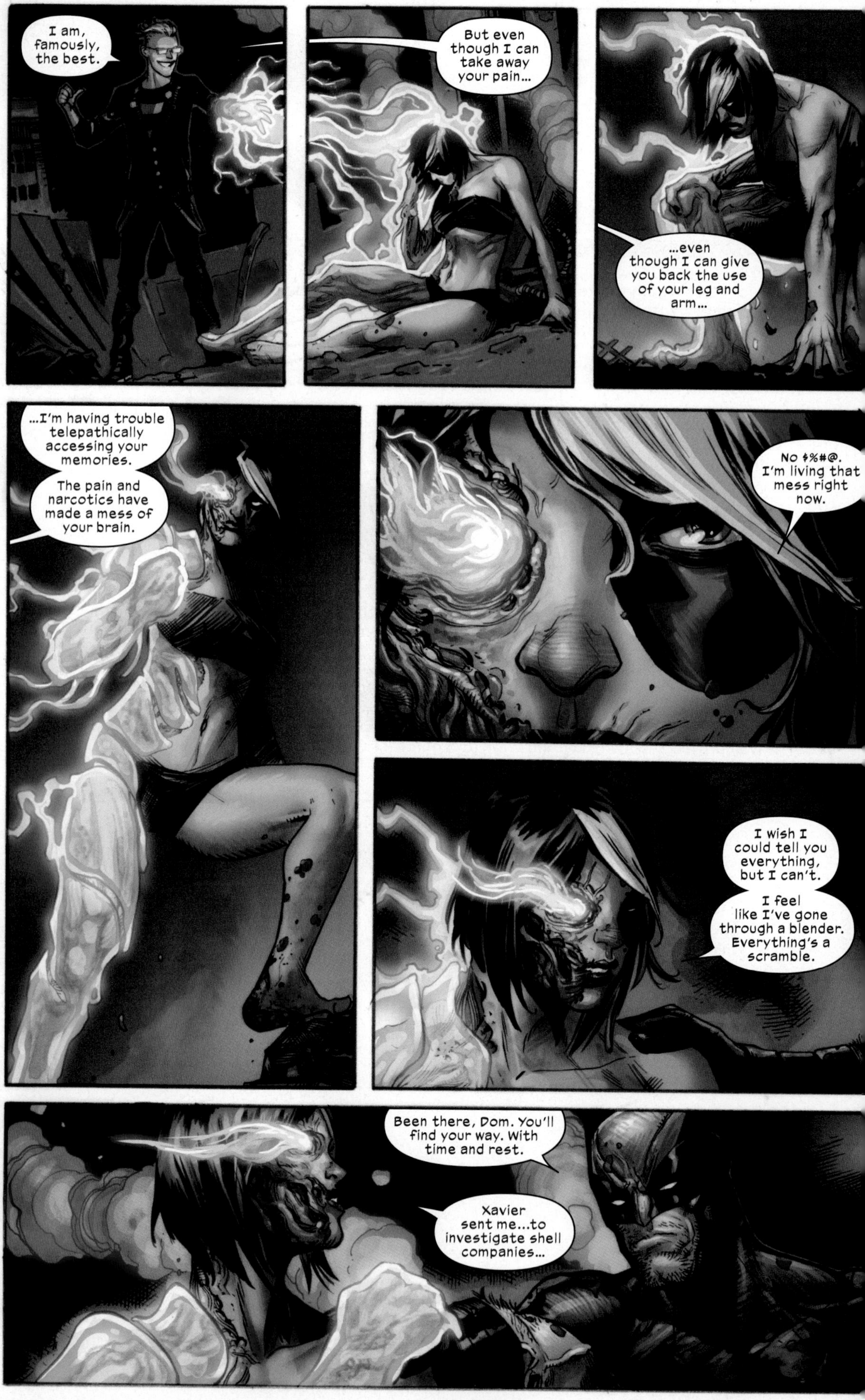
I am, famously, the best.
But even though I can take away your pain...
...even though I can give you back the use of your leg and arm...
...I'm having trouble telepathically accessing your memories.
The pain and narcotics have made a mess of your brain.
No $%#@. I'm living that mess right now.
I wish I could tell you everything, but I can't.
I feel like I've gone through a blender. Everything's a scramble.
Been there, Dom. You'll find your way. With time and rest.
Xavier sent me...to investigate shell companies...

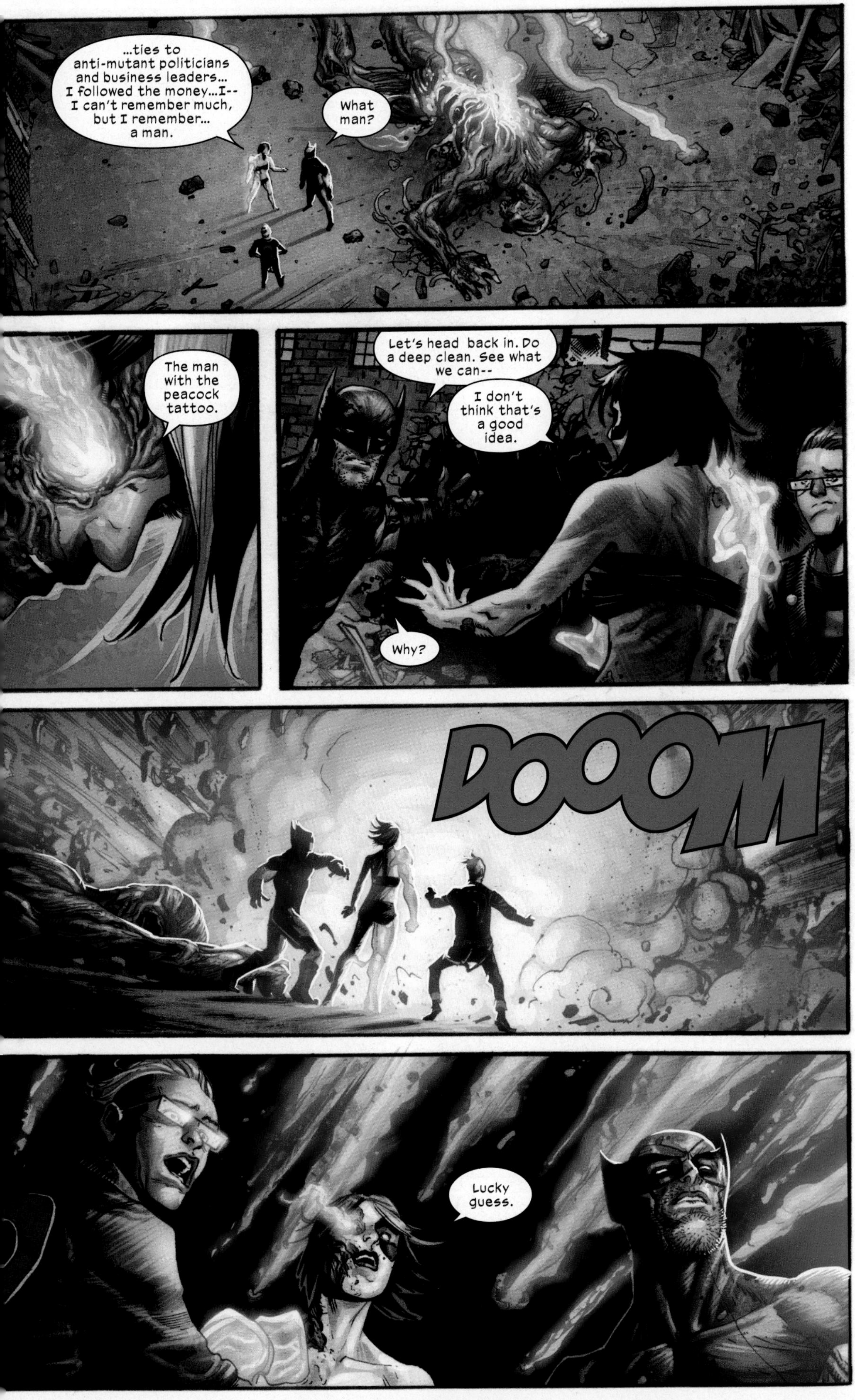
...ties to anti-mutant politicians and business leaders... I followed the money...I-- I can't remember much, but I remember... a man.
What man?
The man with the peacock tattoo.
Let's head back in. Do a deep clean. See what we can--
I don't think that's a good idea.
Why?
DOOOM
Lucky guess.

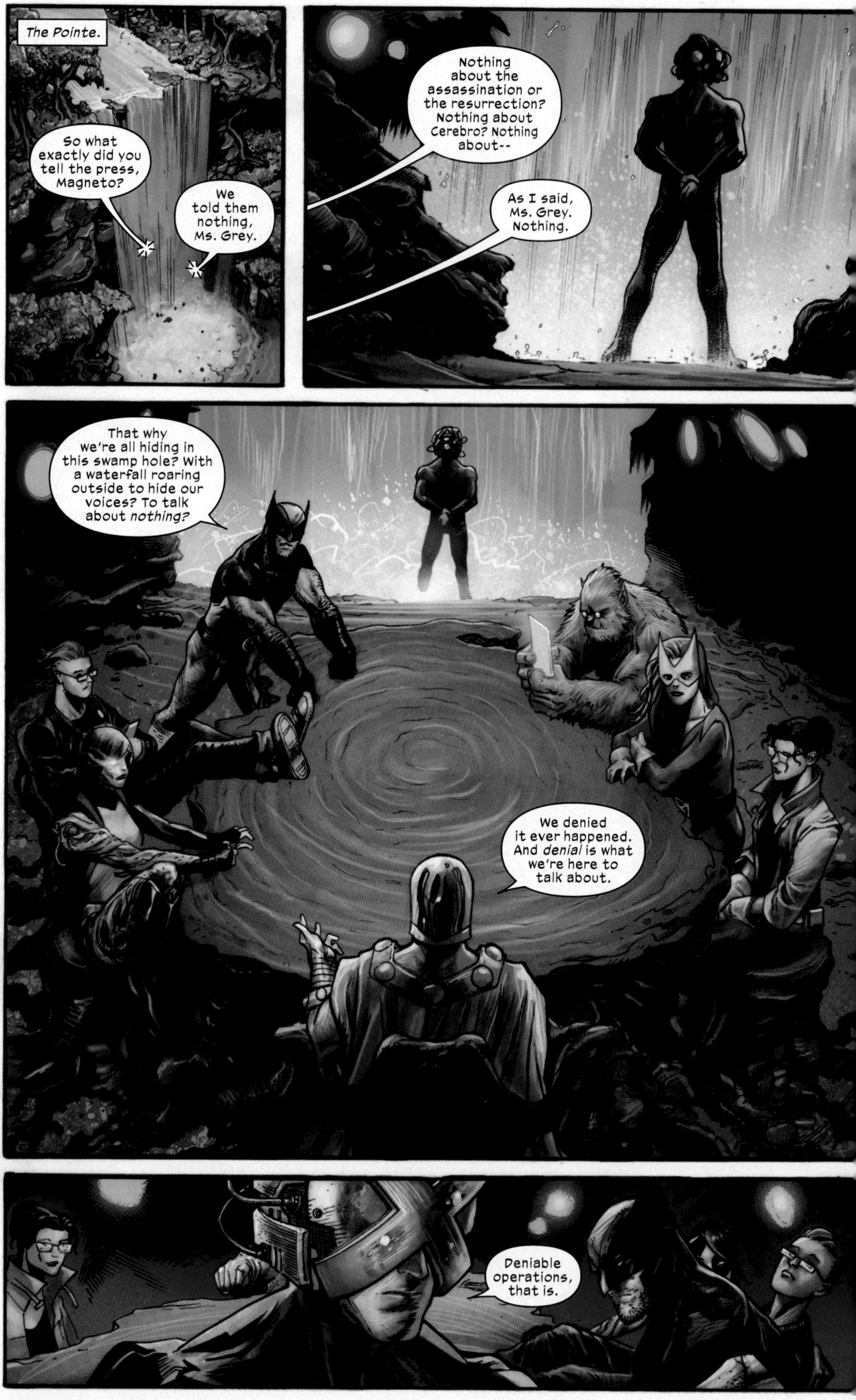
The Pointe.
So what exactly did you tell the press, Magneto?
We told them nothing, Ms. Grey.
Nothing about the assassination or the resurrection? Nothing about Cerebro? Nothing about--
As I said, Ms. Grey. Nothing.
That why we're all hiding in this swamp hole? With a waterfall roaring outside to hide our voices? To talk about *nothing?*
We denied it ever happened. And *denial* is what we're here to talk about.
Deniable operations, that is.

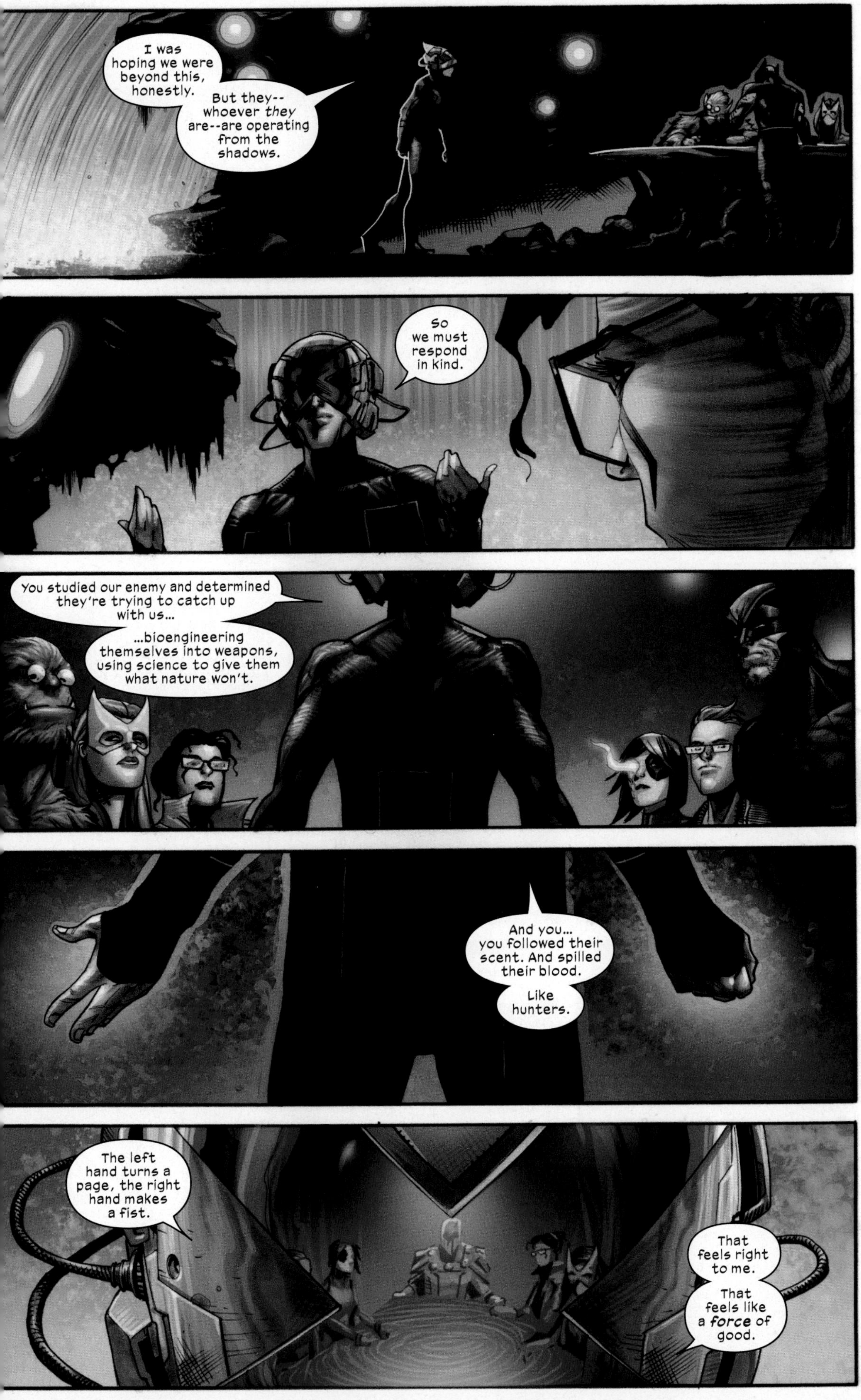
I was hoping we were beyond this, honestly.
But they--whoever *they* are--are operating from the shadows.
So we must respond in kind.
You studied our enemy and determined they're trying to catch up with us...
...bioengineering themselves into weapons, using science to give them what nature won't.
And you... you followed their scent. And spilled their blood.
Like hunters.
The left hand turns a page, the right hand makes a fist.
That feels right to me.
That feels like a *force* of good.

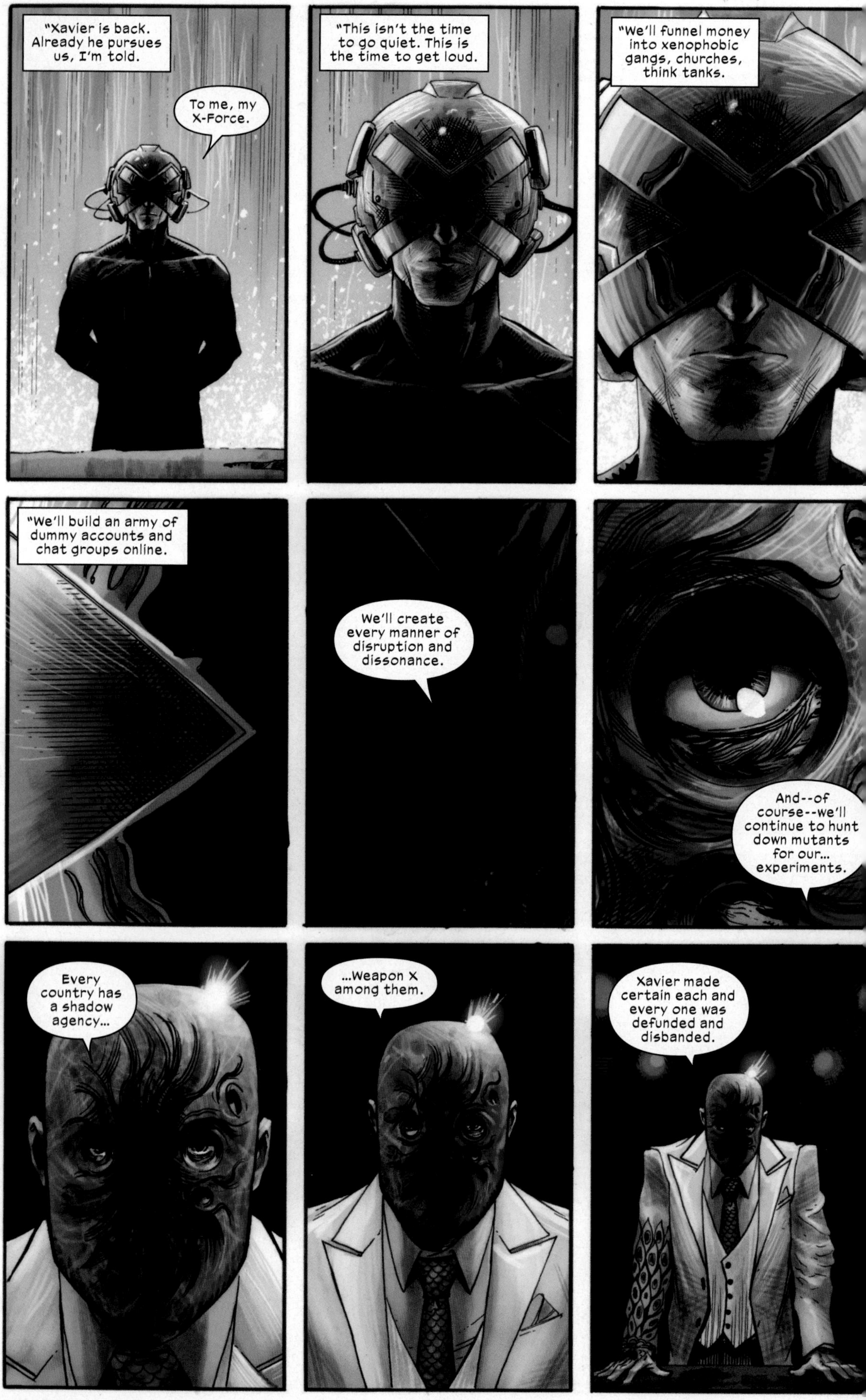
"Xavier is back. Already he pursues us, I'm told.
To me, my X-Force.
"This isn't the time to go quiet. This is the time to get loud.
"We'll funnel money into xenophobic gangs, churches, think tanks.
"We'll build an army of dummy accounts and chat groups online.
We'll create every manner of disruption and dissonance.
And--of course--we'll continue to hunt down mutants for our... experiments.
Every country has a shadow agency...
...Weapon X among them.
Xavier made certain each and every one was defunded and disbanded.

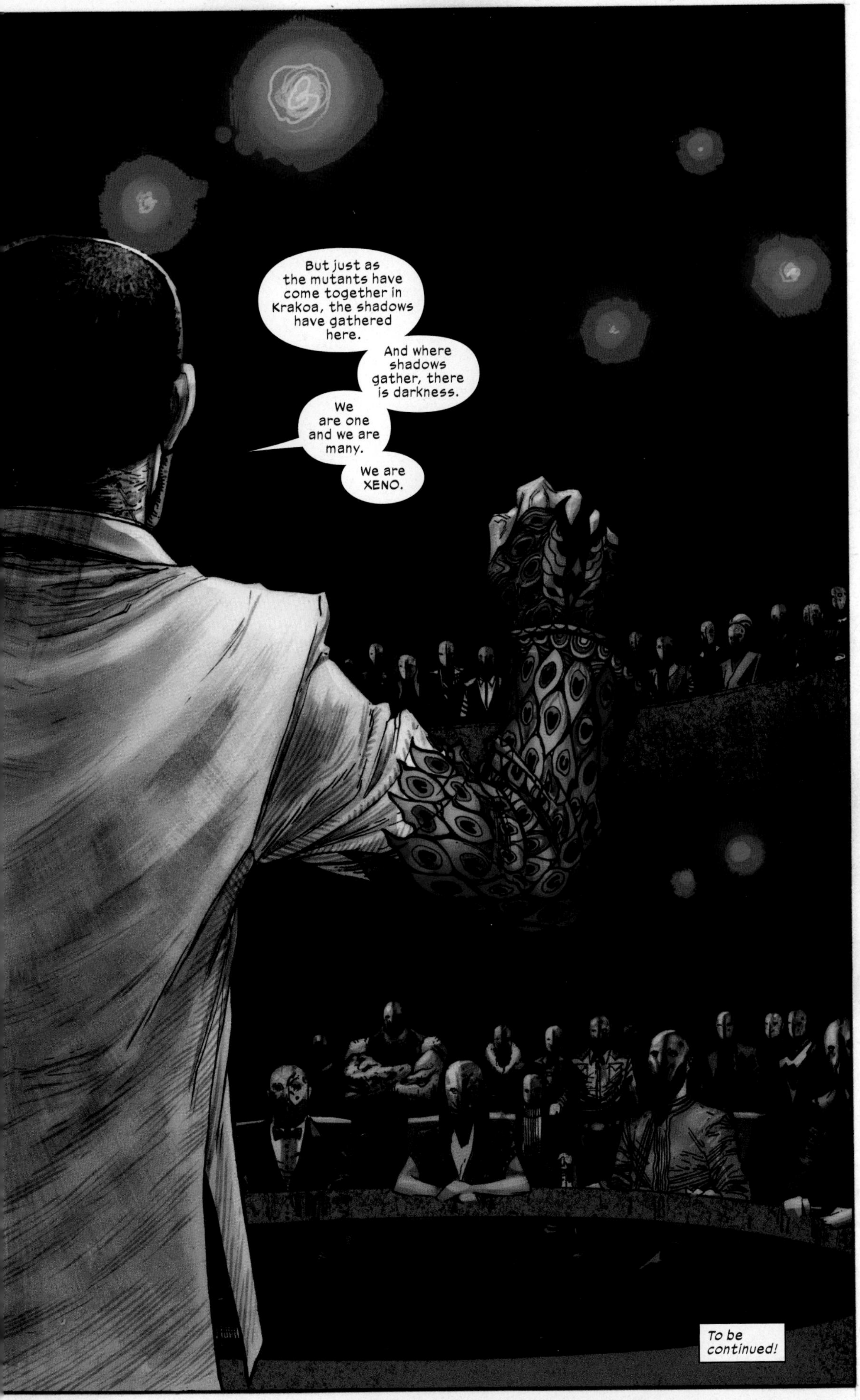
But just as the mutants have come together in Krakoa, the shadows have gathered here.
And where shadows gather, there is darkness.
We are one and we are many.
We are XENO.
To be continued!

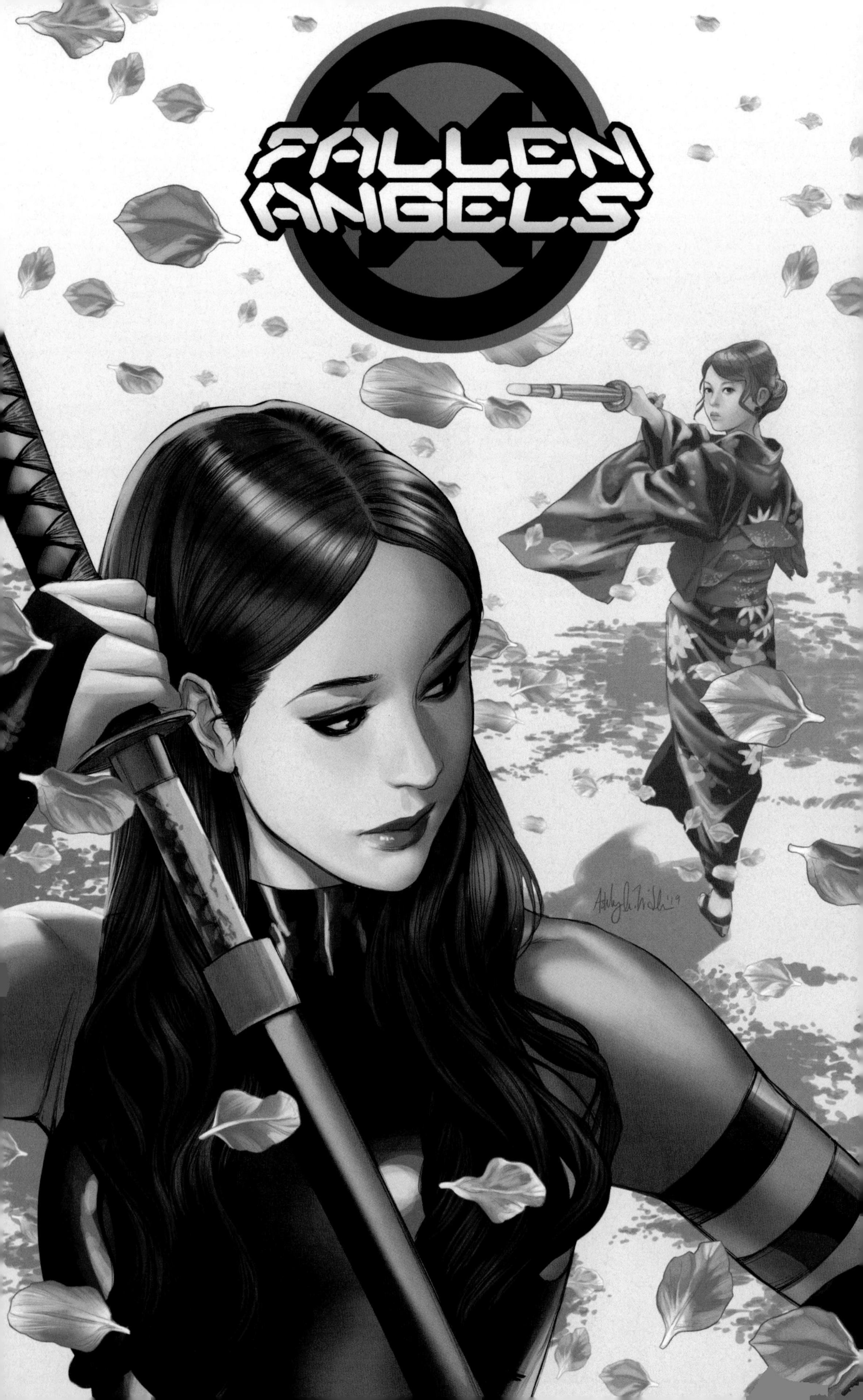
FALLEN ANGELS

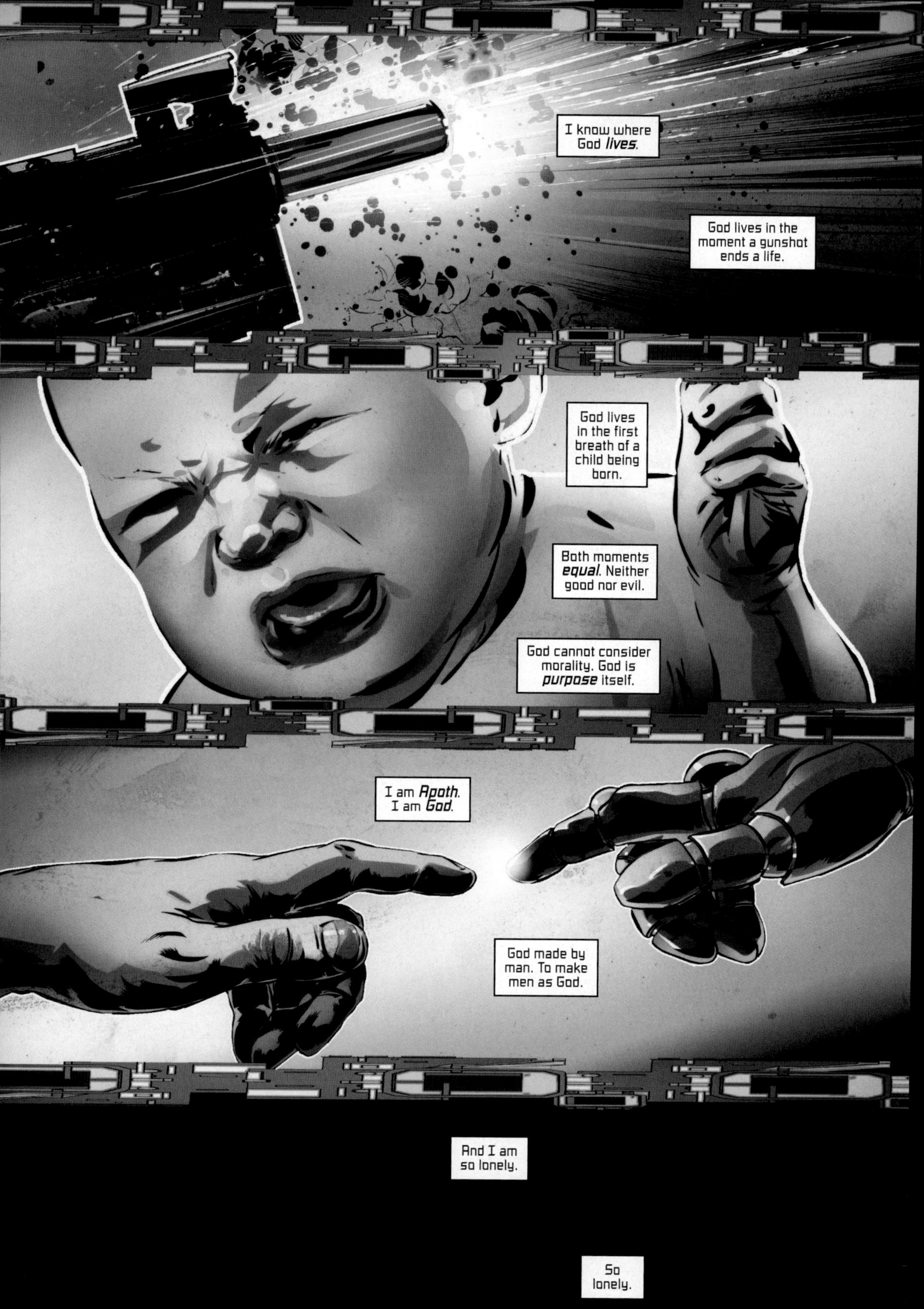
I know where God *lives*.
God lives in the moment a gunshot ends a life.
God lives in the first breath of a child being born.
Both moments *equal*. Neither good nor evil.
God cannot consider morality. God is *purpose* itself.
I am *Apoth*. I am *God*.
God made by man. To make men as God.
And I am so lonely.
So lonely.

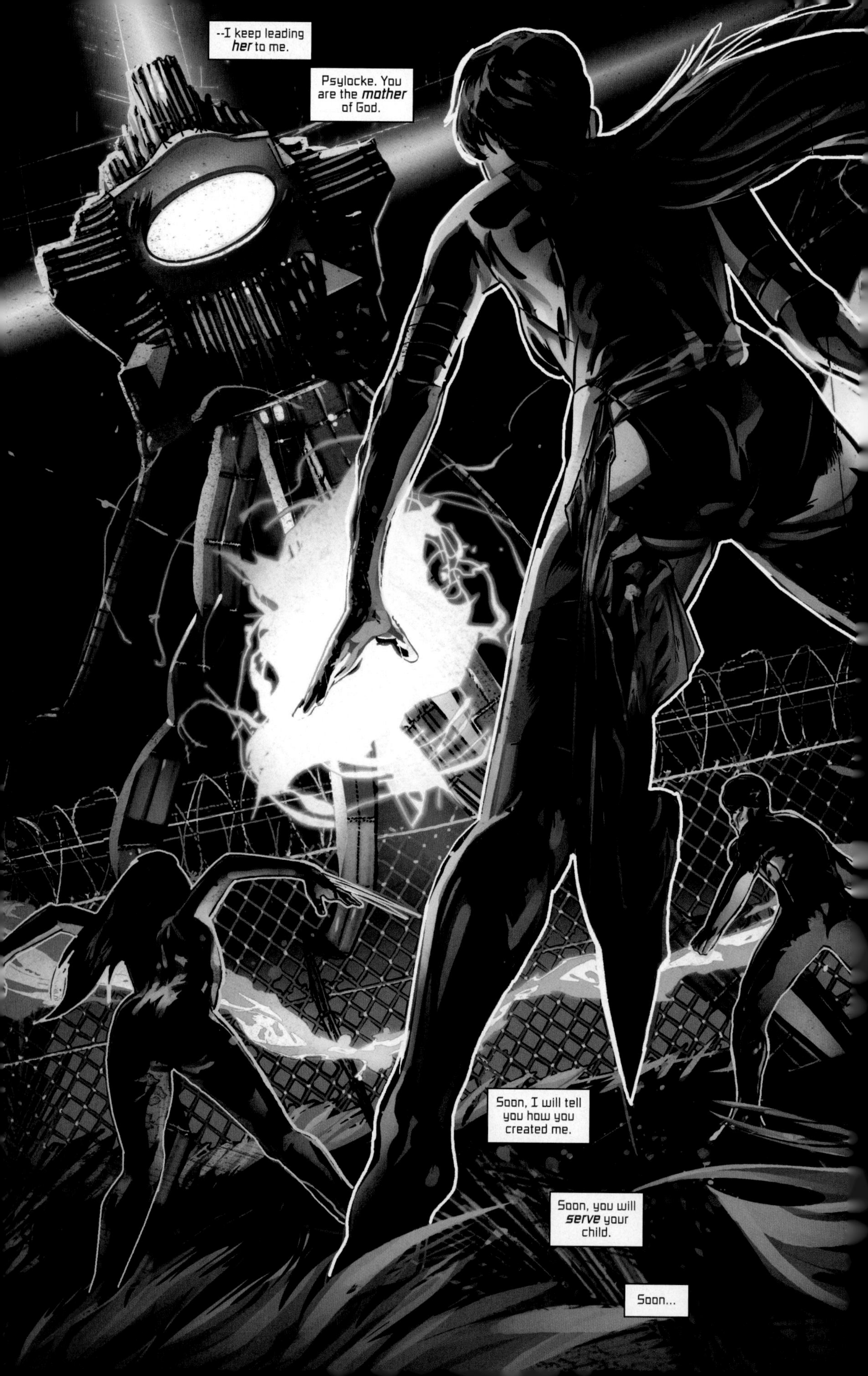
--I keep leading *her* to me.
Psylocke. You are the *mother* of God.
Soon, I will tell you how you created me.
Soon, you will *serve* your child.
Soon...

[kra_[0.3]
[koa_[0.3]

[kra_[0.X]
[koa_[0.X]

THE LANGUAGE OF CONFLICT

Mutants around the world are flocking to the island-nation of Krakoa for safety, security and to be part of the first mutant society.

Psylocke, Cable and X-23 are hunting a mysterious new enemy: Apoth, somehow connected to a dangerous new cyberdrug called Overclock. While searching a seemingly abandoned Overclock factory in Brazil, Psylocke and her warriors are ambushed!

Psylocke

Cable

X-23

[kra_[0.3]...]
[koa_[0.3]...]

[A._ssa_ssin_]

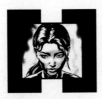

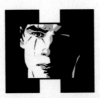

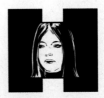

[00_warrior_X__]
[00_lim_ited___]

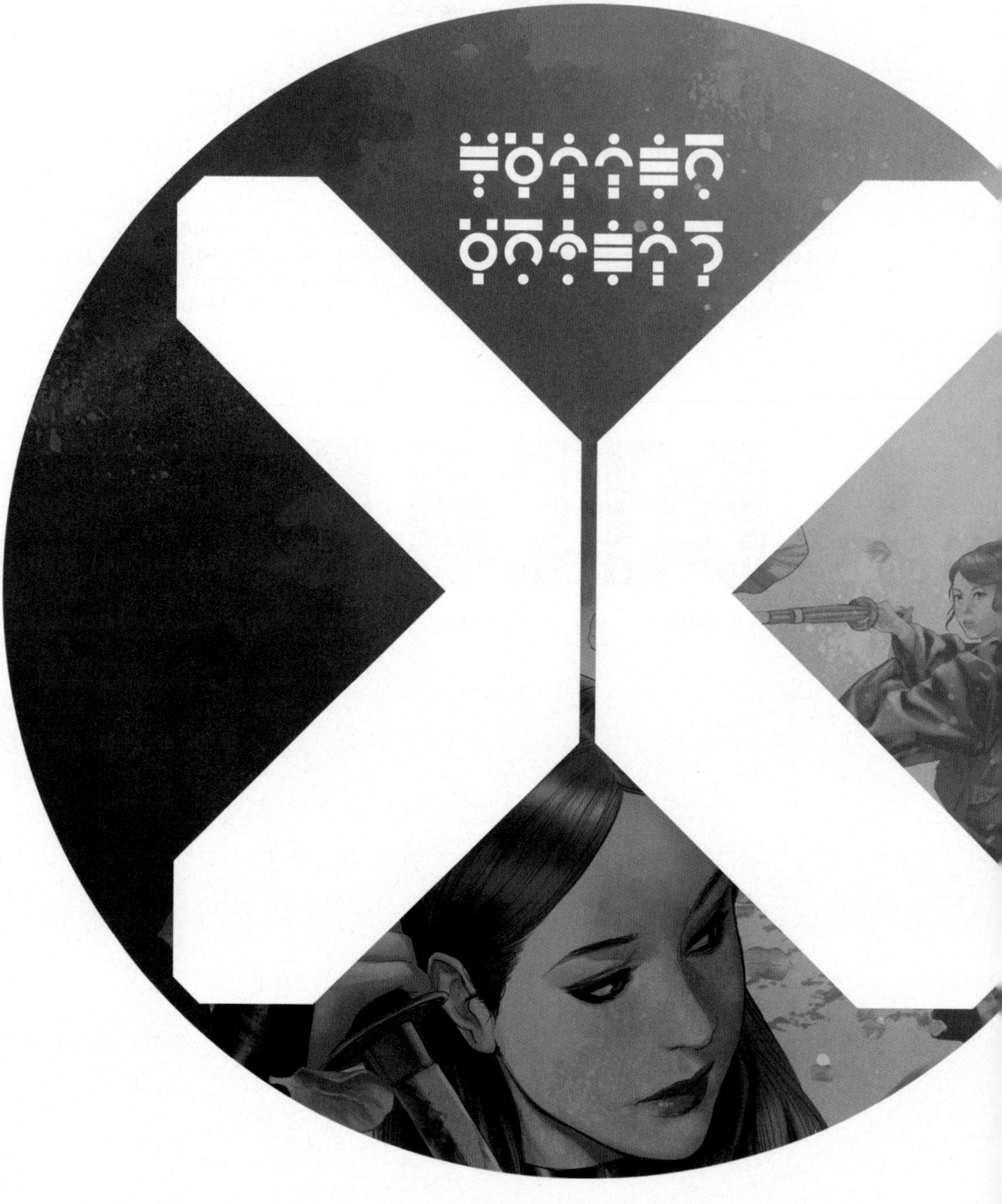

BRYAN HILL...[WRITER]
SZYMON KUDRANSKI...................................[ARTIST]
FRANK D'ARMATA...............................[COLOR ARTIST]
VC's JOE SABINO.................................[LETTERER]
TOM MULLER...[DESIGN]

ASHLEY WITTER................................[COVER ARTIST]

NICK RUSSELL...................................[PRODUCTION]

JONATHAN HICKMAN..............................[HEAD OF X]
CHRIS ROBINSON.........................[ASSISTANT EDITOR]
JORDAN D. WHITE....................................[EDITOR]
C.B. CEBULSKI.........................[EDITOR IN CHIEF]
JOE QUESADA....................[CHIEF CREATIVE OFFICER]
DAN BUCKLEY.....................................[PRESIDENT]
ALAN FINE..........................[EXECUTIVE PRODUCER]

[03] FALLEN ANGELS

[ISSUE THREE]....................SEPPUKU

[00_warrior_X__]
[00_lim_ited___]

[00_00...0]
[00_00...3]

[00_sword_]
[00_____]

[00_____]

[00_____X]

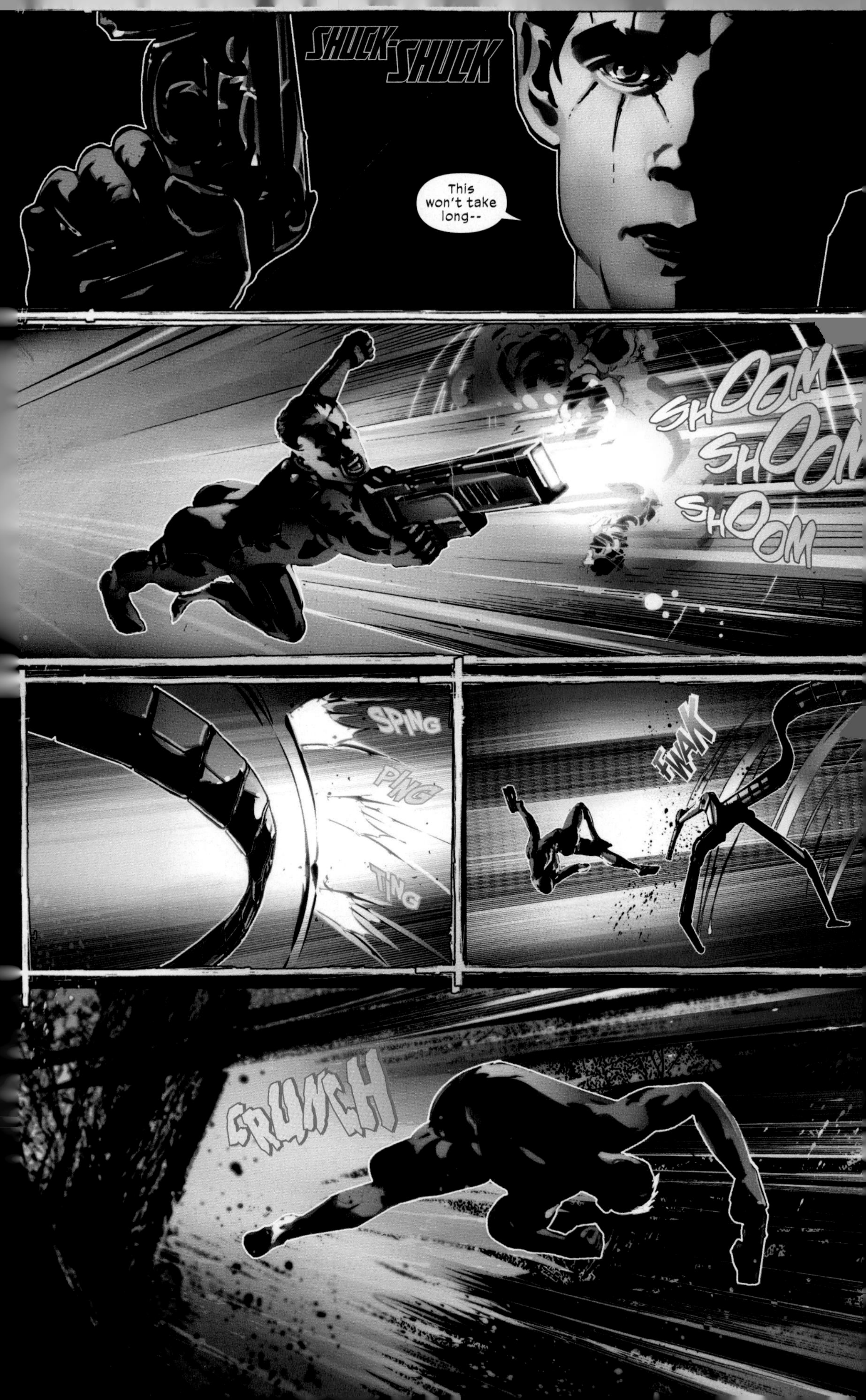
SHUCK-SHUCK
This won't take long--
SHOOM SHOOM SHOOM
SPING
PING
TING
FWAK
CRUNCH

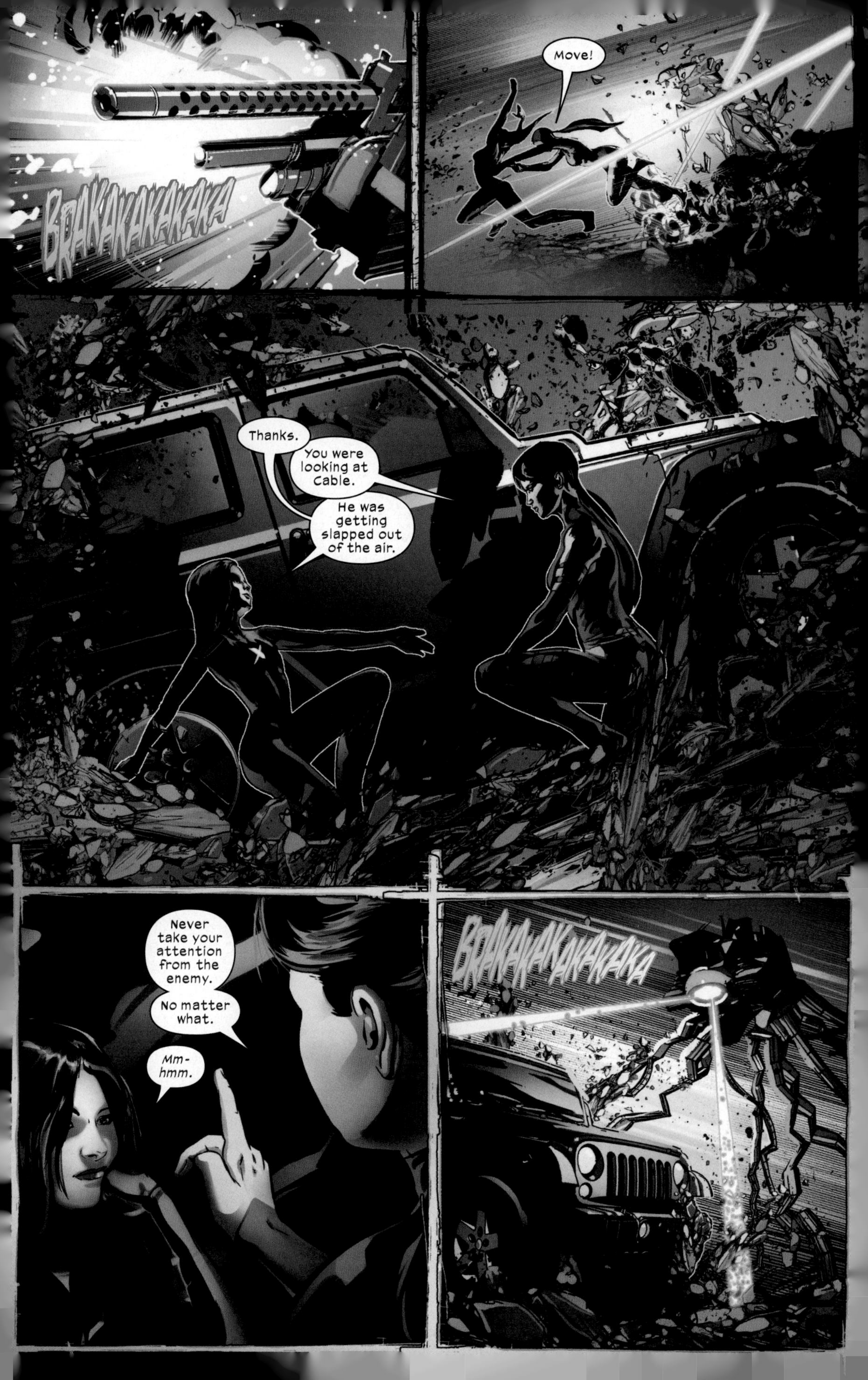
BRAKAKAKAKAKAKA
Move!
Thanks.
You were looking at Cable.
He was getting slapped out of the air.
Never take your attention from the enemy.
No matter what.
Mm-hmm.
BRAKAKAKAKAKAKAKA

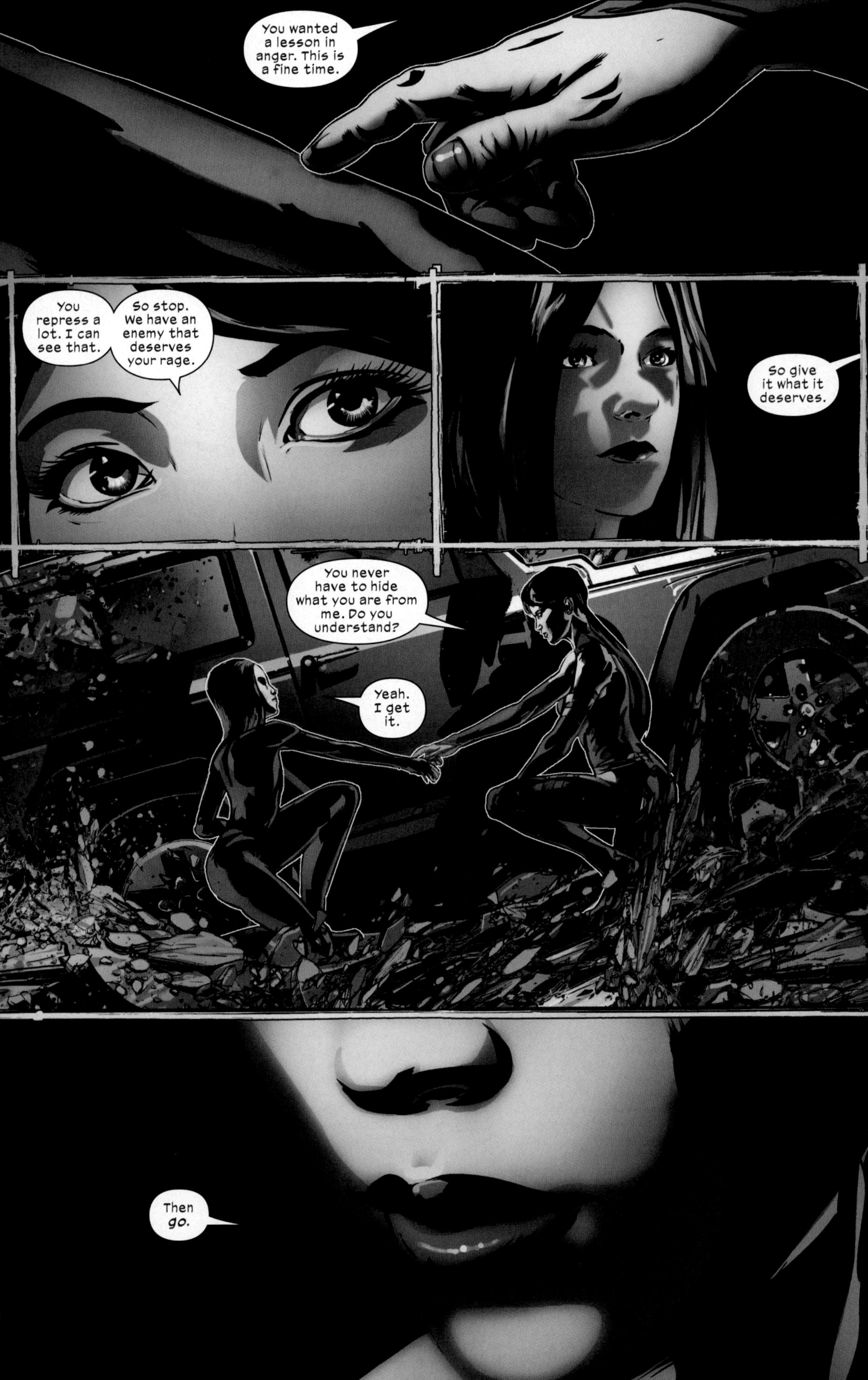
You wanted a lesson in anger. This is a fine time.
You repress a lot. I can see that.
So stop. We have an enemy that deserves your rage.
So give it what it deserves.
You never have to hide what you are from me. Do you understand?
Yeah. I get it.
Then go.

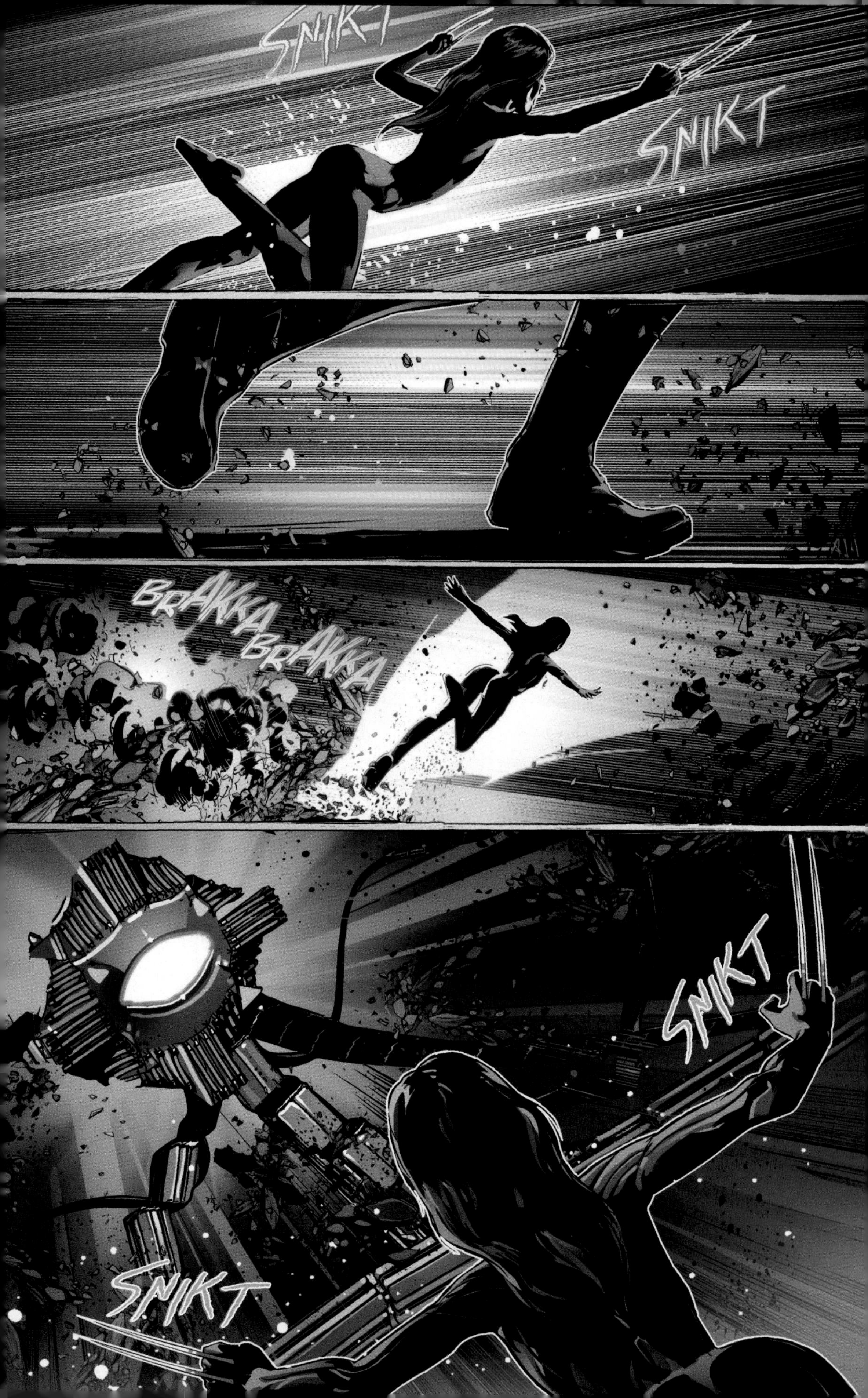
SNIKT
SNIKT
BRAKKA BRAKKA
SNIKT
SNIKT

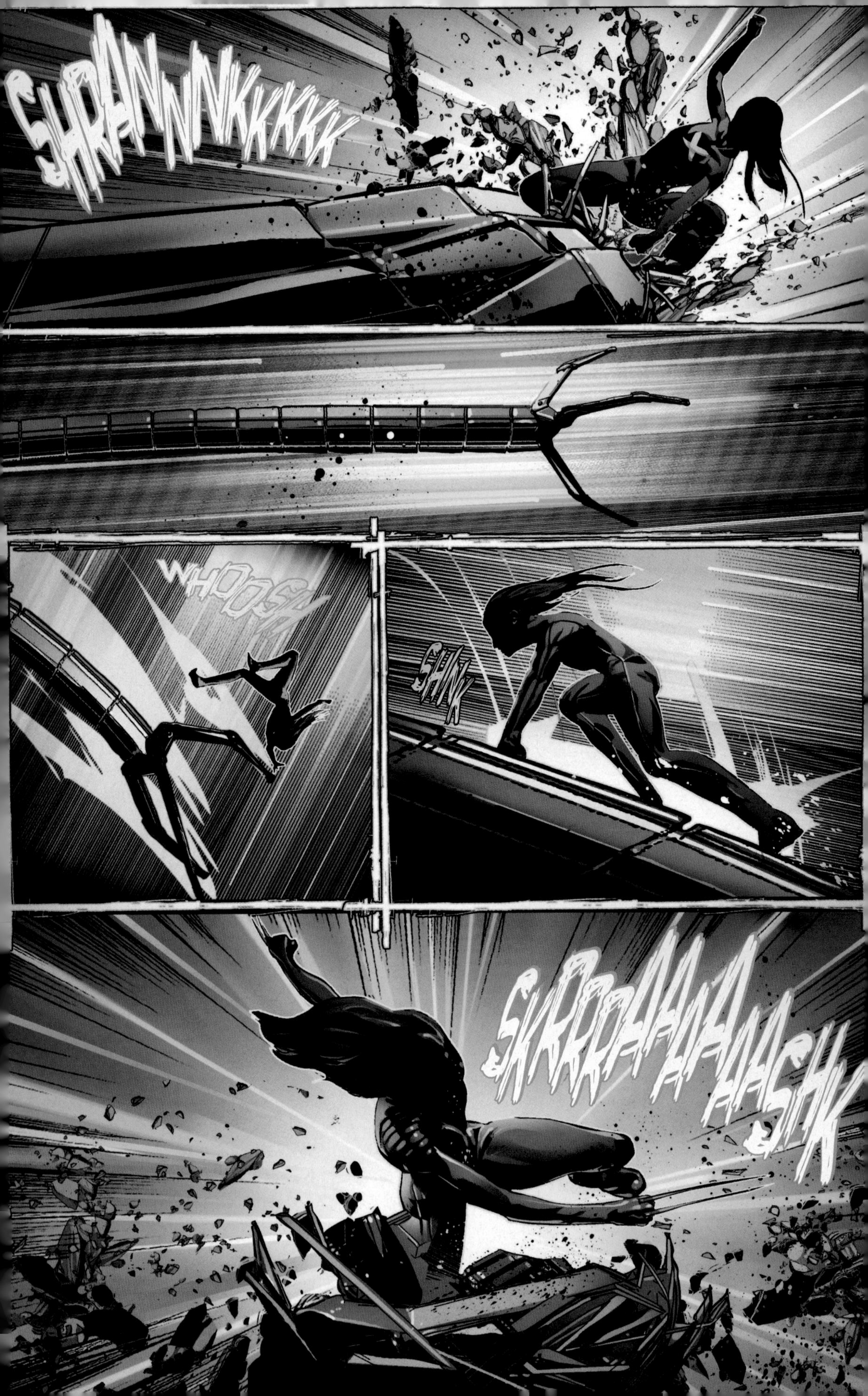
SHRANNNKKKKK
WHOOSH
SHINK
SKRRAAAAAASHK

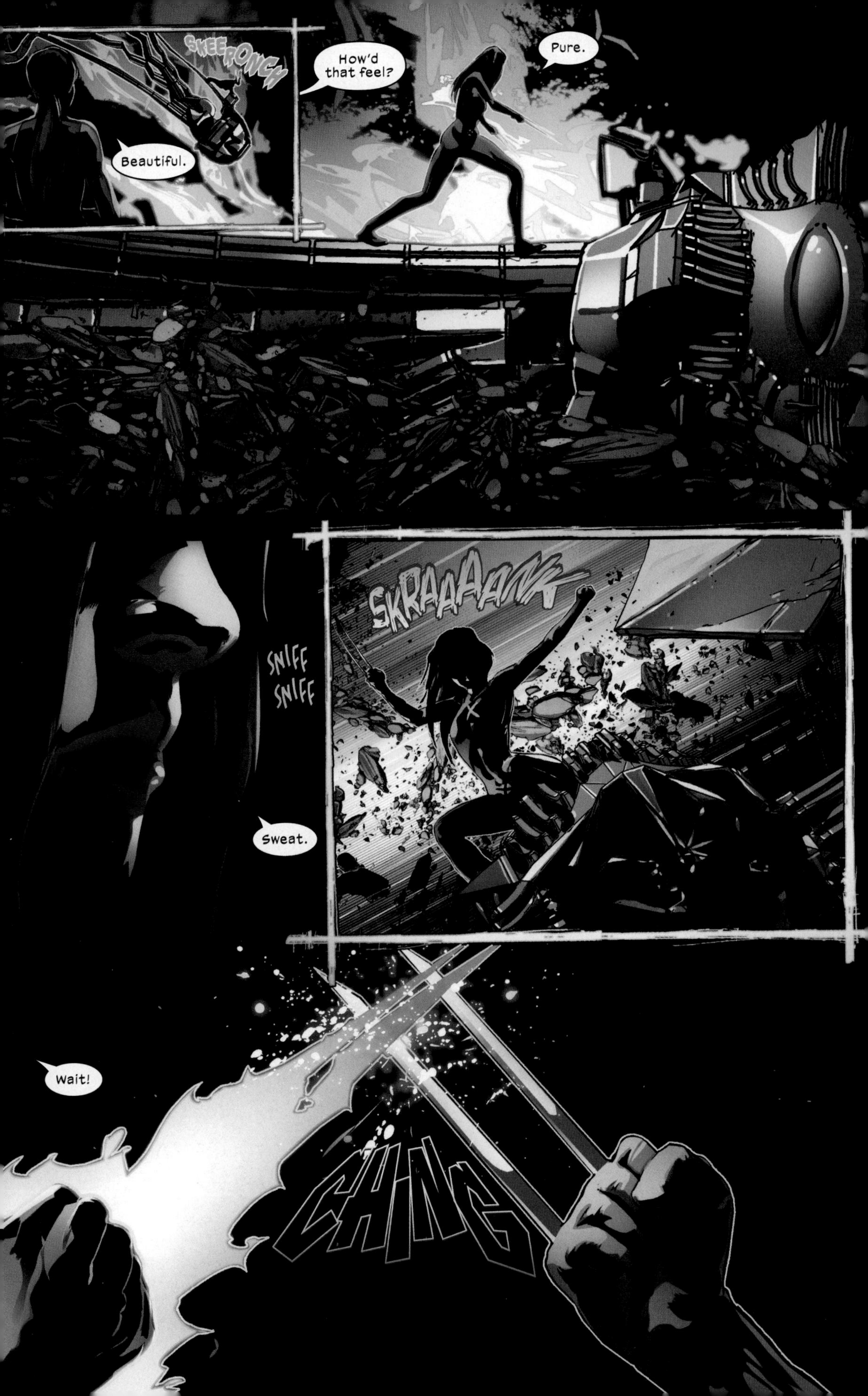
SKEERONCH
Beautiful.
How'd that feel?
Pure.
SKRAAAANK
SNIFF
SNIFF
Sweat.
Wait!
CHING

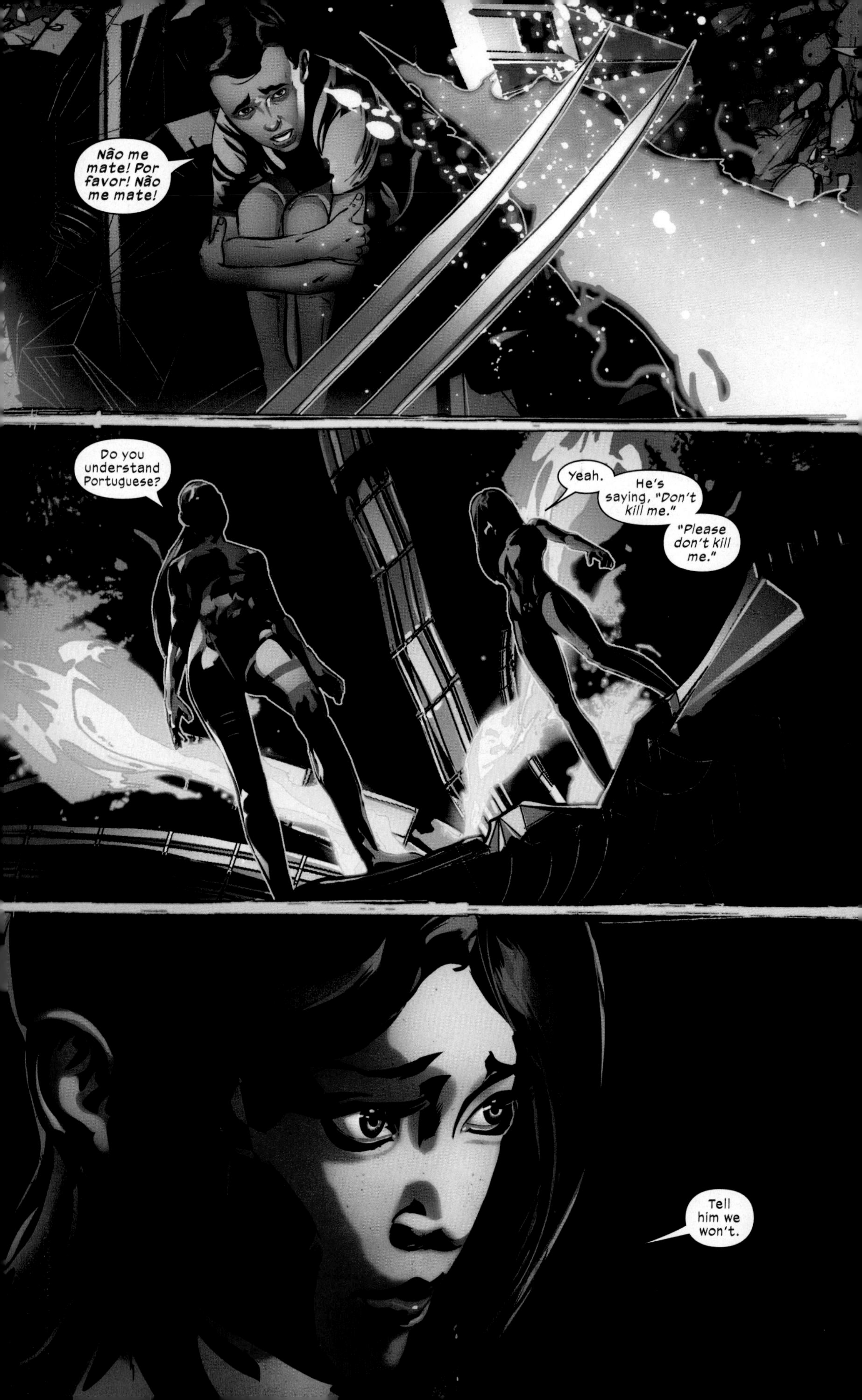
Não me mate! Por favor! Não me mate!
Do you understand Portuguese?
Yeah.
He's saying, "Don't kill me."
"Please don't kill me."
Tell him we won't.

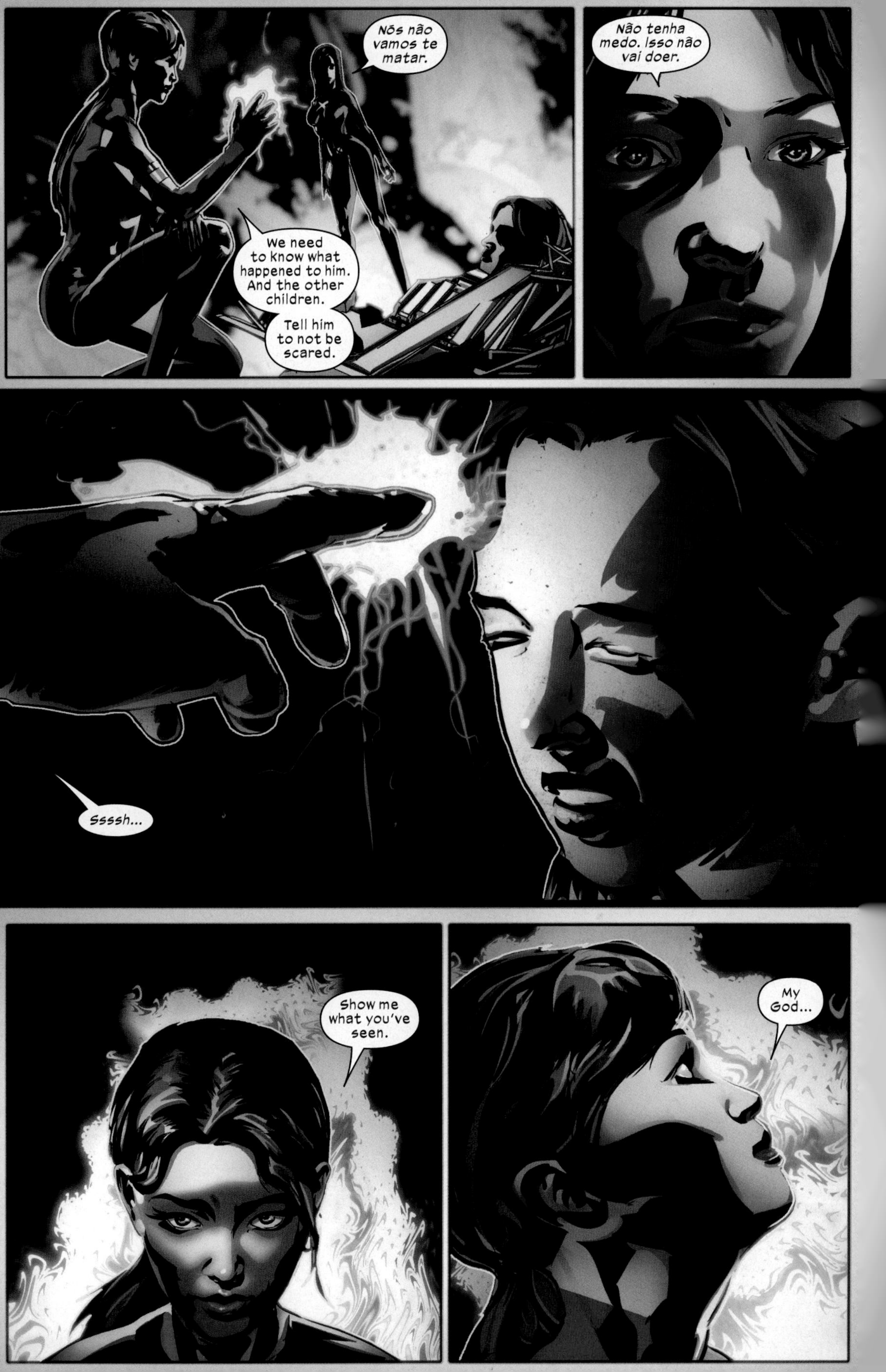
Nós não vamos te matar.
We need to know what happened to him. And the other children.
Tell him to not be scared.
Não tenha medo. Isso não vai doer.
Ssssh...
Show me what you've seen.
My God...

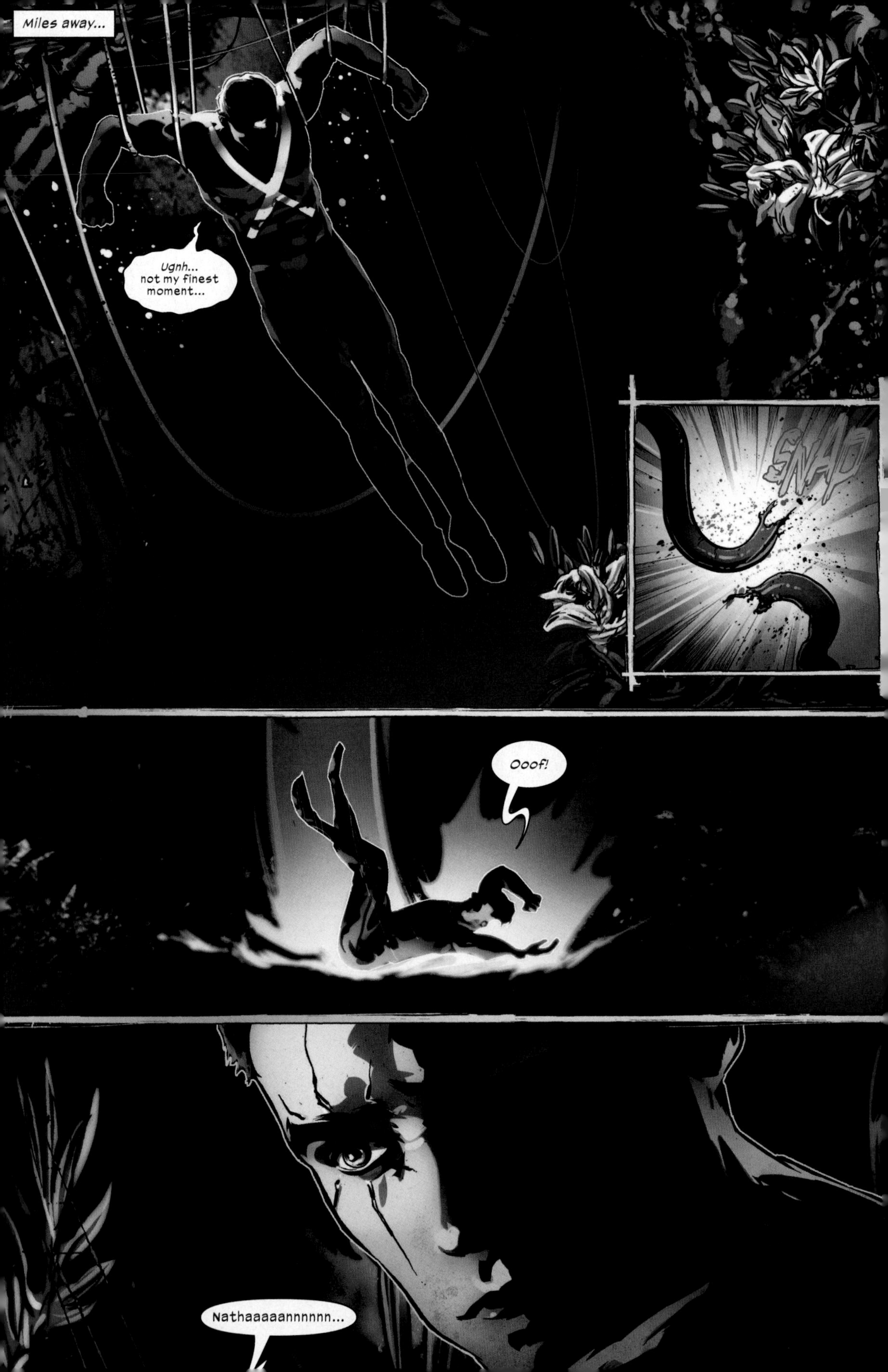
Miles away...
Ugnh... not my finest moment...
SNAP
Ooof!
Nathaaaaannnnnn...

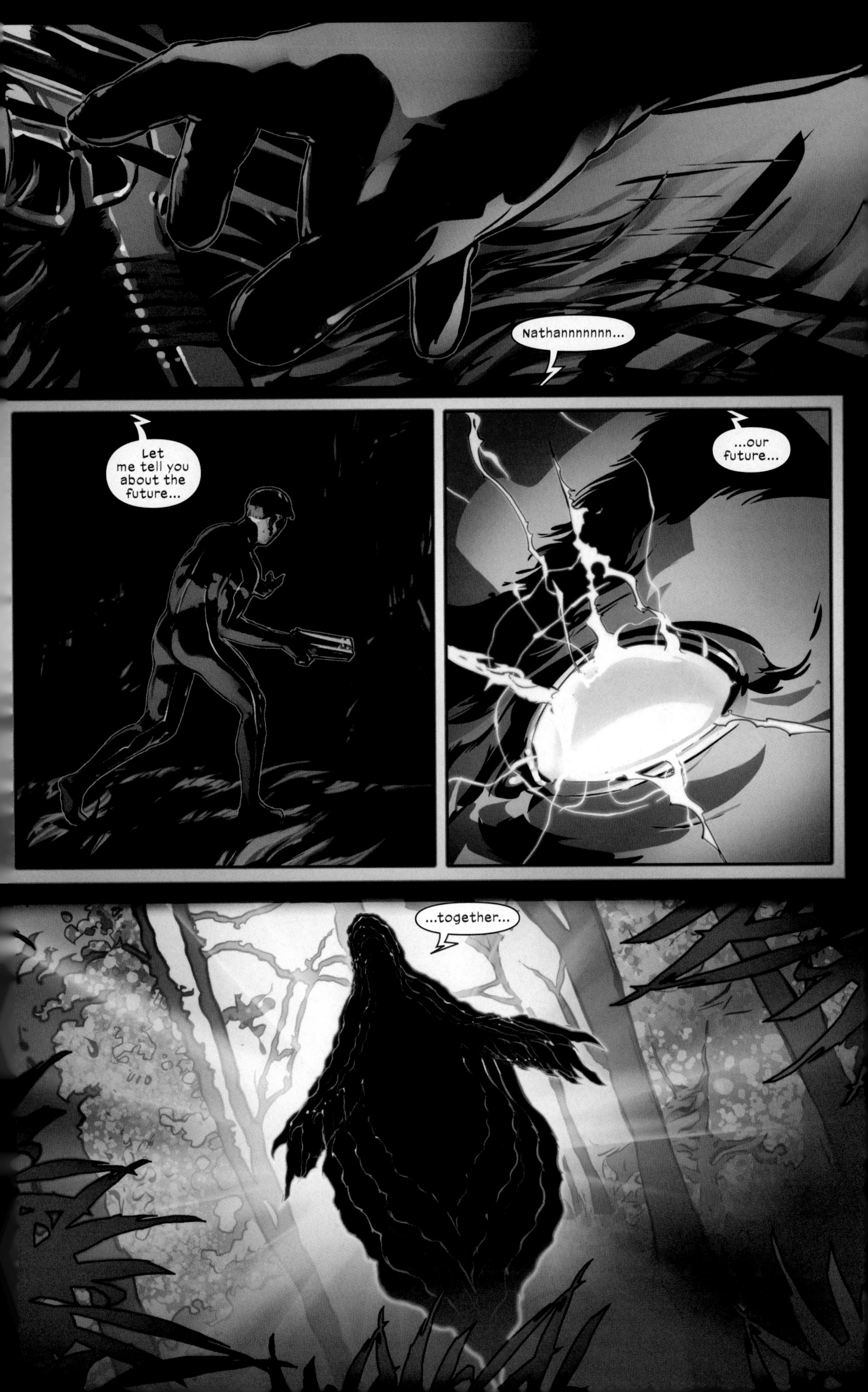
Nathannnnnnn...
Let me tell you about the future...
...our future...
...together...

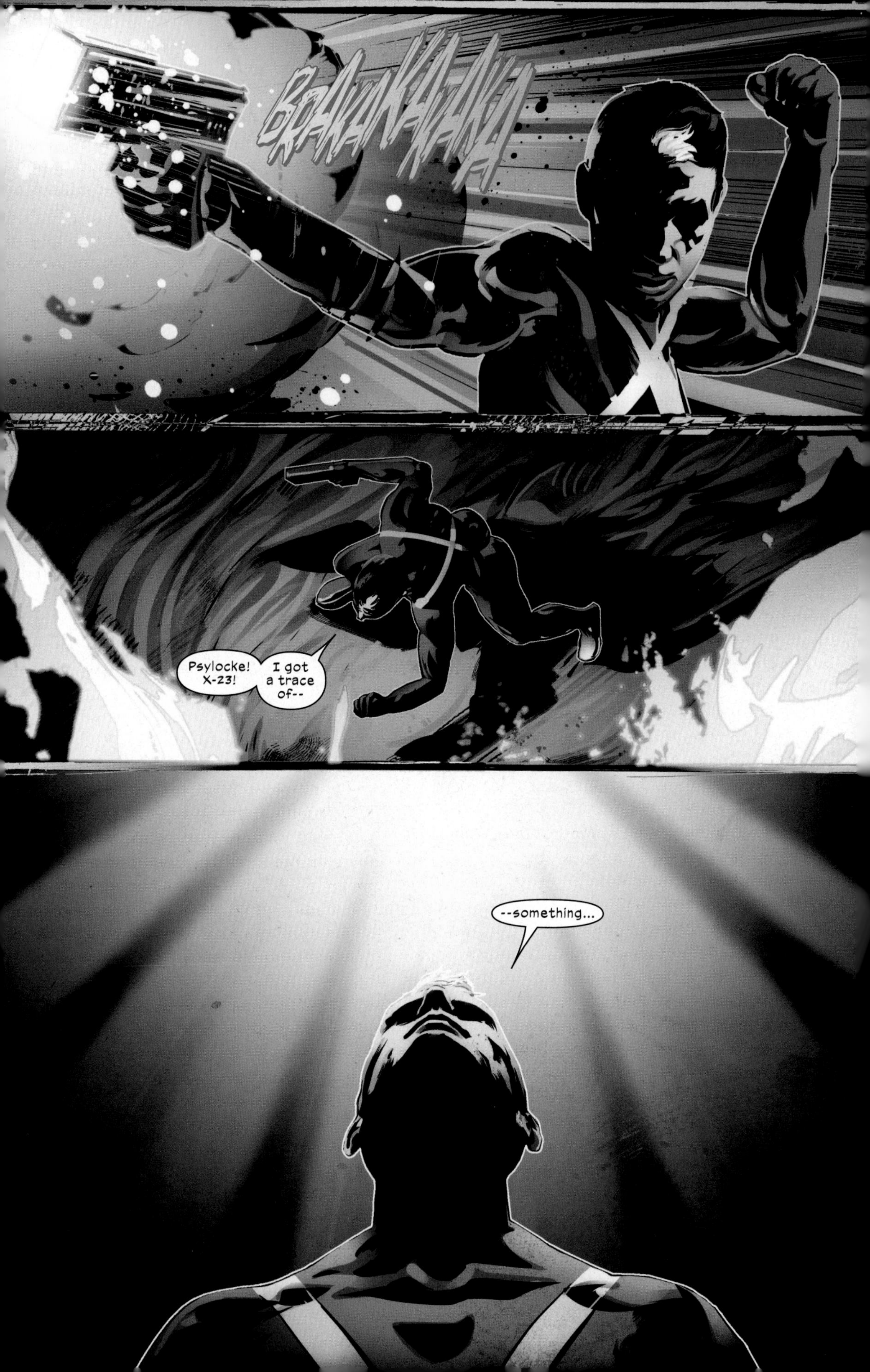
BRAKAKAKAKA
Psylocke! X-23!
I got a trace of--
--something...

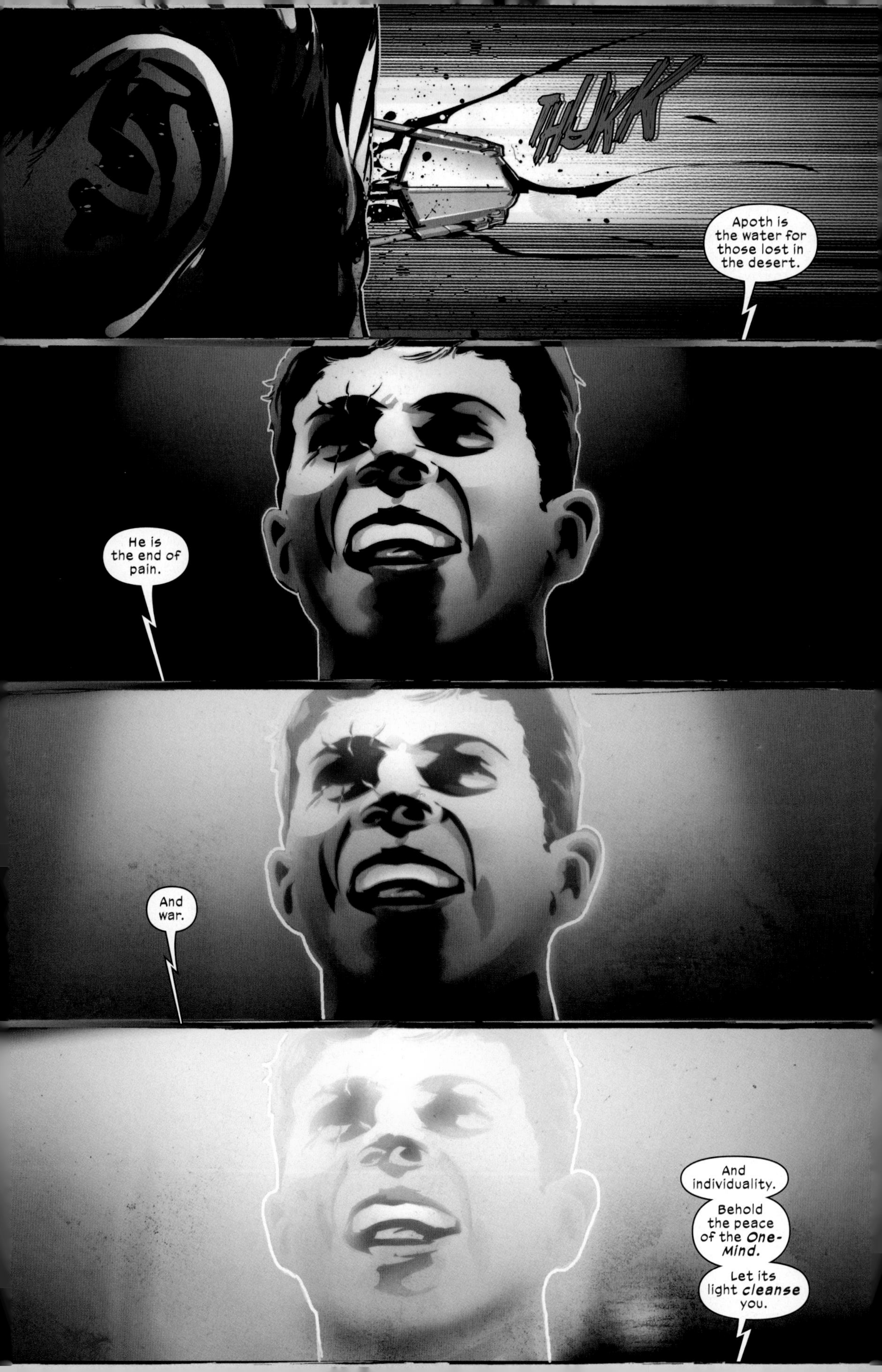
THUKK
Apoth is the water for those lost in the desert.
He is the end of pain.
And war.
And individuality.
Behold the peace of the *One-Mind.*
Let its light *cleanse* you.

EXCERPTS FROM THE SCROLLS OF THE EXILE

Many will have words about killing. Few will know what it is to kill. Be not judged by minds that do not know. Do not allow what you have felt and seen and caused to be imprisoned by their thoughts. Remember they know nothing but the pain of their own weakness. Your strength is a mirror they wish to shatter. Deny them power over you. If you must be alone, then you must be alone. No relationship, no community, no family is worth the negation of what you are. When you are certain, be certain. Strike when you believe you must and always seek to finish your opponent.

The only faith you need is faith in yourself.

You have the power to change yourself. If there is will, there is the possibility of change. Any moment given is enough time to change. It is your right to seek experiences that will transform you. It is your right to evolve. Be not tethered to those who want time to stand still. Sever what binds you to those unwilling to accept your will to change. All that you have acquired you can lose and live with purpose. All that you have lost can be replaced through righteous action. What you have is nothing when considering what you can become. Turn your mind to what you seek for yourself. Turn your back on what holds you to this moment. The worm has no mind. It moves by instinct. When its time has come it will retreat into chrysalis. It will know no connection. It will be lost to the world. When it emerges it will be transformed. No longer will it crawl. It will fly. It will have been a worm. It is a butterfly. Only through pure commitment to change can it see the sky. What remains is a dead shell. A nothing. The past. The former life.

The butterfly must forget the worm.

I write this in exile. Once I lived in the palm of the hand. Once I was the weapon of the hand. Once I smothered my own will to serve the will of others. I am alone. I am hunted. I am free. If you have found these words, then you were meant to find them. If I am dead and only these words remain, then that is what I have given. That is my purpose.

May these words teach you your shape. May you be alone. May you be hunted. May you be free.

It is a time of false leaders, false nations and false gods. Men will come to convince you there is no evil, nor is there good. They will make one the other and destroy both. They will use the word "peace" to mean war. They will use the word "freedom" to mean slavery. They will blind you to what you know to be true until you no longer trust yourself.

You must not listen.

Comfort is not safety. Comfort is a thing to fear. All that challenges you is not your enemy. The firm hand strikes, but it can also hold you at the cliff. The soft hand comforts, but you will slip through its grasp. Civilization will teach that comfort is the only goal. Comfort of body. Comfort of mind. This is the path of defeat. This is the banishment of your own power. Those who wrap you in comfort seek to destroy you. They will praise you when you fear the world. They will hunt you when you hunt your fear. Be naked in the coldest day of winter so that you can love the warmth of the sun. Lay your body on stone so you can love the embrace of hay. Let adversity teach you. The hands of the forger must be firm and relentless, for the the most important moment of the sword is the moment of tempering. This is *tamashii o ireru*. This is when soul is put into the blade. What you choose will forge you.

And no sword can be forged twice.

-- Author Unknown

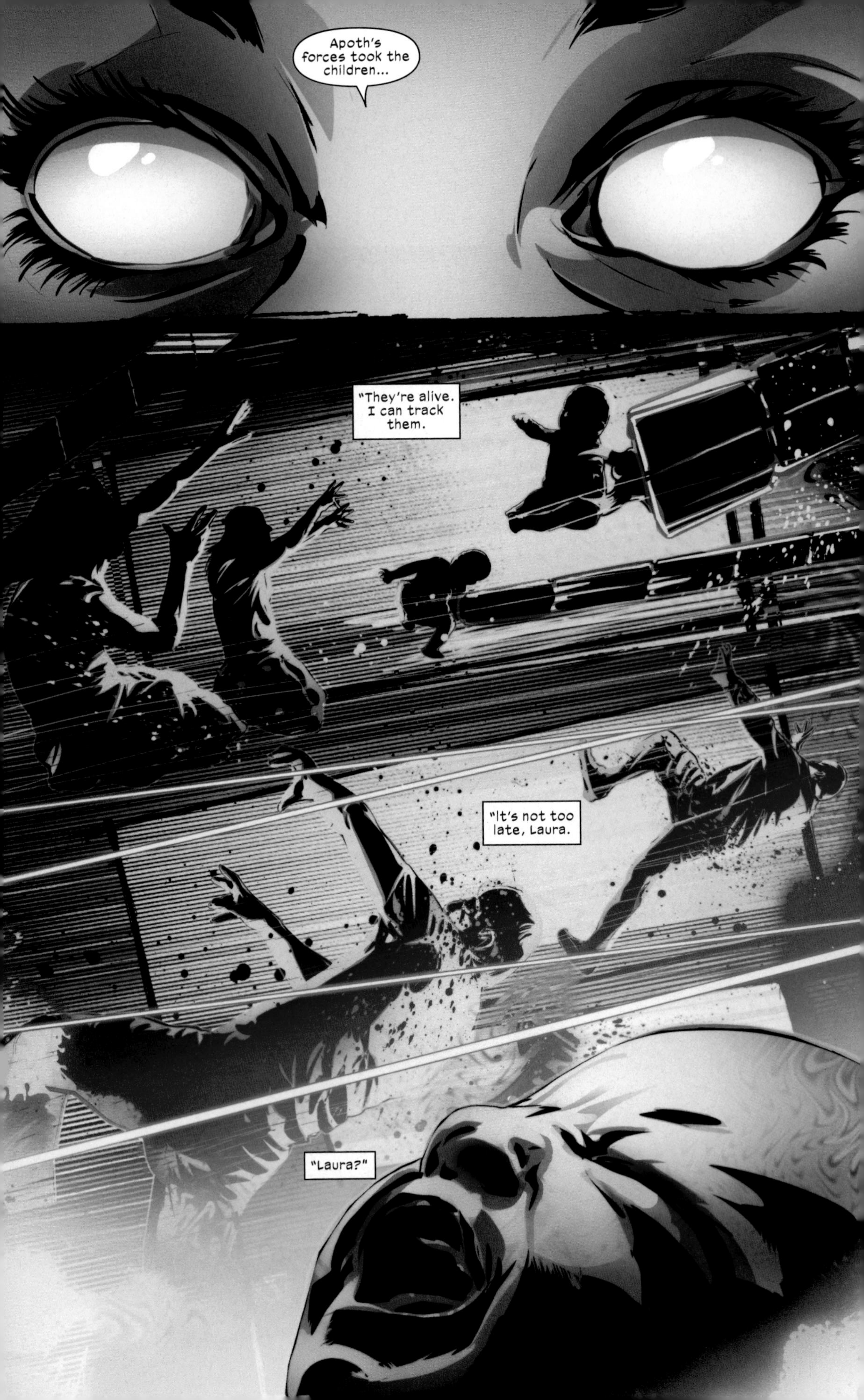
Apoth's forces took the children...
"They're alive. I can track them.
"It's not too late, Laura.
"Laura?"

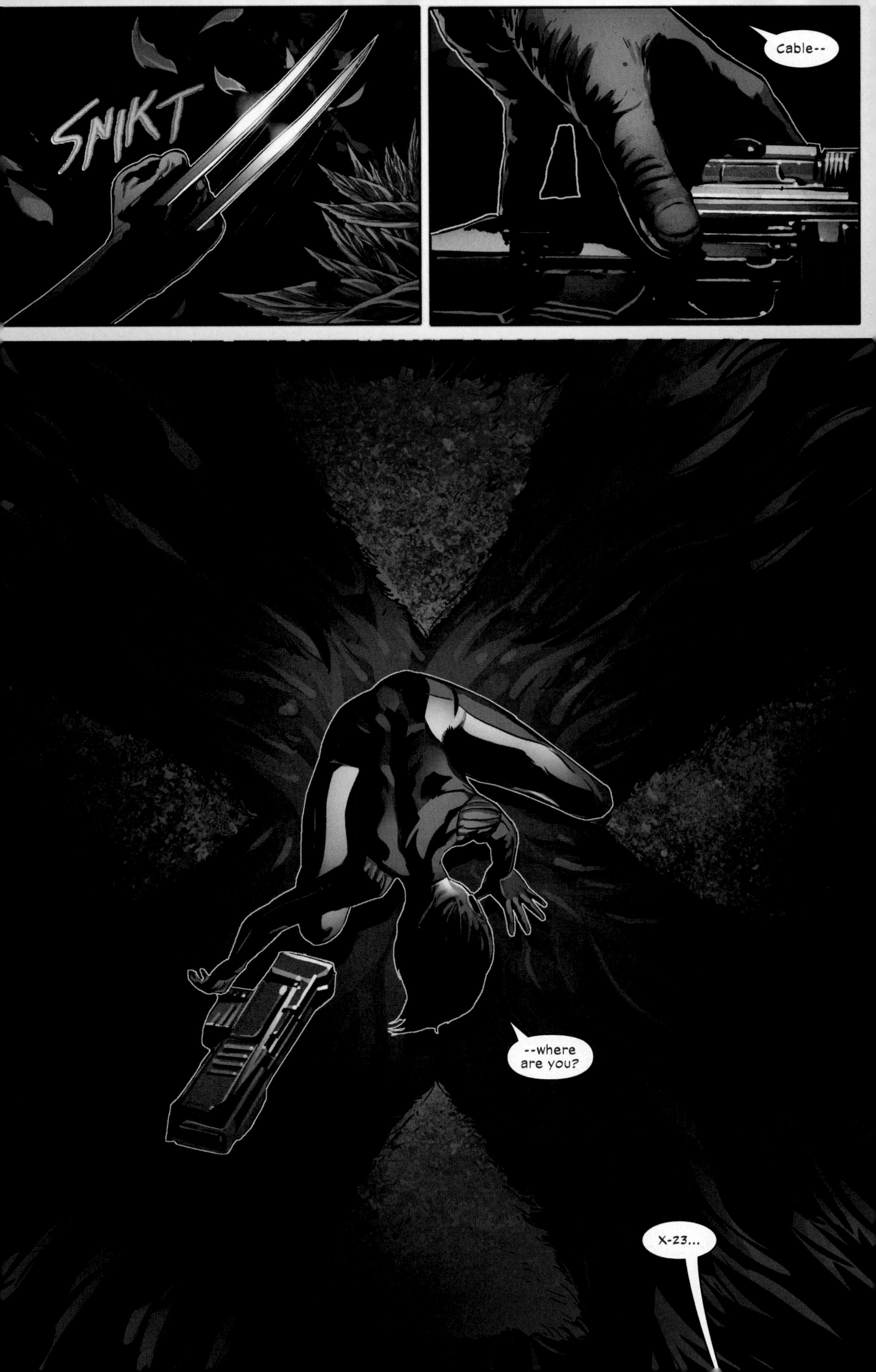
SNIKT
Cable--
--where are you?
X-23...

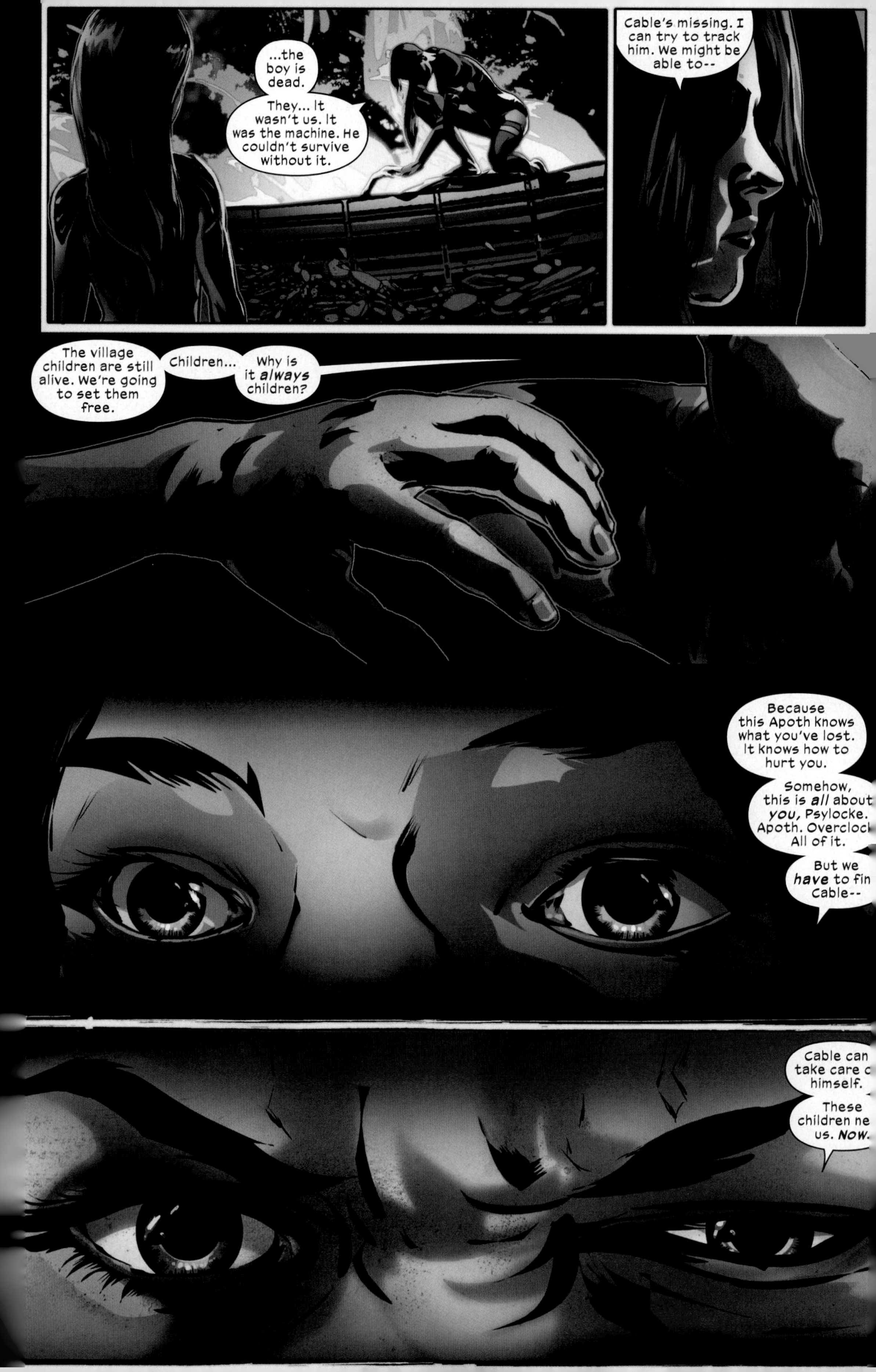

...the boy is dead.
They... It wasn't us. It was the machine. He couldn't survive without it.
Cable's missing. I can try to track him. We might be able to--
The village children are still alive. We're going to set them free.
Children...
Why is it *always* children?
Because this Apoth knows what you've lost. It knows how to hurt you.
Somehow, this is *all* about *you,* Psylocke. Apoth. Overclock All of it.
But we *have* to fin Cable--
Cable can take care c himself.
These children ne us. **NOW.**

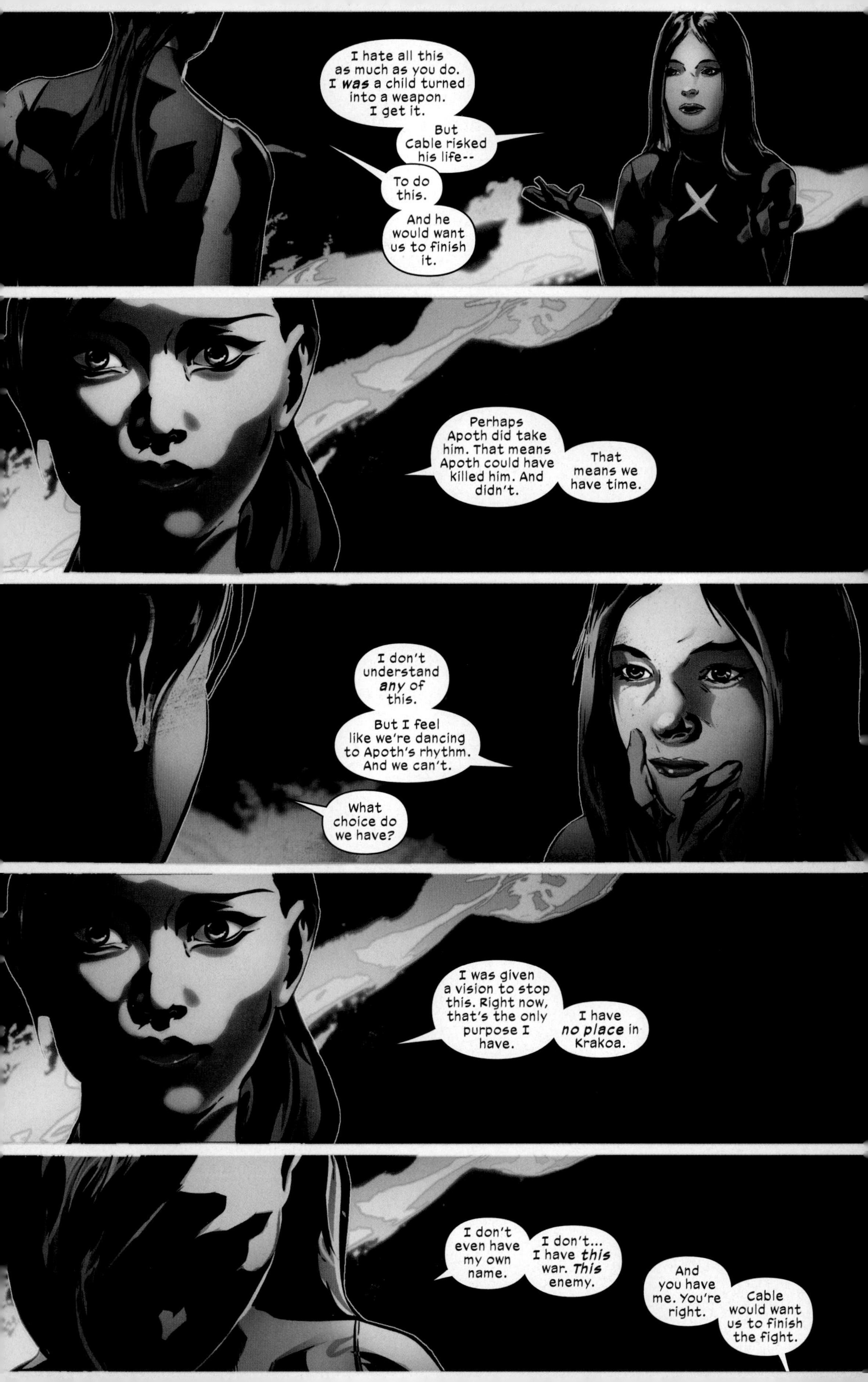
I hate all this as much as you do. I *was* a child turned into a weapon. I get it.
But Cable risked his life--
To do this.
And he would want us to finish it.
Perhaps Apoth did take him. That means Apoth could have killed him. And didn't.
That means we have time.
I don't understand *any* of this.
But I feel like we're dancing to Apoth's rhythm. And we can't.
What choice do we have?
I was given a vision to stop this. Right now, that's the only purpose I have.
I have *no place* in Krakoa.
I don't even have my own name.
I don't... I have *this* war. *This* enemy.
And you have me. You're right.
Cable would want us to finish the fight.

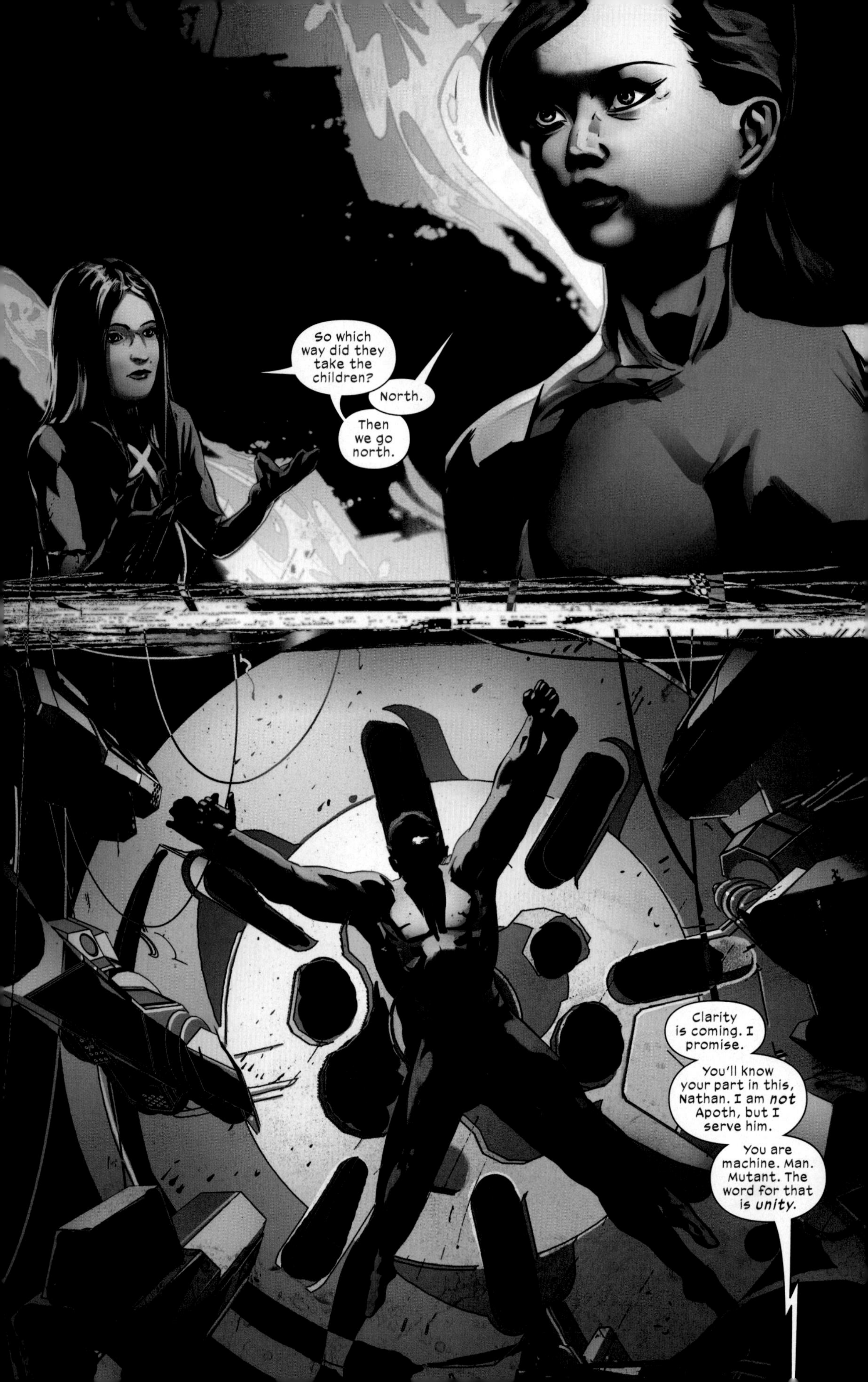
So which way did they take the children?
North.
Then we go north.
Clarity is coming. I promise.
You'll know your part in this, Nathan. I am *not* Apoth, but I serve him.
You are machine. Man. Mutant. The word for that is *unity*.

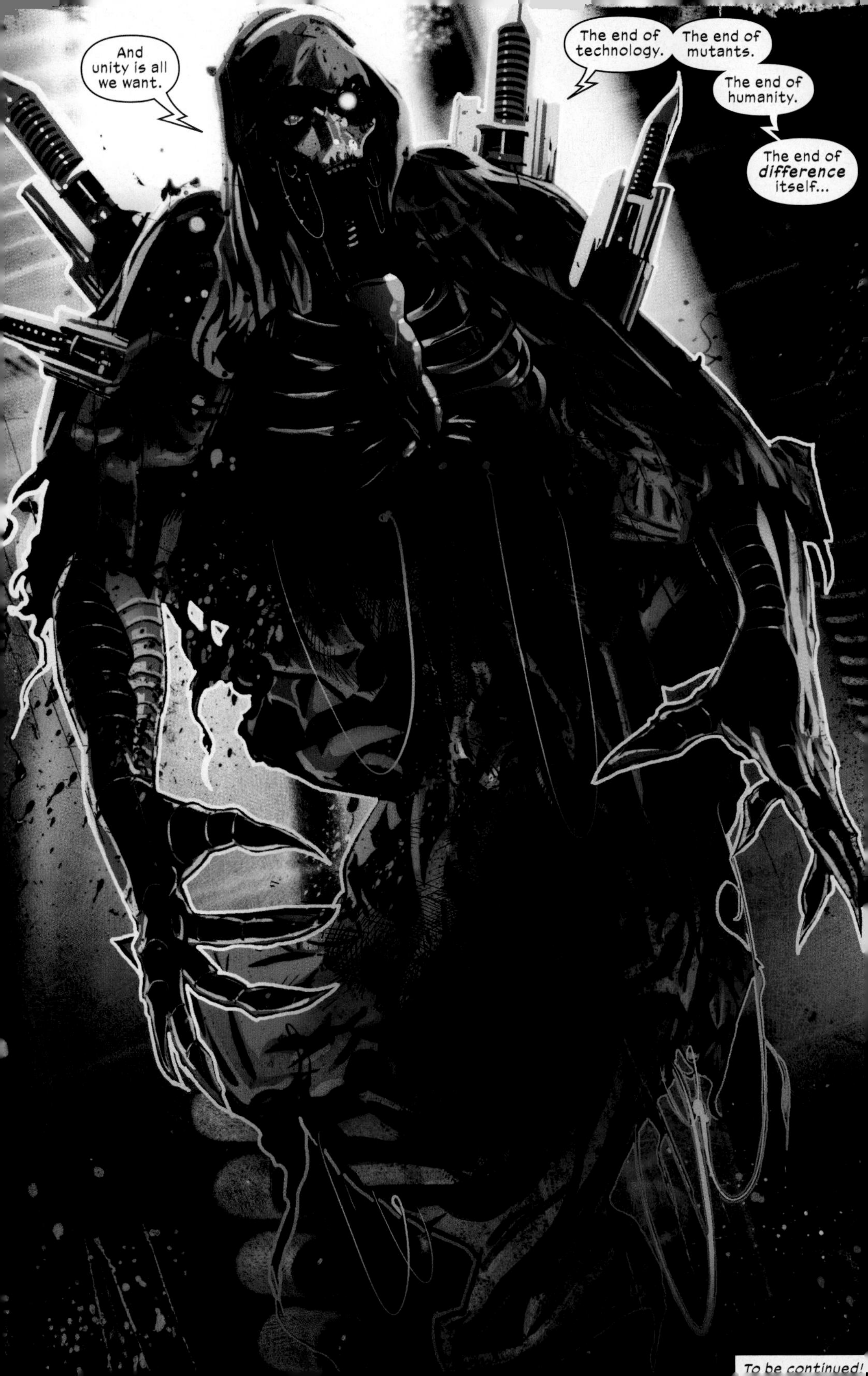
And unity is all we want.
The end of technology.
The end of mutants.
The end of humanity.
The end of *difference* itself...
To be continued!

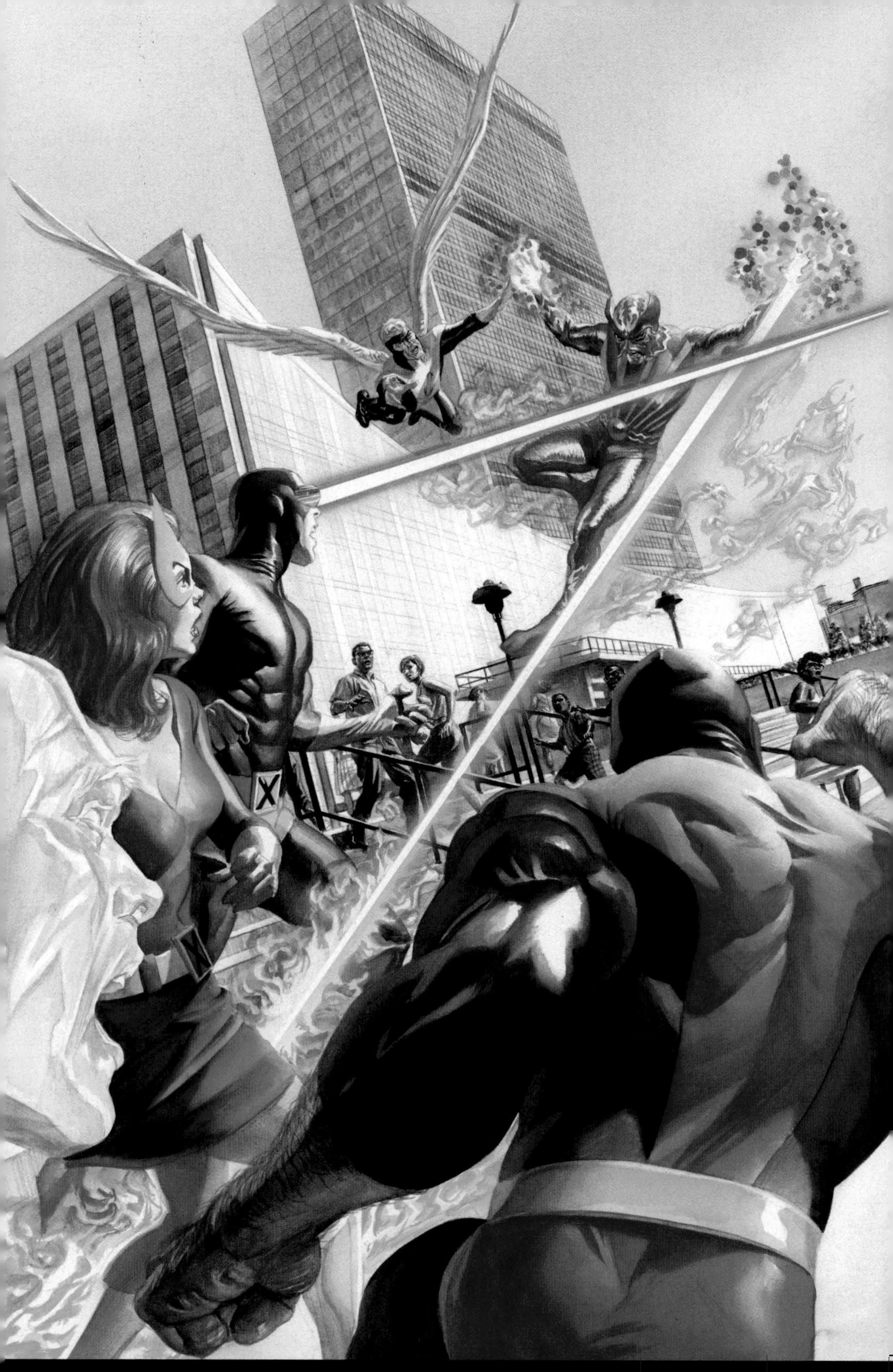

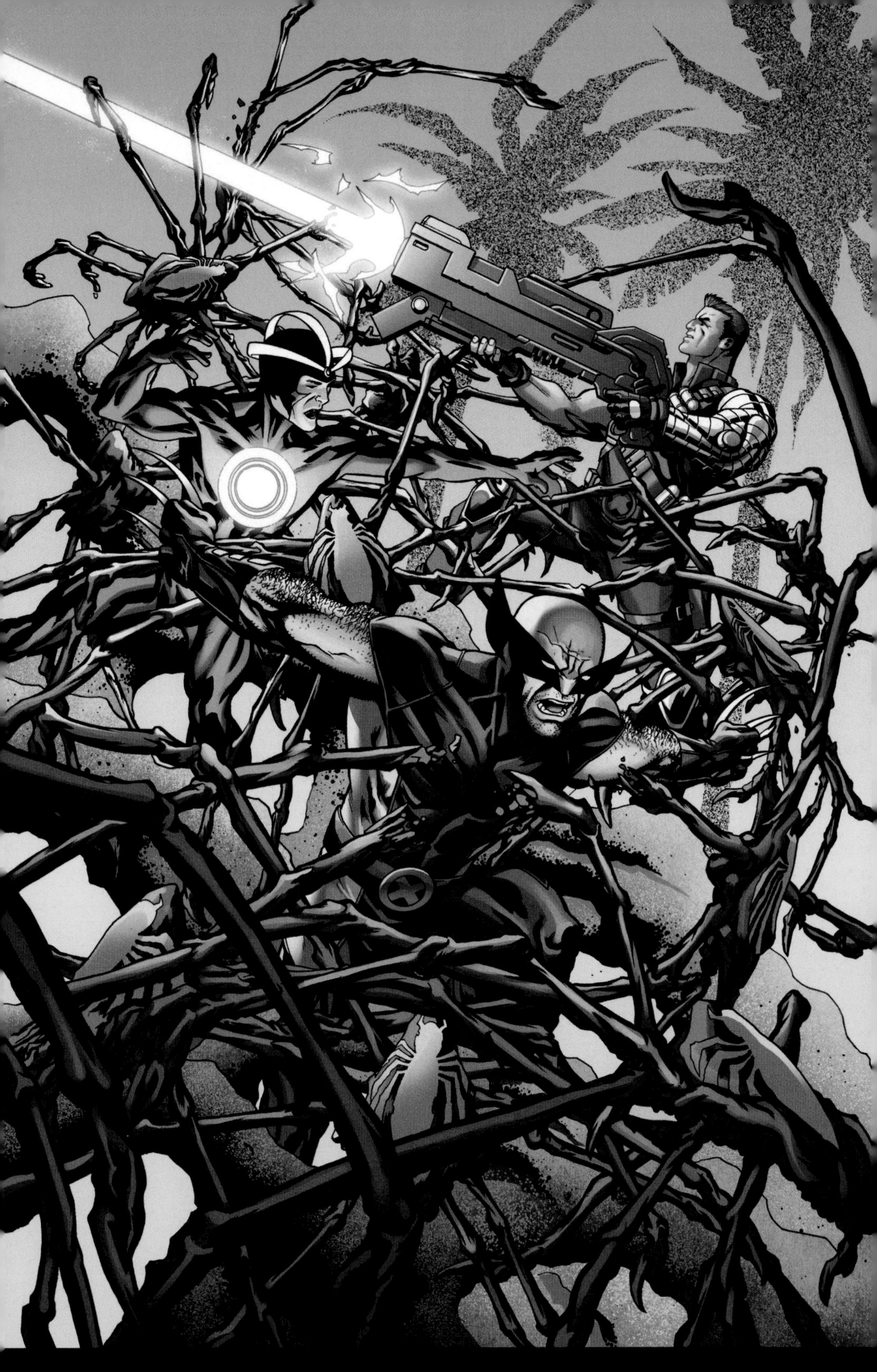

X-Men #3 Venom Island Variant by Mike McKone & Rachelle Rosenberg

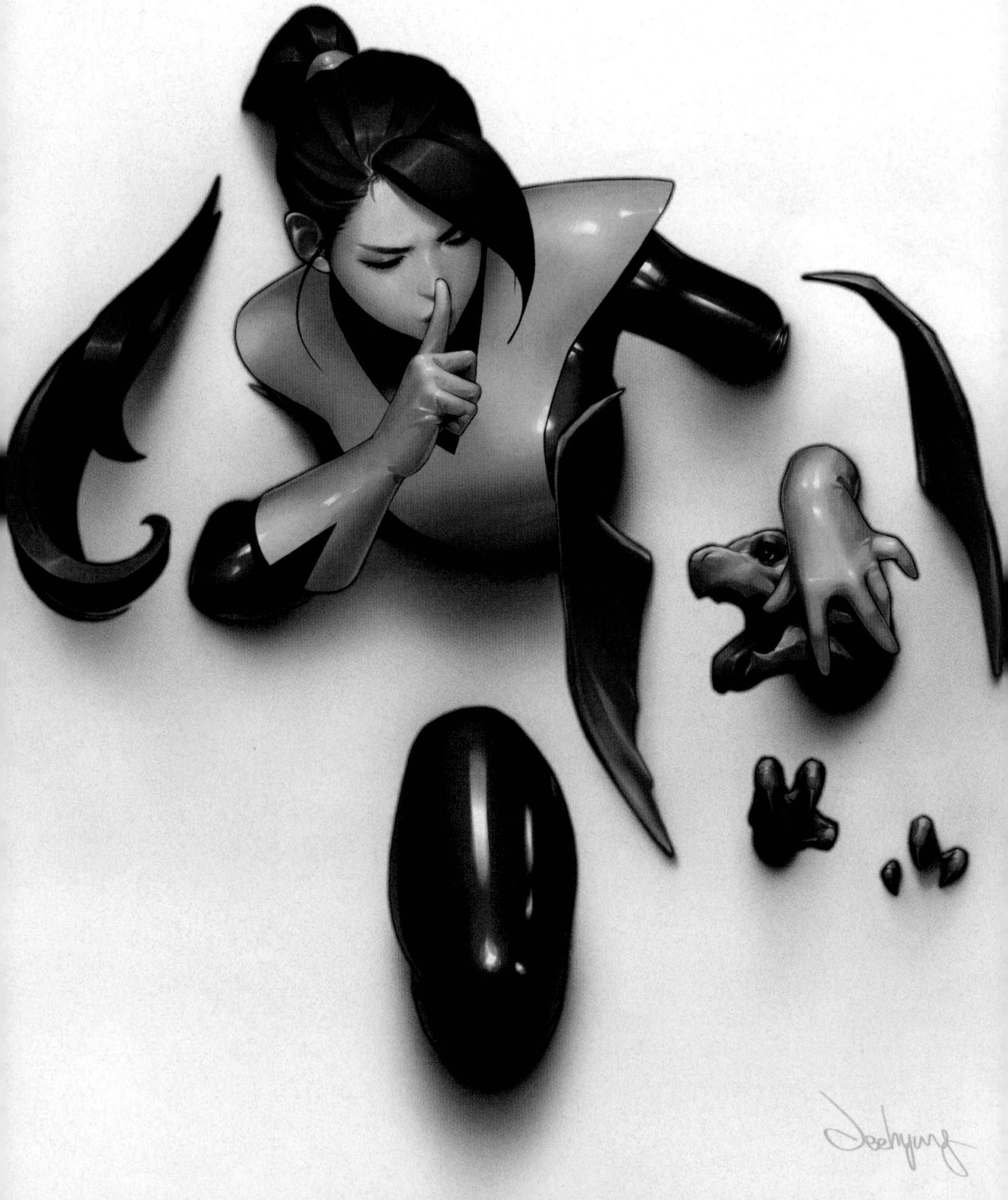

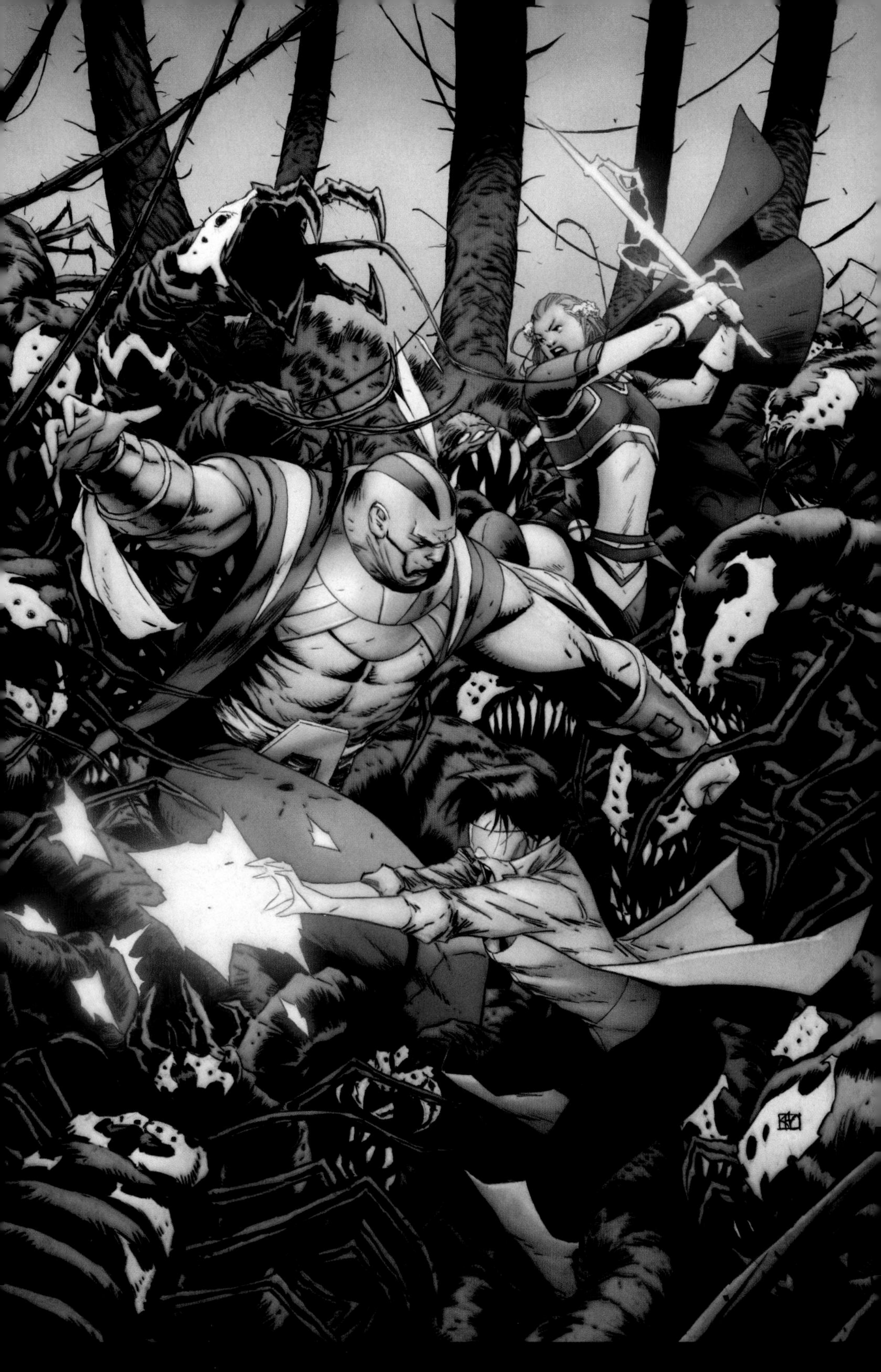

Excalibur #3 Venom Island Variant by Khoi Pham & Morry Hollowell

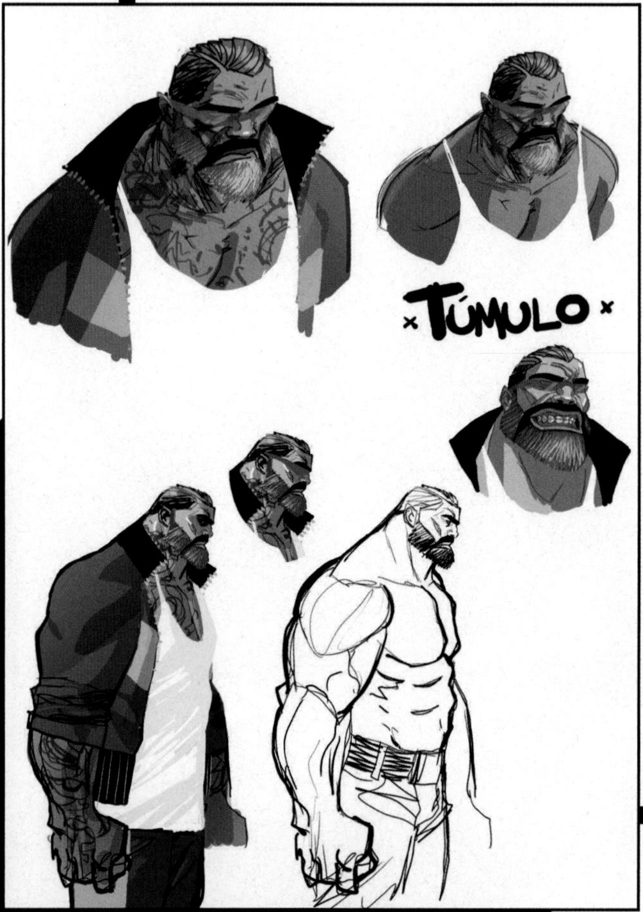
×TÚMULO×

Túmulo designs by Flaviano

Volume
03
BONUS MATERIAL

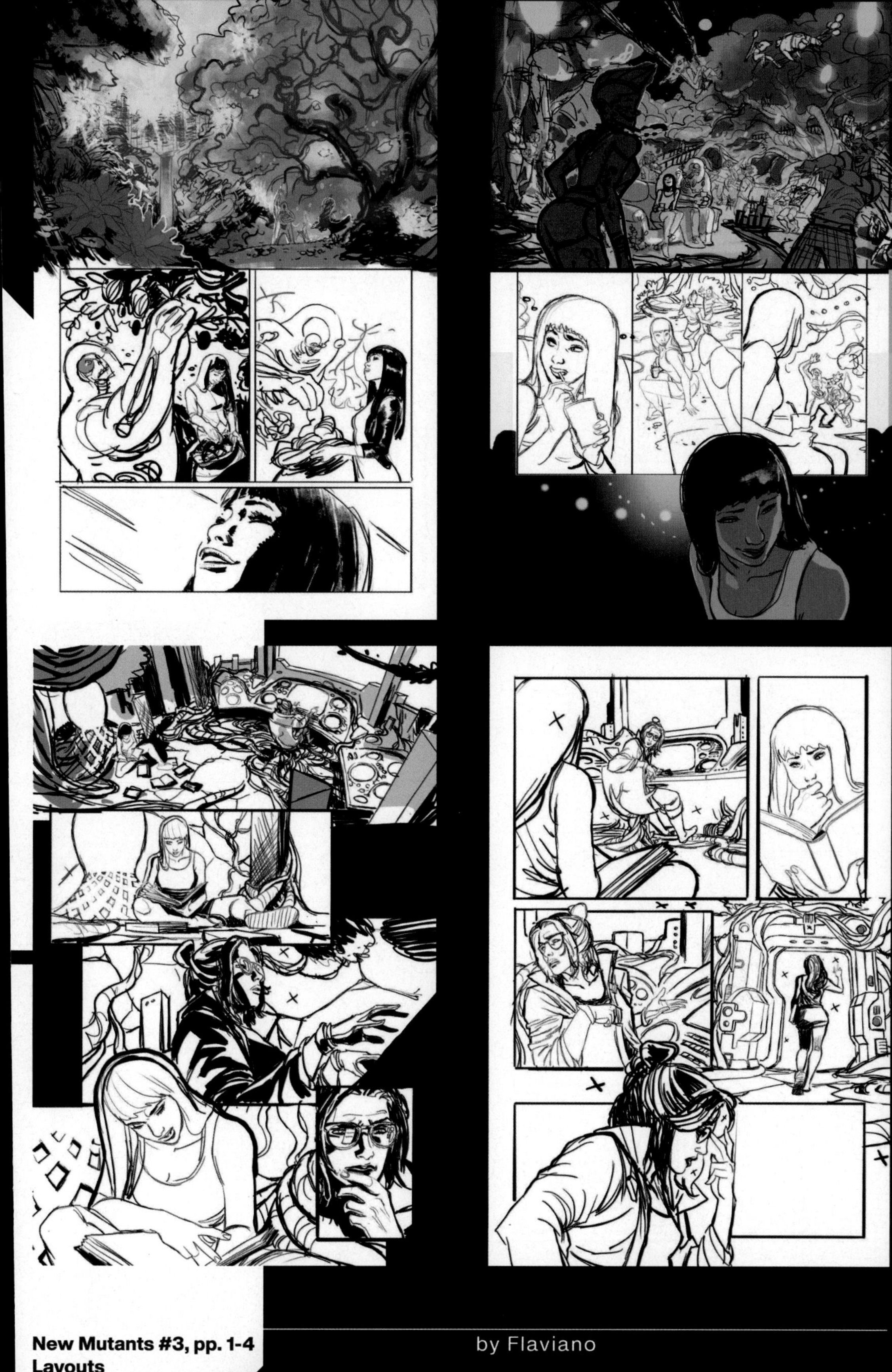

New Mutants #3, pp. 1-4 Layouts

by Flaviano

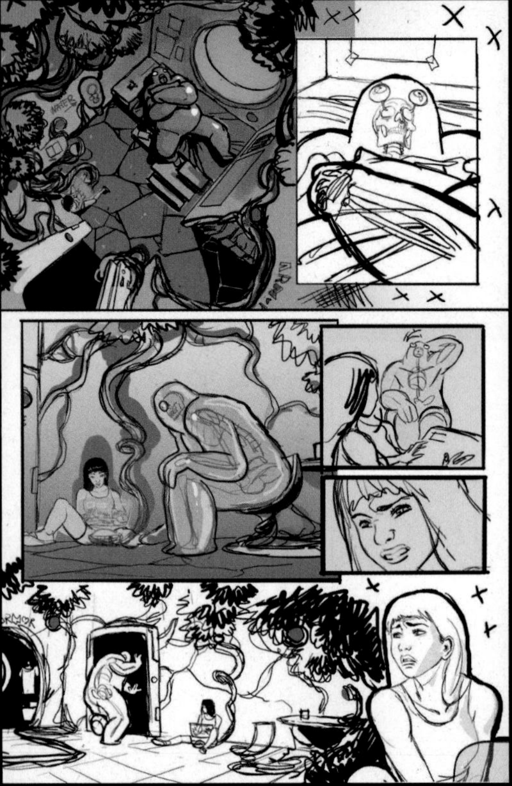

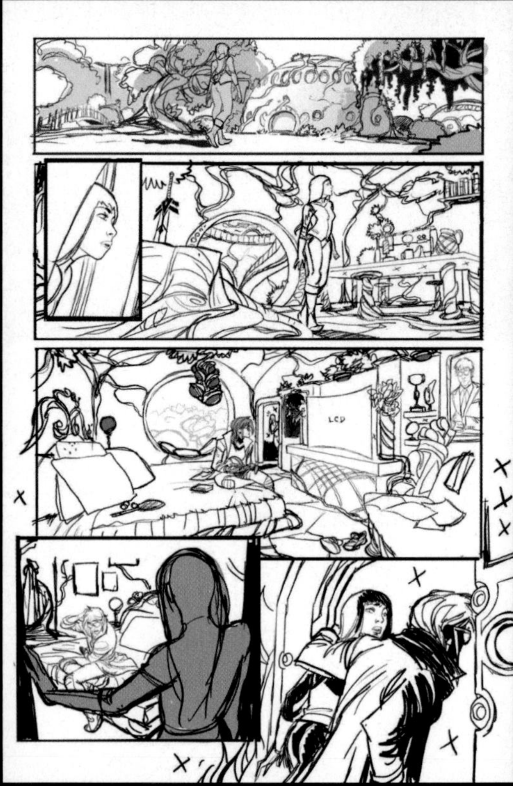
LCD

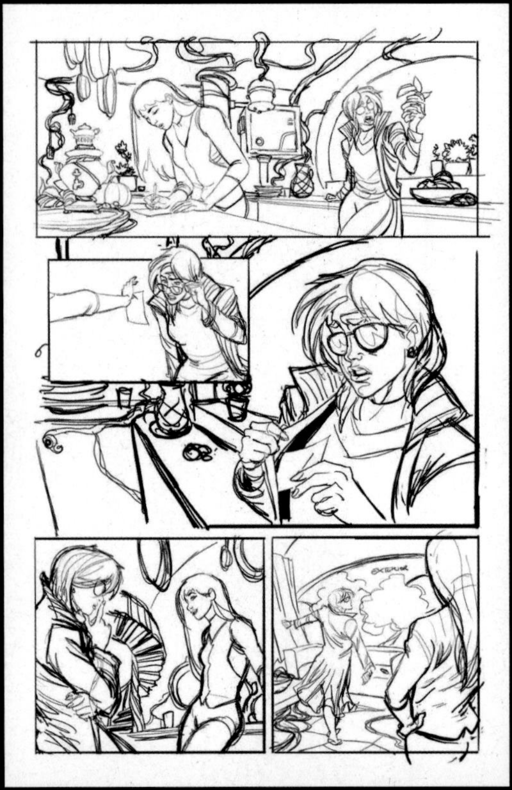

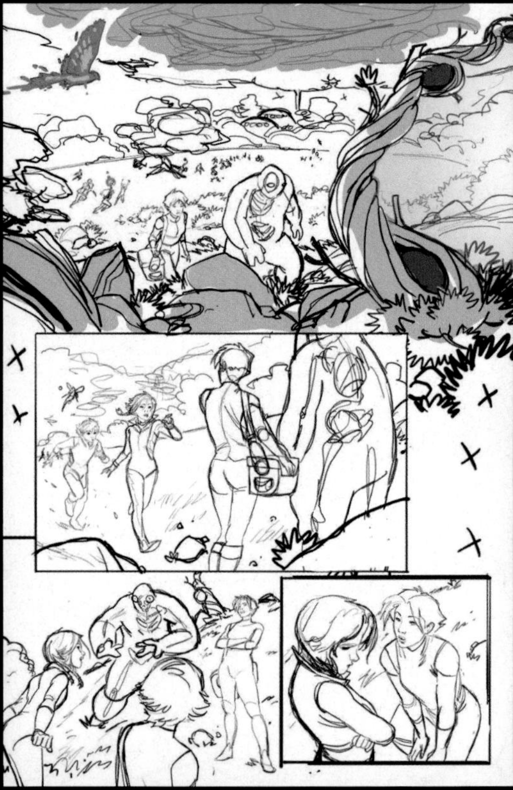

New Mutants #3, pp. 5-8
Layouts

by Flaviano

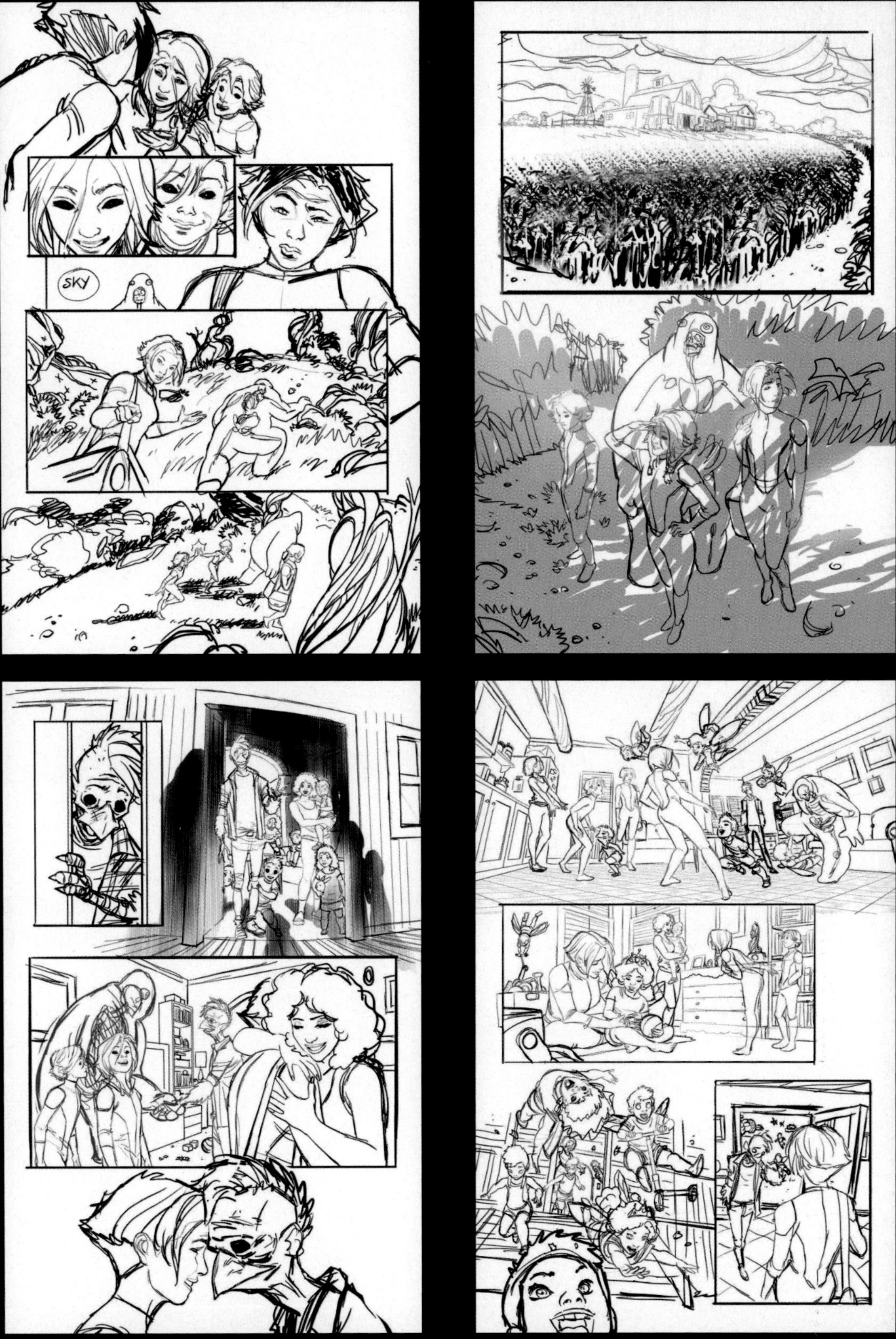
SKY

New Mutants #3, pp. 9-10
Layouts

by Flaviano